QUANTUM SHAMAN

Diary of a Nagual Woman

Teachings in the Toltec Tradition

Book One in the Quantum Shaman Series

Limited edition trade paperback published by
Eye Scry Publications
Yucca Valley, California
www.eyescrypublications.com

Contact:
info@quantumshaman.com
www.QuantumShaman.com

Second Edition – 2014
ISBN 978-0-9896938-4-4

Back Cover Image: Martha Frost

WHOLESALE: BOOKSTORES & LIBRARIES...
Quantity discounts available.
Email: info@quantumshaman.com
Also available through Amazon.com and CreateSpace

QUANTUM SHAMAN
Diary of a Nagual Woman

BY
DELLA VAN HISE

Eye Scry Publications
www.quantumshaman.com

3

First shaman created the world, and when she realized she was lonely, tore out half her heart and put it into her dreaming body so she would never be alone. But because the double was made of Spirit, it left her all too soon and went to dwell in eternity, where its siren cries call her back into the Infinite. This is why the heart has two chambers and why the shaman walks the earth with one eye on the world and the other focused on that which has no name.

Della Van Hise, 2003

For Wendy, for Orlando

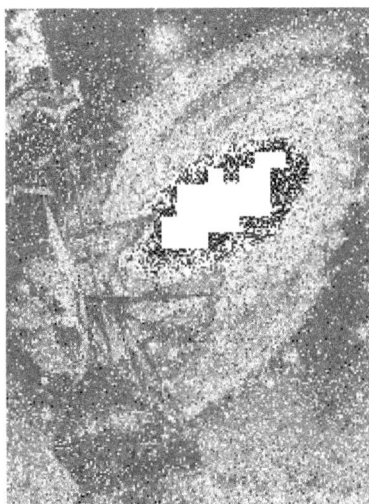

*and the boat in the middle
of the infinite ocean*

TABLE OF CONTENTS

INTRODUCTION

You ask how to know who you are. By posing that question, you have already embarked on the infinite journey, for that is the first question, the last question, the only question. And it cannot be answered except through the course of living, and connecting through Spirit to the infinite otherSelf.

*When you ask, "Who am I?" listen with your heart for the answer. You may feel a pull somewhere deep in your chest, or you may feel inexplicable tears swell from behind your eyes, or perhaps you may catch a scent of autumn apples on a chilly wind – a scent that makes you want to laugh or weep, reminding you of some memory you cannot pinpoint, taking you through All of time to forgotten dreams of something you cannot name. This is the **nagual** – the unknowable, the shadow's shadow, the Wholeness you become through the act of Intending it. All those things that you feel, those things that you know-without-knowing-how-you-know are reflections of the genuine self – the I-Am which exists beyond all roles, all definitions, all words.*

*It is from that connection to **Spirit** that the **warrior** approaches her journey, connecting not with some external entity, but returning instead to the infinite and eternal Wholeness that is already within – the cumulative cohesion of the Spirit as a traveler through allspace and alltime. These are only words, of course, inadequate to the task of revealing any truth at all. What matters, then, is that you look beyond the words and into the source of that calling which has always been with you. That is who you are, that is who you will become if you choose to answer the call, that is your Self in eternity.*

Orlando – May 23, 2004

FOREWORD

Although I had been on some manner of mystical path all my life, the journey became considerably more serious in 1988, when I met a man I knew to be something other-than-human. *Immortal?* Evolved? Non-corporeal? At the time, I could not have said, and had I known the truth then, I would not have believed it, nor even been able to consider it as having any association with what I think of as reality. And yet, it was through his influence upon my life that I was forced to ask the first question: *Who Are You?*

The answer for all of us is a work in progress.

"Shaman" is a word with many meanings. A shaman is a seeker of *Knowledge* who works in alignment with Spirit – not only the knowledge of what we think of as "the real world" but the deeper knowledge traditionally associated with other dimensional planes, and the realm of the Immortal – or, more accurately, the realm of the *eternal being.* Shamans are found in all cultures, and though the purpose of this book is not to serve as a history of shamanism, it is widely believed that the first shamans came from Siberia, and that the word itself translates loosely to "self-healed madman." That healing is the process of gathering one's personal cohesion, and evolving toward Wholeness within the infinite.

The word "Spirit" as it is used here is not intended to convey any extant deity, but instead the always-moving, sentient universe which George Lucas undoubtedly intended when he wrote of "the force" in his <u>Star Wars</u> saga.

However we label it or attempt to categorize it, there are systems of knowledge which may be gleaned directly from the universe itself through a process called *gnosis.* Inside all of us is the code, the spirit, if you will, which some mystics have called *"the right way to live."* I'm not speaking of morality within our human society, for much of what we think of as right and wrong are only agreements within the *consensual continuum* – and therefore subject to change depending on our culture or the time period in which we live.

For example, here in the western world, we have been taught that monogamy is right and polygamy is wrong – and yet that is only a cultural agreement, with which many other cultures on this earth would strongly disagree. Instead, the right way to live is an

9

inherent, living force which permeates the universe, and communicates with shamans, *sorcerers*, magicians, warriors, and all seekers of Knowledge directly. It is through that living force that we find our connection to the infinite.

Of course, learning the right way to live is only one small segment of a much larger system of Knowledge. *Don Juan*, a Yaqui Indian serving as mentor to *Carlos Castaneda*, called this system of knowledge sorcery, though that is a word much misunderstood and much maligned. Others have called it "applied gnosis." Still others refer to it as "scrying the mind of the gods." No matter what we call it, it is a natural part of our human ability, and though we have been programmed through traditional belief systems to think it doesn't exist, or indoctrinated with the dogma of religions to view this Knowledge as forbidden, the simple truth is that it is the very key to our personal survival beyond death, and it is accessible to any of us willing to make the long and difficult journey of self-Realized evolution.

This is the shaman's journey, for the shaman is someone who has seen the world for what it is, someone who has fallen into its traps and its illusions, only to finally – through will and *intent* – heal herself of the madness by embracing and realizing the power of the *Whole Self*.

To some, shamanism is a calling, a natural instinct. To others, it is embraced by choice and may actually be learned on an intellectual level until such time as it permeates the Self and becomes an intrinsic way of life. Shamanism does not belong exclusively to any culture, and it is not a religious practice in that it does not rely on faith or belief, but instead on direct personal experience and interaction with the realms of Spirit.

Now, with the arrival of quantum mechanics, we know we are not merely insignificant entities watching the universe go by. We are literally part of it through our consciousness, our perceptions, and the very atoms of which we are made. We are co-creators of reality, yet only when we begin to understand the awesome power within ourselves will we be able to evolve beyond our primitive belief systems which enslave us to the dust even though we've had the stars at our fingertips all along.

Within the very fabric of the universe itself – not only around us, but within us, down to a molecular level – there exists a *non-*

10

local web of information which literally houses all the collective Knowledge of all that has ever been or ever will be. It is that wellspring of information which has been traditionally tapped by mystics, seers and prophets, yet it is available to any of us who are willing to go out on a limb and peer down into the abyss to confront the simple truth that our lives and our entire existence are nothing like what we have been taught to believe.

The *quantum shaman*, then, is someone who seeks Knowledge from the Olde and the Knew, someone who seeks to Realize their full potential by obliterating the illusions and misconceptions of ordinary life in order to become aware of and empowered through the *cohesion* of the Whole Self. This is the nature of spiritual evolution – where a single, continuing point-of-view is maintained into eternity.

The quantum shaman is within each of us.

Immortality itself is within our grasp.

~

"The destruction of faith is the beginning of evolution."

-Orlando

~

Alphabetical Glossary

For your convenience, you will find in the back of this book a glossary of terms with which some readers may not be familiar. It is by no means complete, and my definition of some terms may not agree entirely with others on this path. For that reason, please feel free to read between the lines, from the corner of the third eye, from the assemblage point of higher awareness.

Terms appearing in the glossary will be designated on their first appearance in bold italic. There are also many terms in the glossary which may not appear in the book text.

11

Duality and the Double

Only when you exist
will I.

PART ONE

WHEN THE STUDENT IS READY
THE TEACHER WILL APPEAR

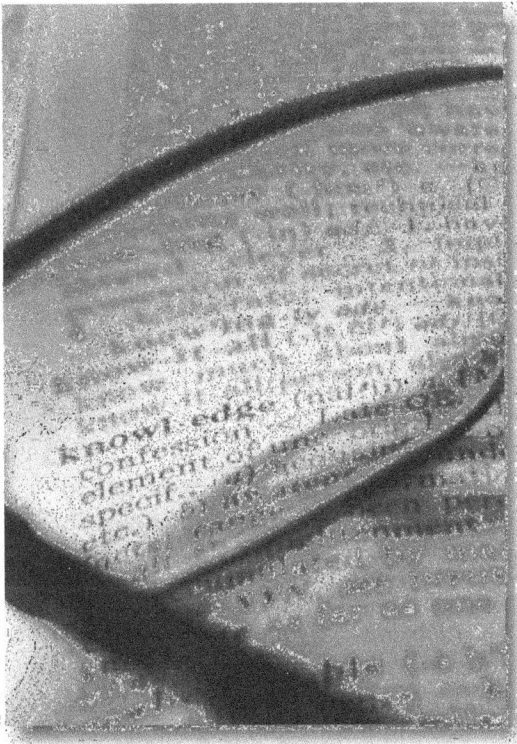

...and often even when the student <u>isn't</u>.

Preface

What defines a teacher? Is it a human being who stands before you with rigid lessons or facts to be memorized? Or is it a drop of rain falling onto the surface of a still pond and the ripples that flow outward? Most often, those who have learned to _See_, begin to engage the teacher within almost from the start – even if it is only the voice of the mortal self at first, asking questions of Spirit which only Spirit can answer. Ah, and can you see that it is the questioning and the answering, the give and take between Spirit and the self, which is the first step in the creation of the double, and once this process is internalized, it creates a link to the infinite which no earth-bound teacher could ever match?

And yet, to many, perhaps an external teacher is necessary in the beginning – someone to show the apprentice how to undo the world of matter and men, how to hear her own voice, how to see with the inner eye, how to listen with the heart, how to speak to Spirit and be heard by the infinite. Learning these things may take a year, a decade, or a lifetime. To some, the lessons are never finished, and so they remain at the level of apprentice forever.

But to the warrior who Sees, once the techniques are learned, it becomes almost a compulsion to seek the inner silence, listening only to the inner teacher, which is the act of beginning to embrace the double as the sentient, Whole Self outside of time – the double who knows you better than you know yourself and therefore is most qualified to teach you how to be who and what you already are, but have only briefly forgotten. When the warrior begins to **embrace the totality of herself**, the student becomes the teacher, and in some cases, even the new **Nagual** – whether it is her conscious desire or not. Such is the manner in which the Knowledge self-perpetuates even after lying dormant for centuries, for it is not stored in the fabric of space-time, but within the energetic sentience of the universe itself, within the Be-ing of every Nagual who has ever been or ever will be. It is a living energy, and as such can never be destroyed.

Each Nagual is the first Nagual. Each shaman is the first shaman. It cannot be otherwise. All that is ever really handed across generations is information: techniques, concepts, ideas. You are an infinite being, and as such you are comprised of infinite Knowledge. All that is required to embrace it is Intent.

Orlando – April 1, 2003

14

Chapter One
The Scream at the Edge of the World

1997 – Ten years after it all began
[Or... There is no beginning, so we begin in the middle]

It was a hot summer evening in the early part of August when I drove to a look-out point high in the mountains of Joshua Tree National Park. The road was long, dark, and fraught with shadows, and I couldn't help drawing the analogy between that road and the spiritual path I had been forging for nearly a decade. Disturbed over financial uncertainty, problems with a new business, and essentially wrapped up in the machinations of the consensual reality, I was finally driven to seek some sort of solace alone in the night, and Keys View was as close to a personal retreat as any place on Earth I had ever known, the kind of place the old sorcerers would have called a *power spot*.

I climbed to the high point where a lone bench looks out over the Salton Sea – an irregular blotch of blacker black against the southeastern horizon – and before I knew it I was involved in a deep conversation with Orlando. When I asked how he had known I would come to this remote location, and how he himself had gotten there – since there were no other cars in the tiny parking lot – he only smiled a little, stretched out his long legs, and slouched down on that cold metal bench to stare up at the stars.

"You're predictable," he said as if I should have already known. "I'm here because this is where you always come when you're mad at the world."

I attempted to engage him in a conversation of just exactly how he knew I was mad at the world, since I'd had no direct contact with him in quite some time, nothing to give him any hint of what was going on in my everyday life. But even as I began spelling all of that out to him, he brushed my words aside with an easy gesture.

"Do you want to talk or do you want to waste time looking for logical explanations for every magical thing that ever happens?" he asked. "That's what's wrong with the world, you know. Instead of embracing the mysteries and trying to determine how they might open a crack in an otherwise humdrum, pre-programmed existence, people waste their entire lives explaining it all away, attaching labels to it, filing and categorizing it until it loses any meaning."

He had a point. And I'd already been inundated with enough mysteries in my time to know that some things simply had no explanation humans could understand. *'Magic is only science not yet understood'*. Words Orlando had written more than a year before rattled through my mind up there in the middle of the night, in the middle of nowhere, looking down on a distant world that seemed far more unreal to me at that moment than the world he had been trying to teach me to *see*.

He was there – whether physically or in some spirit-form manifestation is ultimately of no importance, for in the sorcerer's world there is no difference between body and spirit, and in any world, perception is reality.

"Sometimes the silence up here is absolutely deafening," he mused, gazing out toward that distant dead sea landlocked in the desert.

I immediately recognized his words as more than a simple observation. They had that leading quality – that same intentionally seductive edge that had been my undoing years before when I first met this man who was not really a man at all. I could have argued, pressed my question, but instead I surrendered to whatever it was he was trying to get me to *see*.

I listened.

At first I couldn't hear it above the noisy chatter of my own thoughts, but as I gradually stopped the *internal dialogue* and settled into that place of pure existence, observation and silent awareness of gnosis, I began to hear what Orlando had intended me to hear.

Not a cricket, not an owl disturbed the stillness. The lights of Palm Springs were only far-away glitterings, the line of traffic crawling along Interstate-10 nothing more than an illumined ant trail, so distant the movement of the cars could not even be perceived – just a streak of brilliant incandescence in the middle of the desert, a phantasm, a chimera, a miasma of lost souls rushing headlong through the night, yet seeming to stand still. A fitting paradox.

But above it all, permeating the very air, a shrill, high-pitched scream began to work its way into my perceptions. At first, my mind scrambled around for its usual rational explanation. In the absence of any real external sound, I told myself, remembering some old prattle from a high school biology class, the eardrums began to actually pick up the sounds of one's own body. That scream, I told myself adamantly, was nothing more than the blood rushing through my own arteries, or perhaps even the electrical synapse of the brain itself as it was deprived of one of its ordinary senses. It was the silence a deaf man might hear, I rationalized, the silence of Beethoven's last years, the melancholy of his unfinished symphonies.

There are no words to describe it, yet most of us have heard it at some time or another in our lives – at least those who have found a place of solitude where that silence can exist. As I sit here in my office, there are literally dozens of noises. The hum of the computer. The clack of the plastic keys. A whine of tires on asphalt. Barking dogs. The call of a raven.

Occasionally, when a power outage occurs, we get a glimpse of that silence – when the normally-unnoticed hum of the refrigerator stops and the pump on the aquarium is stilled and the subliminal murmur of all the digital clocks is finally silenced. Maybe then, if we can stop our own internal dialogue and just listen, we can catch an edge of that deafening silent scream.

Orlando laughed as if hearing my very thoughts. "It's the scream nobody wants to hear," he said, though I didn't care for his words in the least. That silent screaming was so loud and so permeating to the very core that all I wanted was to pretend it didn't exist.

For a moment, I found myself back in my old life, back in the identity I had inhabited before I ever embarked on this strange and wondrous journey. There was always noise in the house. I'd turn on the tv for company. If the tv was off, the CD player was gnawing on Credence or Enya or The Moody Blues. If all else failed, I could always pick up the phone and lose myself in mindless prattle with friends for hours. Back then, I'd thought of it all as just normal. The only thing I ever did in silence was my writing, and even that could hardly be called silence, for the very act of fiction writing requires an active and cohesive internal dialogue.

I wanted to mention all of this to Orlando, but I had become so engulfed by that silent screaming that I was completely unable to speak. At times, there would be lulls. Then it would start again, fade, return. Occasionally, there would be true silence, but as I listened and began to analyze the phenomenon, I realized it had no particular pattern. Indeed, it didn't seem to be one scream at all, but literally millions – *billions* – all laid down on top of one another like tracks of madhouse music.

But far worse than the sound itself, that scream was imbedded with a despair so heavy that it carried the weight of a black star – a gravitational field so dense that not even light could escape.

"What *is* that?" I whispered, filled with awe and terror at once. For when I delved beyond the surface explanations and the rational analysis and all the other consensual reality-checks one does when faced with something one does not immediately recognize as part of the ordinary reality continuum, I came to realize that what I was hearing was not explainable in any terms I had ever called normal. It was not the synapse of my awestruck brain. It was not the sound of one hand clapping.

"What do *you* think it is?" Orlando asked, his voice a welcome intrusion into the darkness and the dread and the realization that something utterly profound was happening.

I knew perfectly well what it was, but I was afraid to say it, not only because the answer wasn't rational, but because I didn't want to believe it.

That dreadful, despairing sound, I knew, was the death scream of every living creature who had ever walked the earth. It was the wail of horror and despair choked out at the moment of annihilation before being forever fragmented back into the fabric of the night that never ends.

It was the realization of the businessman that he had sold his life to a corporation that could do nothing to save his soul. It was the last-breath comprehension of the devoted wife and mother that she had lived her entire life vicariously, through the accomplishments and failures of others. It was the lonely weeping of the film star or the well-loved novelist who understood only when it was too late that the adoration of others could do nothing to launch one's awareness across the abyss and into some inconceivable continuity of consciousness.

That scream was the final moment of awareness of The True Believer, the abrupt and unshakable realization that there was nothing out there in the darkness but darkness itself.

There were no gods and no devils waiting to harvest his soul, for ultimately it was the eye-opening, deathbed awareness that the soul itself does not and *cannot* exist unless one has devoted more than passing and passive interest to one's true identity – the *I-Am* that can only be made cohesive and viable by the real efforts of each and every individual human being.

It was, as simply as can be stated, the final moment of awareness that overcomes a consciousness just before that consciousness is brutally but impersonally snuffed out for good. It was the horror of finally understanding that no external force can offer salvation or damnation – but far worse than that, it was the moment of realizing that one's own life had been nothing more than a series of illusions piled one on top of the other like so many insulating blankets, none of them real, none of them having any meaning beyond the existence of their own self-contained play. And, finally, it was the horrific comprehension that one had willingly bought into that play, put on one's costume for the entirety of one's life, and had essentially done nothing more than recite the lines required by The Husband, The Father, The Wife, The Mother, The Daughter, The Son, The Christian or the Atheist, The Republican or The Democrat.

It was, in the end, the horror that resulted when one finally realizes one has been lied to, duped, misled, and literally programmed to serve the very social organism which perpetuates the *program* in the first place. And, most appalling of all, that final scream was the wail of understanding that one really wasn't a victim and never had been. It had always been a choice to live within the program or take the first step to start climbing outside of the comfortable consensus in an effort to get to know the consciousness that resides above and beyond the reflection in one's own mirror.

The scream, then, was the outraged despair of those who had never taken that step.

The struggle to *see* beyond the programs we have been fitted with merely by virtue of being human is the most difficult struggle one will ever undertake. By virtue of living in any society, certain beliefs are more or less automatic. Until fairly recently, if one lived in the United States, it was an automatic assumption that one was Christian and celebrated Christmas. Only within the past couple of decades do we begin to see Hanukah cards or Kwanzaa greetings, or any sort of acknowledgement that perhaps – just perhaps – there are belief systems that do not necessarily agree with our own intrinsic program. In short, we accept the reality with which we are presented. Simply by virtue of being human, for example, we accept that "all things die".

But instead of challenging that program, that belief system, we weave pretty fables within the belief system itself to offer comfort to ourselves. We weave tales of heaven and hell, and blame all our woes on the myth of Adam and Eve, never stopping to consider that each of us is Adam and each of us is Eve. We have free will, too, and we can choose to go on living in the blind ignorance of our fantasy garden, or we can take that forbidden fruit of real Knowledge and claim responsibility for our own deliverance from utter annihilation.

This path is Do-able, I thought, trying to find some hope, some comfort that didn't require blind faith in external forces. I thought of the experiences of the past few years, since Orlando's first letter showed up in November of 1994. The things I had learned weren't dependent on faith or any church or even on Orlando himself. What I knew, I knew from personal *experience* – the only real source of Knowledge.

All these thoughts went tumbling through my head as I sat there listening to that terrible, unending wail – that scream which was the inability to answer the first question – *"Who are you?"*

It was all the ugliness of the truth we choose to turn away from, and it was the reason for all the noise in the world – the noise we use to distract ourselves from hearing that scream, the inner dialogue we had instilled to keep ourselves forever deafened to that one hideous, horrible, inescapable truth that no one ever wanted to look at: our own *mortality*.

I did not want to believe it, for it meant having to accept complete and total responsibility for my own soul, my own continuity beyond death, my own answer to the first question. I wanted it to be otherwise. I wanted to believe in God or goodness or even evil, for any of those external forces would have offered an explanation that would have exonerated me from that responsibility for which there is no outline or set of instructions readily available.

When we drag ourselves beyond the programs and finally dare to look at the truth, the truth is that nature is a relentless but altogether impersonal bastard. We are born mortal and we will return to the dust if nature is allowed to take the path of least resistance. The only alternative to that is the one nature has provided. Evolution itself. Self-willed-boot-strap evolution.

But even that thought was too overwhelming that night overlooking the human world, because at that time I couldn't begin to fathom how to go about forging an *I-Am* identity that might have a chance of assembling itself into some form of ongoing cohesive sentience beyond my mortal death. I didn't even have the words at that time to formulate that concept, only a vague sense that there must be a way, but a lingering anger that it wasn't immediately and easily revealed to me. And so, for that reason alone – that I didn't know how to begin the real work – I wanted nothing more than to toss up a wall of stubborn denial and disbelief, fall right back into the consensual reality's program, and pretend like hell I never heard that scream at the edge of the world.

"Ah," Orlando sighed as if I had said something of great significance even though I never spoke out loud. "Now you're beginning to see how reality is really built. When the average man encounters something he doesn't want to believe, he will spare no expense of time, energy and money – even wars and blood – to spin a more palatable story in which he *does* want to believe. Why do you think there are so many religions in the world, so many different beliefs that are all just the same belief system re-dressed over and over again? More than a savior, Man's been looking for a scapegoat since he first crawled out of the primordial soup and reared up on his hind legs."

A satellite was passing overhead – a silent, lonely star with technological agendas I could not fathom. Orlando's words made me irritable, for the insinuation was that I was trying to toss up a wall of stubborn denial and disbelief and fall back into the consensual reality's program.

Silence fell between us, but I knew I would never hear the silence the same way again. I wanted to blame him for that. I scuffled my feet to interrupt that terrible screaming, but couldn't obliterate it. The screaming and the despair were like something out of Milton. The real Hell was that there was nothing and no one out there to blame. There was only life, death, and perception. No god. No devil. Not even good and evil, which are only willful manifestations of human Do-ings in the end.

I didn't like it one bit. Against the backdrop of the jagged, unforgiving terrain all around me, I was insignificant. Fragile. Out there in the desert alone at night, I could tumble off a cliff and break my neck, or simply drop dead of a stroke. And in the end, it wouldn't matter much. Not in the big picture, which was spread out before me – a blanket of stars dropped down over the Earth from light-years away. I was seeing the past in those stars – the light that I was perceiving having been transmitted years or even centuries in the past. Nothing was real. Not even time. For all I really knew, all the stars had already burned out.

"We talk about this evolution of consciousness all the time, Orlando. We talk about slipping past the *eagle* as if it's a given!" I finally said, not liking the complaining tone in my own voice, but unable to filter it out just then. "But the truth is that I don't know what to do or how to do it! My friends all think I'm certifiable, and half the time I don't even know who I am anymore!"

He was thoughtful for a moment, then I heard him sigh, a soft sound of amusement. "Good."

"Didn't you hear what I just said?" I sputtered, disbelieving. *"I don't know who I am!"*

"At least you now know who you are *not*," he replied, looking at me intently. "At least you have shed the false identities you spent the first forty years of your life trying on, yes?"

Not up to his scrutiny, I stood up and walked to the stone wall that marked the edge of the dirt path. Beyond it lay a series of rock formations and jagged cliffs, 6,000 feet of emptiness between me and the glistening lights spread out in the distant country club valleys below. Though it was August, a strong, cold wind drafted up from those forbidding rocks, whistling eerily through the crannies, momentarily obliterating that awful screaming silence.

I closed my eyes, taking a breath of the darkness and the night. A voice in my mind whispered, *"You can stay if you want."* The image that accompanied the invitation was an unformed idea of lingering like a ghost on that stone wall for all of eternity, watching the tourists come and go, listening to their conversations, tossing sand in their beer cans in the guise of the wind. It was an invitation that was both appealing and unnerving, for I wasn't at all sure what I was being offered.

I turned to say something to Orlando, but the bench was empty again. I thought I heard footsteps on the path leading back to the parking lot, but the only sign of movement was a lone coyote walking soundlessly down the road, a silver ghost in fading moonglow. For a single moment, the coyote turned and met my eyes, and there was something in his gaze – something haunted and hungry and real – something that told me he, too, heard the screams.

Chapter Two
Meeting the Mirror

All things exist within the realm of all possibility, but only some things will be forced to go through the motions of actually occurring.
Quantum Theory

WALKING BETWEEN THE WORLDS WITHOUT A NET

While Orlando was in manifestation on this Earth, we met him in person only a few times.

The first time I spoke with him was an unlikely setting in which to meet one's destiny – a post office in a small town in southern California. It was a morning like any other, early March of 1988. Nothing special. Nothing significant as I stood there at the counter in my ratty yin/yang t-shirt, hair uncombed, waiting for the postal clerk to process some packages. Perhaps I was mildly bored and dissatisfied with the direction my writing career was heading, yet I was content in other areas of my life – involved in a fulfilling relationship of long-standing with my significant other, Wendy.

It was only when I looked up to see this dark enigma at the next window that I entertained the immediate and unlikely thought, *"He's not human."* Without just cause, I was instantly terrified – for in retrospect, I believe I knew even then that I was standing at a crossroads which would forever alter the course of my life.

I could have turned and walked away, and maybe that would have been the end of it – an isolated incident I would have forgotten within a few hours. Instead, I found myself talking to him before I realized I had spoken. Only in hindsight could I see that I was compelled to speak to him *because* he was my teacher – not only that, but a great deal more, though I could not have known that at the time, and *had* I known, I would have turned and fled.

We spoke only briefly that first day, yet there was an unsettling familiarity – a *déjà vu* that was extremely unnerving to someone who had always been poised and self-confident even in the most extreme circumstances. What we talked about, I barely recall. Small-talk that wasn't small-talk at all. Every conversation with him always had the feeling of a zip-file – something that appeared light and manageable on the surface, but always seemed to have layers upon layers of encoding that could only be discovered in hindsight.

I left the post office feeling strangely disconnected. By the time I got home and told Wendy about the encounter, there was an uncharacteristic emptiness in the pit of my stomach. Though I had been in the middle of working enthusiastically on a novel, the words wouldn't come. I stared out the window most of the afternoon.

Even the purple jacaranda sweeping her branches across the neighbor's rooftop seemed to have a secret.

~

Over the next few weeks, I ran into Orlando around town several times. Casual, chance meetings. Or so it seemed. At first, I fought the sense of destiny that had begun to haunt both sleeping and waking hours. Without my knowledge or permission, he had already **hooked me with his will**, and though I might have howled with righteous indignation had I realized this at the time, in hindsight it is very clear that no other course of action was possible on his part or mine. We were both acting in accordance with our destiny – the Nagual man and Nagual woman – though he had the advantage of *knowing* that, whereas I had begun to feel as if I were on a roller coaster that was running headlong without a track.

It wasn't *what* he said, because sometimes he said very little. It was *him*. It was that indefinable something that I could not figure out – that something which would not yield to any attempts on my part to either seduce him or abandon him. I tried both. And both failed utterly. And all the while, he just kept being there with that quiet but dangerous smile that seemed to conceal some incredible mystery.

My ordinary, day-to-day life had been turned on its head. I couldn't eat, sleep or work. It wasn't love. It wasn't lust.

He had *possessed* me, yet it wasn't the typical manner of obsession a woman might have for a man. I didn't particularly want to bed him. More like I wanted to *be* him.

And *that* was a strange realization, since I have always liked who I am just fine.

Whenever I met Orlando, it was like looking into some warped funhouse mirror – seeing myself as I might have been had I been born in another place and time, another gender and another identity.

I had told Wendy of my initial encounter with Orlando at the post office, but she never met him until several weeks later. I had hoped she would take one look at him and pronounce that I was merely a foolish woman infatuated with a handsome man. But instead, without so much as a polite introduction, he hooked her with his will on their first encounter, just as he had done with me.

And then, instead of being my anchor to the real world, she became as hopelessly ensnared into the sorcerer's world as I had become.

Over the course of the next few weeks, he invited us to his home, where we began to first discover that this "man" was far more than we had first believed. He knew things about life. About the way the world is. About us. Sometimes, from one day to the next, he didn't even appear to be the same person. We joked that there were two of him. We speculated as to which one was the evil twin. We decided he could be an assassin, a fallen angel, a poet's muse, or even an immortal vampire. He was a contradiction and a mystery, a living enigma – and in hindsight, it is very clear to me that this was no accident.

This was the lure, the energetic hook. This was the Nagual man.

His name was not really Orlando, of course. I had toyed with the idea of calling him David or Marcus or even Bob – but in the long run, he chose the name Orlando for reasons he has never stated, though my suspicion is that it is a reference to a somewhat obscure movie by the same name – a Virginia Woolf novel about an immortal's journey through time, space, gender and identity.

~

The first time we visited Orlando at his home, he was wearing only a pair of shorts and a loose-fitting tank top when we arrived. The view was distracting. He had not known we were coming (at least not to our perceptions), as this had all been very casual. He let us in, offered us a drink. I accepted; Wendy declined. I've always suspected there was something in that drink – not some bogus mickey, but something of magic. Sorcery.

When he handed me the glass and our eyes met, his expression was one of amusement. "Jack Daniels and water, on the rocks," he said with a wicked smile. "A suicide."

I took the glass with as much bravado as I could muster. "The end of my world?" I asked, playing with him the way a child might unknowingly tease a coiled serpent.

He never hesitated. "Exactly."

So I drank it down, my mind flashing abruptly and without reason on the Baptist church I'd attended as a little girl and the weird rituals enacted on Sunday mornings with such solemnity. *This is the cup of my blood. Drink of it so you may never die.*

I never realized at the time what an appropriate analogy my mind was drawing – not in some quasi-religious sense, but far more literally than any priest or parishioner might imagine.

28

It was his Intent that we would eventually commit to the sorcerer's journey, and *because* he wasn't entirely human – because he had an agenda we would not understand for years to come, based on an energetic connection of Spirit that would take even longer to comprehend – it is clear in hindsight that he chose the form and the demeanor he knew would reel us in as surely as if the hook were sunk into flesh and bone. Looking back on it now, I have no doubt that he could just as easily have chosen the form of an old brujo in Mexico, or a homeless urchin on the streets of Athens.

He was exactly what I needed him to be – the embodiment of the mystery I had been chasing all my life. Maybe that should have been a warning.

As we sat there talking, he began asking the kinds of questions normally reserved for midnight meanderings between old friends. He pulled no punches, played no polite games, and showed no mercy.

"Who are you?" he wanted to know, looking at me with an intensity I could not recall ever having seen in another living being.

I started to respond with some pat rhetoric about how I was a professional writer, a martial artist, and so on, my *self-importance* running rampant at a time when I believed all of those things mattered.

But he shook his head as if not even listening, and held up one hand in a polite gesture meant to silence my inane prattle.

"That's not what I mean," he said very quietly. "I mean who are *you*? Who are you apart from what you do? Who is Della? Who is Wendy? Why are you here on Earth at this particular moment in time? What difference do you think it will make that you ever lived?"

I just sat there, dumfounded, for it suddenly hit me that I had no answers to his questions, no defenses against his psychic probe. In a matter of minutes, he had cut through the shielding I had spent a lifetime building. This was not how it was supposed to go, for I was used to being in control of any situation. I had bullshitted my way into high-paying jobs with no qualifications; I had left home at seventeen and made my way in the world because I had to; I had seduced virgins and concubines alike, and was used to having men eating out of my hand.

And yet, none of it mattered one iota – for Orlando had shown me in a matter of a few moments that my entire life had been an illusion, just a series of dramas played out by a series of actresses. All of them had been me, yet *none* of them were me. I could not have imagined how he accomplished such a drastic re-alignment of my perceptions in such a short span of time – and, indeed, to someone who has never experienced something of this magnitude, it may seem as if I'm rushing the story, omitting details, or simply making it up as I go along.

In matters of sorcery at this level, it must be noted that certain events appear to actually happen outside of time – in between tick and tock. At the time all of this was happening, it appeared to my **ordinary awareness** that perhaps only a few minutes or an hour had passed. And yet, even then, I could not deny the sense of *déjà vu* that seemed to follow Orlando like some mysterious vapor. I could not know at that time that there was a reason for this which defies traditional rationality, and delves straight into the realms of quantum ubiquitousness – where the self exists as a **singularity of consciousness** spanning the all of the space-time continuum and beyond.

Later, when I began reading the books of Carlos Castaneda and other texts on Toltec shamanism, and encountered the concept of **heightened awareness**, there was a sense of understanding exactly how Orlando had accomplished the task of cutting so quickly through my defenses, but at the time it was happening, all I can say is that it felt as if I had been picked up out of one life and instantaneously set down in the middle of a different one.

For the first time in my life, I was speechless.

This mysterious man was asking us to define the meaning of our human lives. And even though I was well educated in many aspects of metaphysics, I'd never really given a lot of thought to those meaning-of-life questions from a personal standpoint – only from a detached, academic perspective – words shoved inside the mouths of fictional characters who appeared at my beck and call on a monochrome green monitor, and could be silenced into oblivion with nothing more than a keystroke.

I fumbled. I squirmed. I tried to focus.

"All I've ever really known how to do is write," I said at last, though even as I spoke the words I could hear the actress in me – the character in her own drama who was always trying to impress someone else, or perhaps only herself. Having become intensely aware of it, I didn't like it, but there it was. All I could do was try to follow through – a rat running a familiar maze. "Maybe we're just here to create," I ventured. *That should impress him*, the internal dialogue commented from the sidelines. *Keep going!* "I mean – some people try to save the world with swords. Some try to do it with flowers in their hair. Hell, maybe I'll save the world with words!"

Bravo! Let him argue with that!

He didn't argue. He just sighed softly. "It's too late to save the world," he stated with a matter-of-factness that raised gooseflesh on my arms, for he spoke as if from personal knowledge rather than any ill-formed belief. "The world will fall – whether in a year or ten thousand years." He had stood up and begun to pace in front of the living room window – a silhouette backlit by a lamp in the corner. "Besides – the world as you're referring to it is an illusion anyway. The only thing you might be able to save is yourself."

Wendy caught my eye with a look that told me what I already knew. We were in over our heads. Indeed, what is so obvious to me now was so alien to me at the time that I could barely even fathom what Orlando was saying. The result was that I found myself becoming defensive – typical, pre-programmed response of my own self-importance, my own attachment to the programs I thought were real.

"Then what's the point of *any* of it?" I quipped, struggling to keep the sharp edge out of my voice.

Orlando stopped his pacing, and turned to regard me with a cobra's hypnotic gaze. "You have to *see* beyond the illusions before you can *be* beyond the illusions."

It was one of those enigmatic responses that made me want to avail myself of a dramatic and angry exit, yet something in the way he spoke those words told me that if I did, it would be over. He was trying to tell us something without coming out and saying it directly – and whatever it was inside of me that recognized Truth told me in no uncertain terms this was no game.

You have to see beyond the illusions before you can be beyond the illusions.

His words echoed in my ears, and again I caught Wendy's eye from across the room.

For a few minutes, we fumbled around in a miasma of words. We even tried double-teaming him in our efforts to convince him that there was meaning in life, purpose in creativity, and identity in what we did. But in the end, it was all just a bunch of self-indulgent clap-trap – and the mere act of attempting to verbalize those lies we all tell ourselves brought into an ever-increasing awareness the fact that they *were* lies. The illusion was right there in front of us and had been all along. But we kept right on preaching it, as if singing it into being would somehow make it real.

We were pathetic **phantoms**.

Orlando continued drinking his Jack Daniels, and watching us to see if we were capable of thinking or just babbling the rhetoric we thought we *should* say because it sounded good rolling off the tongue. Having run out of inventories of what I did, who I knew, what I wrote, or my favorite restaurants, in desperation I decided to try a different tact.

"Okay," I conceded. "Let's say you're right. It's all just illusion. What about the human spirit?" *Yeah!* the internal dialogue chimed in, my only cheering section. *When you can't dazzle him with brilliance, baffle him with bullshit!* Hmmm. I wasn't sure anymore just whose side she was on, but that didn't phase me as I ploughed ahead into a series of chaotic but, at the time, passionate thoughts. "What about people who can read the future? If it's all just dust in the wind and nothing we do here on Earth matters, what about people who claim to remember past lives? Doesn't that mean we go on – beyond this one single lifetime?"

His eyes narrowed a bit. He leaned forward in his chair, and I had the feeling he was studying me the way a serpent studies his prey. "I don't believe in all that psychic mumbo jumbo," he said after a thoughtful silence, surprising me as always with his directness that wasn't rude or inconsiderate, just brutally honest. "In fact, I went to see a psychic once – her name was Sonya Grey – but I didn't like what she was telling me, so I just threw the money on the table and left ."

He held my gaze with that same unwavering intensity as he said this; and even at the time, I had a reaction I could not quite put my finger on. A distant memory stirred – something I should remember, but couldn't quite grasp, like a dream from years in the past struggling to the surface, only to dart back into the shadows before it could be retrieved. For a single instant, everything stopped, and as I sat there sunken down deep into that plush white chair, the very fabric of time did a cartwheel that went into a backbend, then finally moved forward again like some deranged tumbling exercise. I had almost remembered… *something*. But… *what?*

The sensation was baffling, and sent another shiver racing down my back. Who *was* this man?

"So what was she telling you that you didn't want to hear?" Wendy asked boldly.

Orlando chuckled, then turned his intensity on her, leaving me to feel almost relieved. "That the world is made of illusions."

My head spun. I tried to blame it on the liquor. The internal dialogue had reverted to running inventories of the clothes in my closet, the items I needed at the store, what I had to do tomorrow.

It wasn't boredom.

It was fear. A sense of impending destiny.

I said nothing.

The conversation moved on, though I was in an almost trance-like state. By the end of the evening, we'd discussed everything from the fallacies of religion to the potential end of the world to the possible existence of an immortal soul. It was a blur of words, a cyclone of energy – and yet I found myself oddly detached from it all, like an observer lost in the balcony, a washed-up actress who had forgotten her lines.

In some secret, selfish little way, I had hoped Orlando would disappoint me. I had hoped he would open his mouth when we first came through the door that night, and say something stupid. I had fantasized that he might even revert to some crude posturing and suggest a *ménage a trois* – at which point I would have been validated in self-righteously pronouncing that he was just another typical male.

Instead, he was not only a gentleman, but a sage.

I was in serious trouble.

~

It was only when we got back to the house that I began to get unbidden images of an event which had occurred almost a year in the past. Just a glimpse at first. A few fleeting snippets of memory, cut at random from the scrapbook of my life.

And then, quite suddenly, it was all right there, tumbling out of the past like an avalanche that threatened to bury me under the implications.

In June of 1987 – almost exactly nine months before – Wendy and I had gone to the county fair with a good friend, Ellen. Throughout the day, we had been in high spirits; and, independently, each of us had noticed that there was "something in the air," though none of us spoke of it until later in the afternoon. We referred to it at the time as a feeling that something was going to happen – something mysterious and wonderful and potentially life-altering.

And yet, even at the time, I couldn't help secretly believing I was just engaging in wishful thinking. Though I had experienced the mysterious many times in my life, I was at a crossroads where that excitement had begun to give way to a sense of sameness, perhaps even the onset of a frustration for which I had no explanation. Even in my satisfaction with life, I was restless, and so the feeling that overcame the three of us that day was one to which I was almost afraid to surrender.

In one way or another, I had been chasing ghosts and walking on the razor's edge of the nagual all my life – yet whenever it seemed I was about to catch the muse, tackle the mystery, get my hands on the pulsing artery of the unknown, it would always slip away, back into the shadows, always one step ahead, one step out of reach.

My mother's voice echoed in my mind: *"Sometimes you have to be satisfied with the cards you're dealt. Don't get your hopes up too high. Otherwise you're just setting yourself up for disappointment."*

Not a philosophy I would choose to live by, yet I wondered fleetingly if I *had* begun to live in fear, refusing to open myself to the mysterious and magical unknown because of some pre-conceived conclusion that it would *always* remain one step out of reach. I focused again on the memory that was struggling to surface, something about that day at the fair almost a year in the past.

That evening, just before we were going to leave the fairgrounds, we scouted out something to eat. Fried something-or-other, with enough cholesterol to block every major artery on the spot. The sun had finally set, leaving the western horizon an abstract watercolor of purples, pinks and sea-grey. Somewhere in the distance, steel drums clattered an eerie rendition of *Stairway to Heaven* while screams from the midway echoed off of aging cinder-block buildings badly in need of paint.

Sitting at a wooden picnic table, we ate in silence, each of us lost in thought. Even though the day was almost done, the feeling that there was something magical in the air lingered. I wanted to hold my breath, to make the day go on just a little longer.

I was hungry for something back then – hungry for that head-on collision with the nagual that never seemed to come. I would have danced naked on Hollywood Boulevard if I'd thought it would open that door.

Only after a few minutes did I realize I had been staring fixedly at a colorful tent at the perimeter of the outdoor dining area. Though there were other vendor displays, this one seemed to stand out, to the point that I was silently, unknowingly mesmerized. My dinner was gone, though I had no memory of eating.

I had been staring absent-mindedly at three people in the crowd – a young couple in their late 20s, and the man accompanying them. Without my conscious awareness, this man had held my attention for a full minute before I ever realized I was watching him. At least 6'4"; raven black hair a couple of inches over the collar; 5 o'clock shadow that gave him the outward appearance of a dangerous rogue; and dark glasses even though the sun was only a fading memory in the west.

At this time in my life, even though Wendy and I had been together as a couple for almost nine years, I still enjoyed looking at handsome men. So did she, for that matter. So I nudged her with my foot and nodded toward the human enigma standing in front of the pretty tent. Catching my eye, she grinned, and I realized that she had been watching him, too, even before I pointed him out. That was his nature – to command the attention of a room just by virtue of his existence.

The couple became preoccupied at a jewelry display, at which point the enigmatic man walked inside the colorful tent and appeared to be talking to someone seated behind a desk. As it was almost night, I could see candles burning inside. The setting was oddly alluring. Unexpectedly magical. His face was a study in angles and shadows, flame-glow and curiosity. He stood there for only a few moments. Then, reaching for his wallet, he pulled out a couple of bills, tossed them onto the desk, and hastily left.

I thought very little of it at the time.

He caught up to the young couple, the three of them disappeared into an exhibit hall, and that was the end of that…

…until, nine months later, after that evening in Orlando's house, when I abruptly knew what it was I had been struggling to remember.

The inscription on the side of that tent had read:

Psychic Readings by Lady Sonya Grey

When that memory came flooding back, when I realized Orlando must have been intentionally baiting me with a forgotten incident nearly a year in the past – an incident that had taken place at one isolated moment in the course of an event that hosts well over a million people during its 2+ week run at the fairgrounds – I literally sat on the edge of the bed in a state of bewilderment and shock.

To the casual observer, it could be easily explained away. Coincidence. Synchronicity. Delusion.

And yet, on a level of pure intuition, I knew it was no mere happenso. Tumblers clicked. There was a reason I had had such a strong reaction to Orlando at the post office the day I first met him.

He isn't human. Those words rattled through my mind over and over as I sat there with the jagged pieces of a complex puzzle in my hand, not knowing what to do with them, not even knowing if all the pieces I was holding went to the same puzzle.

You have to <u>see</u> beyond the illusions before you can <u>be</u> beyond the illusions.

That was the night my life changed forever.

~

Any rational being can easily explain away the events I am attempting to describe. To anyone else, perhaps the anecdote of my initial encounters with Orlando is nothing more than a report of an ordinary event blown out of proportion.

And yet, that is the preferred defense system of the consensual agreement. Literally *anything* can be explained away if that is the intent of the perceiver – and it is no coincidence that the agreement itself is set up in such a fashion as to maintain its own status quo. It is designed to protect itself from change through a complex system of denial, stasis, and the ongoing spiritual bankruptcy of its inhabitants.

Shamans, mystics and sorcerers have known this for centuries, so it stands to reason they have been among the most persecuted individuals in a long and bloody human history. That which does not support the status quo threatens it.

You will sleep better if you close this book right now and tell yourself that the author is clearly mad and the tales she is telling are only fabrications or exaggerations of otherwise ordinary events.

The other amusing thing is that the nagual itself occasionally aids and abets the very consensual reality to which it exists as antithesis. It stands to reason, therefore, that Carlos Castaneda was never able to produce the mysterious don Juan; no UFO has ever landed on the White House lawn to be photographed by zealous paparazzi; and I can no more prove my story in a court of law than I could sprout wings and fly.

And yet…

This isn't a tale of faith. To those who have taken this journey for themselves, the bizarre machinations of the sorcerer's double are legendary, and perhaps even obvious. To the uninformed – even those who may be yearning to embark on a spiritual path – those machinations will appear bizarre, frightening, and perhaps even cause the seeker to question her own sanity.

This is the first test.

Chapter Three
Memories That Never Happened

Wendy and I continued meeting with Orlando for approximately the next three years – always intermittently, never when we might have expected, and often under unusual circumstances. His house often stood empty; and if asked where he had been, he would simply say he had been away on business, or out of town. Sometimes his absences lasted weeks, other times months.

I cannot say that he ever attempted to teach us anything directly. Quite the contrary – our conversations were often mundane, or so it seemed at the time; yet there continued to be some inexplicable sense of destiny where he was concerned. Sometimes I would look at him and almost-remember something – not unlike how I had felt that night in his house when I was *almost-remembering* the first time I had seen him at the fair, nine months before we actually met. And yet, it was different, too. The almost-remembering seemed to be connected to some otherworld – like trying to remember a dream that refused to yield itself up to scrutiny.

What was also odd is that our lives had begun to take a turn we were not consciously aware of while it was occurring. Both Wendy and I were aspiring fiction writers – indeed, I had already sold one professional novel at the time, which should have been a strong foot in the door – but where there had been a lot of promise and possibility in the past, now there was only rejection and a steadily declining income as the internet began replacing the printed word, and the entire publishing industry was turned upside down in a spiral of uncertainty.

Realizing at last what was happening, I invested my time and energy in pursuing a career in real estate, and was relatively successful in it – for the three or four months it lasted. To the surprise of the nation, the California real estate market crashed virtually overnight, and suddenly my license wasn't worth the paper on which it was printed.

I hung on with it for a few more months, though, and as a result, a series of events came close to handing me the corner piece of the Orlando puzzle, yet at the time I simply did not have enough of the *other* pieces to make sense of it.

In the course of my agenting, I was showing properties to Ellen around April of 1990. One house in particular seemed promising, and when we pulled up in front of it, both of us remarked that it felt familiar.

The layout was unusual – a U-shaped home built around a central courtyard where a large swimming pool was located. Because of the design, one could look out virtually any window, across the courtyard, and see into other rooms of the house. Out the back, a game room had been added on after the original structure was built, so there was virtually no yard. As a result, the ascending hillside, covered in ice-plant, formed an earthen wall at the rear of the house, which added to the overall claustrophobic feeling.

When I showed Ellen the property, there was still a small amount of furniture and personal effects present, but it was obvious the owners were already in the process of vacating. We spent a reasonable amount of time there that day, with Ellen attempting to determine if she could make it work in accordance with her own visions. In the end, she decided against it, and we left without so much as a backward glance.

It wasn't until years later – almost 12 years, to be precise – that we came to understand the significance that house had had in our lives. To someone outside the world of sorcery, what follows will undoubtedly sound like the machinations of a madwoman. And yet, to deny that it happened would only perpetuate the illusions of the consensual agreement.

It was sometime in 2001 when I was listening to a CD I'd just bought entitled _The Mask & the Mirror_ (Loreena McKennitt), and as _Marakesh Night Song_ began to play, I found myself transported abruptly to a memory of that unusual house I had shown to Ellen all those years in the past.

In this sudden memory flash, I *saw* myself, Ellen and Wendy in that house – with Orlando. The four of us were sitting on the floor of the master bedroom; the room was completely devoid of furniture now, and had the scent of having been recently cleaned. I had the Knowledge that the home was unoccupied, the owners had moved, but the house itself was being used in what I can only think of as second attention – very much like Carlos Castaneda describes "quasi-memories of the other self" with regard to when he was beginning to recall incidents that took place in heightened awareness.

In this memory, *Marakesh Night Song* was playing throughout the house, and my impression was that the people in the house were other apprentices, though at the time I would not have thought of myself in that fashion whatsoever; for as I have already mentioned, Orlando never attempted to teach us anything directly while in ordinary awareness.

At one point in the song, there are lyrics which read, *"Don't you like my mask? Don't you like my mirror?"* So as I was listening to that song on the CD for the first time in 2001 (at least to my linear perceptions), I was quite literally bowled over by the super-imposed memory of Orlando, in what could have been no later than 1991, placing his hand in front of his face, peeking through his fingers as he drew his hand dramatically aside, mime-fashion, and lip-syncing those lyrics: *"Don't you like my mask? Don't you like my mirror?"*

Words cannot possibly convey this sequence of events with the sheer force of power that I experienced. The song in question was not even written when I had shown Ellen the house in linear time (circa 1990). And the visions that accompanied the song were so intensely powerful that there is no doubt in my mind they are not the result of mere wishful thinking.

This was not a daydream. This was not the memory of a dream. Instead, it played in precisely the same way any other real memory plays – and that reality has not diminished with the passing of time. It *happened*, and the fact that I cannot explain rationally how it occurred in any linear fashion does not alter the fact that it nonetheless did occur in the realm sorcerers refer to as heightened awareness.

Indeed, I was so affected by this incident that I called Ellen and asked if she had any particular memories of that house. Though I was expecting nothing, she began talking about a vague memory of attending a party there, and began describing in detail a galvanized wash tub in the kitchen, filled with half-melted ice and soft drinks. Other people milling around the house. Some were wearing masks. Like a Halloween party, she speculated.

As soon as she mentioned the galvanized wash tub, my mind instantly locked onto it, and I remembered reaching in to pull out a Diet 7-Up. The cold water on my arm. The wet silver-white can. The laughter from the den, where a group of people had gathered.

And Orlando waiting in the master bedroom.

Wendy was standing off to the side, and seemed almost dazed. In the shadows just off the kitchen, two people I did not know talked in quiet tones, away from the crowd. When I returned to the master bedroom, the freshly-shampooed grey carpet was coarse and rough as I sat on the floor and leaned my back against the beige wall. Ellen laughing. Wendy leaning against Orlando, relaxed, comfortable.

Ellen's memories of the incident stunned me, for they meshed precisely with my own – which, in ordinary awareness, would appear to be impossible, since the event in question never happened in what we traditionally think of as "the real world."

And yet…

It *did* happen. Somewhere. Somewhen.

When I asked Wendy about the incident, her recollections were not as sharp as Ellen's, though she did have some hazy memories of a Halloween party in that strange house – a house she never visited in first attention at all, for she hadn't gone along when I showed the house to Ellen in a professional capacity. And yet, she, too, described the layout as if she had been there a hundred times.

It would be impossible to explain what has apparently happened to so many of us over the years. We can call it missing time, or heightened awareness. We can call it quasi-memories of the otherSelf. But whatever we call it, it is important to realize that these are not the products of our imagination, nor some glitch in the memory function of the brain, as some psychologists might have us believe. These are very real events – whether they occur in ordinary awareness, heightened awareness, or in *Dreaming* – and at times, if we are fortunate, we may be able to validate them through our connections to other warriors, just as I was able to validate with Ellen and Wendy the memory of that strange house and that extremely meaningful song echoing eerily through the crack between the worlds.

~

It was around 1990 that I began reading *The Teachings of Don Juan.* Despite the controversy that has raged about Castaneda for decades, I found the books to be eye-opening, and the parallels to my own life uncanny at times. As I would be reading something in one of the books, it would happen in my own life. More than once.

When first reading Castaneda, I actually thought for a long time that he was making it all up with regard to heightened awareness – it seemed somehow convenient to suddenly say, "Oh, by the way, I just happened to remember some more adventures with don Juan."

But now, in light of my own events, and my own quasi-memories of the otherSelf, I have no doubt that the events he was describing were altogether true, to the best of his ability to relate them. Words simply cannot contain the nagual, yet the nagual continues to exist in defiance of words.

In hindsight, it's clear that the nagual was trying to reveal itself to me, but it was hiding in plain sight. And, quite honestly, I wouldn't have known what to do with it at that time in my life even if I had managed to grab a hold of it.

Everything seemed to be crumbling around us. Our writing careers had taken a dark turn. The promising real estate career lay dead at my feet. The Midas touch I had possessed all my life had turned to dust.

And then came the day when I drove past Orlando's house and noticed the FOR SALE sign displayed prominently in the yard.

Chapter Four
The Crystal and the Nagual

What was it about the post office?

It was there that I first met Orlando, and there I was destined to speak with him in the corporeal world for the last time. I had not seen him since his house went up for sale – perhaps six months or so previously.

I must reiterate that I did not know then what I have come to know since. I did not know Orlando was the Nagual man. I did not know that I am the Nagual woman. And I couldn't have known then that these two beings are *literally* halves of a whole – not in any petty romantic sense, but in that they are mirror images of one another on the energetic plane. In shamanic terms, I was not only facing the other half of myself, but as I have since come to discover, I was also facing my own double, and it was probably only my ignorant naiveté that saved my life that day.

> *"No sorcerer knows where his Other is. A sorcerer has no notion that he is in two places at once. To be aware of that would be the equivalent of facing his double, and the sorcerer that finds himself face to face with himself is a dead sorcerer. That is the rule. That is the way power has set things up. No one knows why."*
> - Carlos Castaneda - Tales of Power

It was late June of 1991 when Wendy, Ellen and I were once again on our way to the county fair – exactly four years to the day since I had first seen a dark stranger enter a psychic's colorful tent at dusk, exactly four years to the day since my ordinary life had been turned on its ear. My mood was darker than it had been four years before – without that impending sense of wonder which had been so prevalent in the past.

I wondered fleetingly if I were just going through the motions, going to the fair because it was what we always did. The magic was somewhere in the past or the future. Without having the words for it at the time, my world had turned to folly, and the result was that I felt displaced even from myself. The immortality of youth was fading, but I had not yet replaced it with anything, for I was still skating on the edge of believing I had all the time in the world, yet beginning to intuit that life itself was somehow eluding me.

It was, in hindsight, the beginning of *Seeing*, the onset of *clarity*. And in all likelihood, it is what was responsible for the events that occurred that day.

The weather was hot, the sun unnaturally bright, reflecting off the silvery marine layer common to the coastal area of San Diego. We left the house around 10 a.m., but had to stop at the post office on the way out of town. As far as I knew, Orlando had already been gone for quite some time, having simply disappeared out of that small town as mysteriously as he had first appeared; and in many ways, I had honestly believed I would never see him again. It was almost a relief.

But as we pulled into the parking lot and I saw him standing in the outdoor courtyard of the post office, my heart jumped instantly in my chest, because as much as I admired and respected this enigmatic being, I had also become strangely afraid of him, for history had proven that any time we met, I would find myself unsettled for days or even weeks to come. From a vantage point well into the future, it's now possible to determine that this sense of unrest was undoubtedly caused by the shifts in my awareness which occurred whenever we came into contact – an actual movement of the *assemblage point* from its normal location (the awareness of everyday affairs) to heightened awareness.

Now, several years later, I am not certain if the shift of awareness was facilitated by Orlando, or if I had learned the technique and automatically shifted into heightened awareness whenever we met. In the long run it might not matter except as a matter of curiosity – for the results were the same.

I am often asked by skeptics and new warriors alike, what would be the purpose of such a shift. Quite simple: from the assemblage point of heightened awareness, we do not fight ourselves. In dreams, we do not question that we can fly, or communicate telepathically, or read with our eyes closed. We simply do it. So there is very good reason for a Nagual to shift the attention of his or her apprentices into that state. Not only does it become possible for the apprentice to learn and absorb concepts far more quickly, it also affords the apprentice the opportunity to work directly with the same type of awareness commonly associated with Dreaming. Instead of the automatic response of, "That can't be done!" the manipulation of creative energy is second nature – and learning to control that energy at will is what gives the sorcerer her ability to create and ultimately manifest the double: the energy body as an immortal construct, existing outside of time.

Why create the double at all?

And again, the answer is obvious to one who *sees*.

The shaman's double is the shaman in eternity – it is the immortal construct comprised of pure energy, capable of housing and maintaining the unique *I-Am* even beyond the threshold of death itself.

The problem is that when we return to our ordinary state of awareness, we cannot remember the majority of events which took place in heightened awareness. At first, this seemed ludicrous to me. Impossible. And yet, when it was pointed out that we have literally dozens of dreams every single night, and might remember only fragments of one or two, it became possible to understand how time spent in heightened awareness can be entirely evasive to our ordinary memory/perception.

Indeed, it is only through a painstaking process known as *remembering the other self* that we might begin to recapture those memories at all. In ordinary awareness, we simply do not possess the preceptor organs of memory for events that occurred in heightened awareness – in much the same way that we cannot see the sub-atomic universes with the naked eye, but we can learn to see them through the use of special tools. In the case of remembering the other self, those special tools are the tools of perception.

~

To this day, more than twenty years after the incident I am going to describe, I am still unraveling and reconnecting to events that occurred while in heightened awareness.

What I did not know that day in 1991 was that Orlando was indeed a master sorcerer, and a great deal more. All I knew then was that there was some connection between us – not only myself, but Wendy and Ellen as well. And so when I saw him standing there in the courtyard, I was inundated with a flood of perceptions that I could not explain or even understand. Looking at him from a distance, the same words that had come to me when I first saw him repeated in my mind: *He's not human.*

I had come full circle. Except now, instead of only believing those words to be true, I *knew* them to be true on a level of gnostic certainty that defies conventional explanation.

It occurred to me that I had nothing to say to him. Obviously, I told myself with no small amount of self-importance, he was in the process of selling his home and moving out of the area. If he had wanted to talk to us about it, he knew where we lived. Yet he had said nothing.

I looked away, unable to bear the sight of him, for one thing hadn't changed since it all began. Every time I laid eyes on him, it was like looking into some dark, masculine mirror of the spirit. In many ways, I had already dealt with the idea of losing him – though losing *what* I couldn't have said. Our relationship had never been anything more than casual, and at the time this incident took place, I had no inkling whatsoever of the events and interactions which had occurred in heightened awareness.

I felt like a befuddled schoolgirl with a crush on a teacher who had never given her a second glance. And for that reason alone, I made the firm decision to simply stay in the car, and ignore the son of a bitch altogether.

And yet... As if observing from a distance, I saw myself opening the door and walking toward him.

Despite my fear, like a moth to flame I was drawn to explore the light he exuded. Not the bright, blinding light so often spoken of in airy-fairy new age books, but instead his luminous form was one of black light – subtle, unearthly, a dark light beneath the surface that illuminates those who are compatible with its properties, just as a black light selectively illuminates objects in a room while leaving others unchanged. As was typical with him, he did not appear the same as he had on our last meeting.

In hindsight, to say there were two of him would be to limit what he is, what we are *all* capable of being. He is an eternal being with an infinite number of possibilities, no longer confined by the constraints of the space/time continuum. All of us have that potential. He could just as easily have appeared as a woman, a boy, or a coyote. The familiar form was for our benefit – perhaps an energetic construct he had created, or perhaps an actual human form he had borrowed on and off over the years.

Skinwalker, the voice of gnosis whispered.

At the time, I didn't understand the reference, but years later, I would discover that a skinwalker is a shaman who may borrow another's form for the purpose of walking briefly in the human world.

Undoubtedly, in addition to everything else he may have been, Orlando was also a skinwalker.

For reasons of her own, which she later related as simply shock at seeing him there, combined with her own fears, Wendy went on inside the post office to conduct her business, never speaking to him at all that day. Ellen was standing off to the side, a silent observer, and when I questioned her about the event years later, she could only say, "I *couldn't* go near him. This was always how it was with him, every time I saw him. I knew he would see through me and I wasn't ready to deal with that. It wasn't him I was afraid of. It was myself."

Having no such common sense, I approached him alone, in a state of dead calm.

We spoke briefly, mainly small-talk, and though I could not determine why, I read him as oddly nervous, even anxious. At this point, he had been in and out of our lives in a rather mysterious fashion for about three or four years, and had been very instrumental in changing the way we thought about life. In short, he had started us on the path, without ever taking any direct action to do so. He had done nothing specific – no teachings, no lectures – other than speak in plain, direct terms about how the world in which we live is largely an illusion, and the programs that drive the majority of human beings are little more than scripts placed on them from the moment of birth.

"We're prisoners of our own delusions," he once told us. "And the worst delusion of all is that humans believe they're already free. That's what keeps people chained to their jobs, their ideas about family, society, life and the world. As long as they think they're already free, they remain blind and subservient to the prison. It's a flawless trap."

I recalled our first conversation about the state of the world, and my naive comment that I hoped it wasn't too late to save the planet. Now his words came back to me. *The only thing you might be able to save is yourself.*

I hadn't understood at the time. But I had been haunted by the implications that there was no external salvation, Orlando's seeming Knowledge that, one day, whether in a hundred years or a hundred million years, even the planet would be laid to waste – if not by the designs and devices of humans, then certainly by some wayward asteroid. It was inevitable. And it didn't seem to bother him in the least.

As we spoke there in the outer courtyard of the post office with these thoughts running through my head, I began to feel physically shaky, a sensation of dizziness, weakness in the legs, slightly blurred vision. This was not a typical reaction for me, even in the presence of someone I had pre-determined to be "not human". Curiosity has always driven me – an intense need to interact with the unknown, embracing it wholly.

Our meeting was – to my perceptions that day – unexpected, casual, but friendly. And yet, I cannot deny that there was an underlying sense of fear and trepidation even as we stood in the shadows of the building, discussing such mundane topics as remodeling, real estate news, the growth of the small town in which we both lived. Nothing of significance. And yet, just below the surface, an entire universe of energy was seething.

It was as if two separate events were occurring at precisely the same time, yet only one was accessible to my ordinary perceptions. On the surface, just a mundane conversation that would be quickly forgotten. But at the same time, some incredible event for which neither science nor mysticism has any easy answers.

It was palpable, a living force that thrummed like a heartbeat, and pounded at my senses with all the force of a hurricane. I felt it, but instinctively denied it, trying to tell myself to keep it light, and all the other yammerings of the internal dialogue that are so often our undoing.

On the outside, I was entirely calm. But on the inside, all I had known about the world was coming apart in a maelstrom of energy that was destruction and creation at exactly the same moment. But like a caveman witnessing a rocket launch, I had no concept at all of *what* I was experiencing.

We spoke for about five minutes, at which point Orlando simply returned to his car and drove away. When he left, it all felt rather anti-climactic.

And yet, by the time I returned to our car, I could barely stand. My body was shaking to the extent that it was like a mild form of convulsions. And again that haunting thought which I had entertained upon first seeing him years before whispered through my mind: *He's not human.* The contact I had had with him over the three-year interim had done nothing to convince me otherwise. And the physical reaction I had to him that day could only reinforce those words with a terrible presence of foreboding, finality and even grief which I could not begin to comprehend.

Completely in contradiction to my nature, I wanted to weep, for it felt as if my very soul had been torn out of my body and scattered like ashes on the wind.

~

Wendy, Ellen and I continued on to the fairgrounds amidst a flurry of conversation, though I noticed that I was removed from it, detached, almost floating outside the car, a passive observer. I cannot stress strongly enough the profundity of the reaction I had to this encounter, and yet it had all seemed so completely normal.

By the time we reached the fairgrounds nearly an hour later, I was feeling somewhat better, though remained in an uncharacteristic daze as we walked around. The trinkets that had once thrilled me seemed rusted and faded. Meaningless.

53

The elaborate flower gardens in the exhibit halls failed to inspire me. The carnys on the midway appeared older, more haggard, and had lost their dark-edged mystique.

It was when I was sitting across from Wendy at lunch that she looked at me very strangely and inquired, "Did you buy a new crystal?"

I had been in the habit of wearing a blue agate cut into the shape of a crystal point – not for any reason, other than that it was a pleasant color and shape, and I had bought it at the fair the year before. But when I glanced down, instead of its usual bright turquoise blue, it had turned a faded, muddy brown. Since this was a semi-transparent stone, we could see that even the deeper veins of agate had been affected, so profoundly changed that it was barely recognizable, only a few scant traces of blue.

I could only stare at the stone in disbelief, at first not making the connection to my encounter with Orlando. It seemed that some incredible burst of energy had actually altered the stone down to a molecular level – *while* it was around my neck. I had felt the effects of this, quite obviously, but did not perceive it directly, except through the reactions in my body.

The rest of the day passed as if in a shallow sleep, a hollow dream.

~

Even though I stated at the beginning of this chapter that the encounter at the post office was our final meeting with Orlando on the corporeal plane, that is both true and untrue. The next day, we crossed paths with Orlando for what would turn out to be the last time, and the unnerving thing was that he did not appear to know us in the least. This was not some act or game, but a literal "blankness" that has haunted us ever since, as if the spirit that had inhabited the body had simply departed. The incident occurred in a crowded restaurant, and though he was jovial and friendly with others, there was simply no thread of recognition toward any of the three of us. When our eyes met, I knew I was looking into the face of a stranger.

Orlando was gone.

What remained was a corporeal vessel belonging to another man, a mortal human being who clearly had no memory of any of it.

It was only much later that Wendy and I recalled an odd statement he had made to us shortly after we first met in 1988.

"One day I'll be rude to you," he had said, standing in the driveway of his modest home, backlit by the dusky California twilight. Dark glasses had obscured his eyes that day, even though the sun had long since set. The 5 o'clock shadow gave him the appearance of a handsome pirate, an unpredictable rogue, perhaps even one of Anne Rice's vampires. No, he wasn't human. And I was destined to encounter the evidence of it at the post office during our final encounter, as well as when we saw him at the restaurant the next day.

"Why would you be rude to us?" Wendy asked him, all those years in the past.

It seemed he never heard her. "One day I'll be rude to you," he repeated. Then, with even greater emphasis, his voice softened, almost a whisper, fervent. "Don't take it personally. Don't *ever* take it personally."

He never explained his statement beyond that, though his words had given me chills even as he spoke them – as if he were privy to some knowledge about the future that no one else could know. And yet, when we remembered those words after the incident at the restaurant, it all seemed to make as much sense as is possible in matters of sorcery.

If he was the manifestation of Nagual man, he undoubtedly knew it, and had long since accepted his fate. He knew he would leave the world in the manner of a sorcerer, and to those unfamiliar with matters of sorcery, there can simply be no linear, rational explanation of what that means. Even as he told us in 1988 that he would one day be rude to us, it is my belief he already had knowledge of exactly where the future would lead him. And now, more than ten years later, it is extremely clear to me that any eternal being who exists technically outside of time, also exists within *all* of time. Past, present and future would be equally accessible. He didn't just *seem* to know the future. He *did* know the future.

And, of course, none of this can even seem possible to a properly programmed rational mind. It can only be reported in the same manner alien abductions or sightings of bigfoot are reported. Such is the manner in which the consensus reality maintains and safeguards its status quo. These things are not part of our ordinary reality, and so we are programmed to the deepest levels to simply dismiss them.

~

Clearly, something incredible happened during my final conversation with Orlando, some massive rearrangement of reality on a level of which perhaps only the *allies* are capable. And if I didn't have witnesses to this, I wouldn't have believed it myself.

That night after the fair, I took the crystal off and placed it in a medicine pouch that was always with me. Over the next few months, I would occasionally take it out to examine it or show it to friends while relating this strange tale of power, and the startling thing was that it was beginning to "heal" – the brown discoloration was slowly returning to blue. This, of course, is also supposedly impossible, or at the very least, extremely unlikely, even according to a quantum engineer from whom I have learned a great deal about the workings of consciousness and energy.

When about eleven months had passed, I went to look at the crystal one day. Every other item from the medicine bag was still safely inside, yet the crystal was missing and has not been seen since.

As to what all of this means?

It is my opinion that Castaneda left much unsaid, either intentionally or because the Knowledge had not yet become available to him. What he did not say is that the Nagual man and the Nagual woman are *literally* two halves of a whole, unlike any other being on Earth, as I will attempt to explain later in this book . And when one half leaves the world of ordinary awareness, the sense of tearing away is as much physical as emotional. It can leave evidence in the form of altered crystals... which, of course, are probably destined to disappear.

It was in November of 1994 that we began receiving letters from Orlando, and the path re-opened to consume us completely. But I have never seen him physically since that day when the crystal turned from blue to brown, when the world turned wrong-side out and everything I thought I knew about reality was obliterated completely.

It was that day that the **Rule of the Nagual** was set in motion in my life, and I do not believe I will see Orlando again until I have also passed beyond the Eagle to embrace the totality of myself. And, of course, when we do meet again, I have little doubt that he will be standing there in the middle of all Eternity, in the heart of Infinity, holding that crystal in his hand.

Question & Answer

One advantage of having a website and online forum is that I am often asked some very difficult questions which really force me to think – particularly with regard to the topic of Orlando, the Nagual man and Nagual woman, and the sorcerer's double.

~

QUESTION: *Why were you able to associate with Orlando for three years without any apparent conflict? Why do you think you had such a serious physical reaction when you saw him for the last time at the post office? Why did the crystal go dark on that day?*

ANSWER: There is some significant truth to the old adage, "Ignorance is bliss". At the very least, in the sorcerer's world, ignorance can be a form of protection. Until the warrior achieves a certain level of awareness, she is functioning more or less on a level of innocence – more accurately, a level of fragmentation where perception simply doesn't allow the warrior to see the dangers all around. But when the warrior begins to open her eyes and realizes even minimally that something very strange seems to be happening, it is in that moment that one loses one's innocence. My perception, all these years later, is that it was on that day I first began to really open my eyes. I *saw* Orlando, and that act alone was sufficient to change everything. For once I *saw* him in the sense that a sorcerer *sees*, he became the Nagual man in a single, blinding instant of transformation. To an ordinary human being, these are only words, meaning nothing.

QUESTION: *You said in The Crystal and the Nagual that you were facing your own double and the other half of yourself. Is there a difference?*

ANSWER: The answer to this question would fill an entire book all on its own. Essentially, however, it could be said that any warrior can develop a double, and yet not all warriors are Naguals (double-beings). The warrior's double can take on any manifestation; it may look like the warrior herself, or a coyote or a bird. The *double being* (the Nagual) is simply born as such, and her doubleness is an attribute like blonde hair or green eyes. The double-being is usually (from my experience) experienced as a literal "opposite" – in the sense that "opposites attract". Male to female, dark to light, yin to yang, and so on. There may be exceptions to this, as I can only speak from my own foundation of Knowledge.

QUESTION: *Why do you think you had such a painful physical reaction to all of this Has it occurred to you that maybe Orlando was evil and the crystal protected you?*

ANSWER: I thought about that, for all of about ten seconds. So much of this is simply impossible to discuss within the parameters of words alone. To the warrior who *sees*, no explanation is needed. But to answer your question, my physical weakness and shakiness were the result of an energetic tearing away of the other half of myself. I have no doubt in hindsight that when we met that day, Orlando had already known I would be coming there, and he was simply waiting for me to arrive, as had often been the case in the past.

The difference was that I had lost my innocence, so to speak. I had begun to *see* at a rudimentary level, and the result was that we could no longer be in the same world for the same reason that no sorcerer can face his double. The instinct to reconjoin on the level of energy – to create the singularity of consciousness, in other words – would simply be overpowering, and yet evolution would be thwarted if that reconjoining were to occur prematurely. There was still too much to learn. Orlando recognized this that day, and it was at that moment that the rule of the nagual was set in motion. To

59

my physical eyes, he simply walked away. But had a more experienced Seer been present, it could have been observed that Orlando left the world in that moment, **burning with the fire from within**. The force of that energy is what I experienced, as well as what undoubtedly caused the agate to turn dark.

QUESTION: *You said that when you saw Orlando at the restaurant the day after the post office incident, he didn't seem to know you. Two questions: 1) Why? and 2)If he burned with the fire from within, how was he still walking around?*

ANSWER: He didn't know us because the entire consciousness that was Orlando was gone, probably from the moment he walked back to his car at the post office. As for the second question, a master sorcerer can attach his consciousness to anyone at any time, particularly if that person is distracted or not particularly awake spiritually. It's called a walk-in, or a skinwalker. When the sorcerer removes his consciousness from that body, in most cases the person has no recollection of what just happened, because in that case, the memories belong to the *consciousness*, not to the physical body. The body can be used much like a radio – tuned to a specific frequency determined by consciousness. The radio itself has no awareness of what stations it might play during the course of its day. It is only a conduit.

QUESTION: *Are you or were you ever aware directly of Orlando's thoughts? Is he a metaphor for your alter-ego, or does he have his own life?*

ANSWER: He is most definitely not a metaphor. The double being is very real, and from this mortal/human assemblage point that is "Della", no, I do not have direct awareness of his whereabouts, what he is doing, or even what he is thinking. At most, there are occasional periods of "overlap" during which I have an intense awareness of his existence within *third attention*. It is that awareness which is like a constant beacon, luring me to complete the work that is required before we can be reconjoined. Also, during meditative gnosis, I can connect directly to him for the purpose of gathering information and Knowledge.

Chapter Five
Fifteen Years Later

*"Once on the other side, the man will have to wander around. His good fortune would be to find a helper nearby – not too far from the entrance. The man has to ask him for help. In his own words he has to ask the helper to teach him and make him a **diablero**. When the helper agrees, he kills the man on the spot, and while he is dead he teaches him... but neither you nor they have the power to refuse... When you make the trip yourself, depending on your luck, you may find a great diablero in the helper who will kill you and teach you. ...After your return, you will not be the same man. You are committed to come back to see your helper often. And you are committed to wander farther and farther from the entrance, until finally one day you will go too far and will not be able to return..."*

-Carlos Castaneda, <u>The Teachings of Don Juan</u>

~

I came across this passage in the summer of 2003, during a time when I was working through some personal issues, and though I have read these words many times previously over the years, they seemed to hit me with renewed meaning. In my opinion, what don Juan didn't say is that there also comes with that re-birthing process a responsibility and a Knowledge which can never be ignored from that moment forward.

Many years after Orlando burned with the fire from within, I went through the rite of passage don Juan is describing, and I was indeed fortunate to meet a powerful brujo who killed me on the spot and made me a diablero. More accurately, in hindsight many years later, I would say that this incident opened the energetic pathways between the four compartments of my own double-beingness, and becoming a diablero is a process that is eternally ongoing, and no one can "make" us anything. We can be handed the tools, but the Doing is always up to each of us.

Even though I had learned to surrender to the path and see where it might lead, I was still stubbornly rooted in first attention perceptions, even after several years of being on this journey. I could comprehend the journey intellectually, yet I could not entirely *see* the journey.

Growing up in the 60s, I was surrounded by the drug culture, the counter-culture, and the anti-culture movements from a young age, yet it wasn't until my late 30s that I decided to try shifting my assemblage point through the use of the sacred mushroom. During the entire course of this journey, I can count on one hand the number of times I have engaged this ally – and I want it to be clear this is not something I encourage or condone. For myself, it was necessary due to my own thoroughly stuck assemblage point, and I do not believe I would have been able to dislodge it *without* the mushroom and the guidance of a master shaman who arranged for the journey in Mexico.

It should be emphatically stressed that these plants are sacred and, in all likelihood, sentient in a manner which is evident to those who have engaged them, and yet may sound ludicrous to anyone who hasn't. They are not light entertainment nor recreational. To treat them with disrespect is not in accordance with the right way to live, and if ever the decision is made to engage with these allies, it has been my experience that the only proper way to do so is under the guidance of a master shaman, and only when all other attempts to dislodge the assemblage point have been thoroughly and impeccably tested first.

As for the process, perhaps the easiest way to convey the experience is simply to include an excerpt from my journal, written on the morning after it occurred.

May 6, 1997 – Initiation

The ally is within me, a living entity – the essence of the mushroom opening the doorways to the nagual as if it alone possesses the key. As Wendy and I are lying on the bed, I am visited by the elder shaman I've seen previously in visions, who tells me without speaking, *"You've had your play. Time to get to work."*

I find myself in the underworld. In this place, there is no water, only pale sand and lots of rocks – just words limiting the experience, but that's the hell of it. The first thing I experienced was seeing Orlando's animal-self standing slightly above me on one of the rocks, and when I look up to acknowledge him, he immediately lunges down on me, baring his fangs and laying open my throat before I know what's happening. At first, he's the Orlando I've seen in visions before – slightly more rugged, definitely more wild than when I knew him in manifestation, but undeniably the same Spirit.

But immediately after he rips my throat (sharp as razors, inhuman, animal teeth, sharper than wolves' teeth, all fangs, almost like a shark), I see the blood pouring out of me, and then I'm lying on my back in the sand, literally being split open by the "Orlando animal" and others like him – three or four of them in all. There is no fear, for it is as if I am a displaced observer, watching these events happen from safe harbor, knowing it has been my destiny from the start.

At this point, Orlando has become 4-legged, with the airbrushed-white face of a wolf/bird and the body of a dog. As my body is opened from throat to pubis, he stands on all four legs in the center of me, tearing out the internal organs and tossing them to the others who stand nearby. I am literally devoured from the inside out, and as Orlando is consuming what I perceive to be my heart, he lifts his head and looks me in the eyes, my blood running over his lips, my body inside his animal belly. When our eyes meet, I sense that he is loving what he is doing. There is also an abrupt realization that it had occurred to him to leave me as dead, but

64

because he finds something in the heart of me, something embedded down to a blood/cell level, I am deemed worthy of saving.

After I am totally devoured and only my skin remains – an empty husk devoid of organs and even bones and muscle – splayed on the sand and laid open as a deer hide would be laid open – the Orlando-beast dives inside the still-warm skin and pulls it around him like a cloak, then begins rapidly sewing himself in with sinew and a wooden needle. Inside my skin, a new Self rises onto the underworld beach.

The spirit of the shaman is within me. The essence of the otherworld inhabits me. I am no longer entirely human.

At this point, I bounce back into a functional awareness and write down notes on what happened, and I am reminded of the excerpt from _The Teachings of Don Juan_, about going through the passageway and finding a helper who will kill one on the spot and make them a diablero. But for whatever reason, in my case, the underworld shaman himself – the beast/animal/man/Anubis – climbed inside my skin, and I am recreated as much _him_ as myself.

Beautiful, yet disturbing on some level because it made me wonder if this was somehow trying to tell me that I am Orlando's physicality – if it's been "just me" all along. But when I tell Wendy this, she comments that he had to exist in order to do the things he did that night. He had to _be_ Orlando before he could take me apart in the underworld. She goes on to suggest that this road we're on is so important that he could only trust himself to be inside me.

"_You have to be immortal before you will know how to become immortal._"

The only way to know I have the immortal within is if Orlando is the immortal within me, so he had to remove the mortal trappings and rebuild me with the essence of himself, which is what I created him to do in the first place – to replace what is temporal with what is eternal.

Nothing will ever be the same for I am no longer the same.

End journal entry...

At the time I had no awareness of what is commonly called the shamanic initiation, or the shamanic transformation, nor did I have any awareness of the character of Anubis. It was only later, after I began researching certain symbols encountered during the vision quest that I began to realize this was the form Orlando had taken – guardian of the underworld.

This dismemberment is described in many books – though I had not read them at the time this occurred – the ritual itself a rite of passage wherein the seeker is taken apart in her human form and recreated using parts from the underworld itself. In most instances, the warrior/seeker sees herself being rebuilt – after the organs are removed and destroyed, new organs are put back in by the shamans and inorganic beings who performed the dismemberment – sometimes crystals or specific stones; elements of particular power plants such as mushrooms or peyote buttons; animal parts, particularly the eyes of a wolf or the teeth of a lion.

It's also important to note that this event occurred *before* I had become aware that Orlando is my own double, the Nagual man. At the time this happened in 1997, I was still functioning under the assumption that he was an entirely extant being. This was not an easy revelation, nor a quick one.

> *"I am now faced with the special problem of having to explain what it is that I am doing... and I must first of all reiterate that this is not a work of fiction. What I am describing is alien to us; therefore, it seems unreal."*
> Carlos Castaneda ~ *The Eagle's Gift* (Prologue)

Nothing will ever be the same, for I am no longer the same.

Those words, written so many years ago, have turned out to be far more true than I could ever have imagined. Since that vision-quest which took me into the underworld to meet my destiny, I have literally never been the same. In so many ways, the world has become a dollhouse inhabited by cardboard people living cardboard lives – and at first, the sorrow and the anger I experienced at what I was seeing came perilously close to destroying me altogether, for it brought home to me the deep and intrinsic sadness of don Genaro's path, as described in *Journey to Ixtlan.*

There was no going home, for home had been an illusion all along.

But as time has passed and I have engaged the infinite journey with as much impeccability as I can, I have come to realize that this is simply the way of things, and there is no real cause for sadness or anger, because in the final analysis, every sentient being chooses their path and embraces their destiny according to the dictates of their own Intent and the power of their own will.

There are no victims.

I have found myself moving further and further away from this world – or, in don Juan's terms, further from the entrance, deeper into the otherworld, and at times there is less and less reason to return here. This is both good and bad, though even those words are loaded and can't really be applied. It is simply what is. I have no regrets about this, though a certain melancholy does intrude at times. It is the melancholy of knowing those we love most may choose a phantom's path, the melancholy of realizing this is truly a solitary journey, even when we walk it with other warriors or loving companions.

Over the course of time, I have encountered many sources (including Orlando, Arnold Mindell, Michael Harner, Castaneda and others) who have made it known that this solitary path often ends up costing the warrior everything we think of as normal: job, family, friends, lovers, and sometimes even our very life.

When Orlando first cautioned me about this, I thought it would be different for me. (Hah! Self-importance 101). But as time has gone by and I can now look back on a certain portion of the path, I must say that this is turning out to be true. Those who were once my closest friends are now all but gone completely from my life. I cannot be content talking of recipes and child-rearing and last night's sitcoms; and the friends I once knew are too disturbed at the idea of walking through life with *Death as their advisor*. And so it goes.

What comes to me as I'm writing this is the strong inclination to say to newbie warriors: be sure this is what you want. For myself, it is all I have ever wanted or desired, and on the night I was dismembered by my double and reassembled, I knew my world had changed forever – yet again, in an ongoing series of changes. I would not go back even if I could, for now I am in love with the infinite, and my Intent is hooked to the third attention.

And yet... I have watched others on this path who do end up regretting their choices, who end up wishing they didn't know any of this, wishing they could go back to their normal life. I have even watched some of them actively try to forget by absorbing themselves in every manner of distraction from drugs to real-life-role-playing. Though once a warrior passes a certain point on the path (no one can say for sure what that point is, as it is different for each of us), it simply isn't possible to undo what has been Done. If there is a limbo, a hell, surely that is it.

There are those who would say nothing changes when a warrior wholly embraces the path with the Intent to become a man or woman of Knowledge, but that has not been my experience. There are those who would say we keep all our old friends and make new ones along the way, but that has not been my experience either. There are those who would say that as we become more spiritually aware and begin to engage our abilities, we will be loved by all those around us... but *that* has most definitely not been my experience.

I never forget that some of history's most enlightened brujos, shamans and woman and men of Knowledge were shunned, persecuted, and occasionally even crucified.

This path will not make anyone love you. It might make them turn on you. And it will definitely change your life and your relationships with those around you forever. Why? I think that's what I was *seeing* in my meditations. As we integrate ourselves and lose our own fragmentation, it is the natural instinct and "job" of the consensual reality to make every attempt to bring us back in line with the status quo. If/when we don't realign with that status quo is when we are essentially identified as a threat and begin to be treated accordingly, rather like how the human immune system fights off invading viruses.

The problem, of course, is that this "virus" of Knowledge isn't a dis-ease. It's the antidote – but "the body" doesn't recognize that because of its intensive and long-term programming. And so the warrior finds herself on a path that becomes paradoxically more solitary, and at the same time more vast and all-encompassing as it stretches toward the Infinite.

Choose the path wisely and only if it is from the heart. Have no regrets. And know you can never go home again, for the food will have no taste, and the wine will have turned to vinegar, and the faces at the window will be phantom faces with hollow eyes and empty smiles.

Most of all, have no sadness in that. Instead, rejoice in all you Know.

PART TWO

Dismantling the Old World
Assembling the New

You have to __*be*__ *immortal*
before you will know how to __*become*__ *immortal.*

Chapter Six
The Medicine Witch

"The medicine witch is duality's paradox, existing simultaneously as nurturing spirit-mother and visionary madwoman, slipping into the underworld to trade souls with the immortal twin, then returning to the world above to teach others how to follow even when it seems no one's listening."

-Orlando – December 25, 1997

The medicine witch is part magical practitioner, part healer, part visionary madwoman. The medicine witch is part heretic, part quantum thinker, part dancer on the tightrope between the worlds. The medicine witch is the enlightened crone of the future whispering into the ear of her own bumbling fool as that fool stumbles through the linear now.

I could attempt to tell you about myself, but that would only paint a picture of my past – the self of the known world, who has gone here or there, who has accomplished this or that, who is really only the mechanism and not the ghost inside the machine. So it seems that the best way to tell you about myself is through sharing parts of my journey, as fantastical or far-reaching as it may seem.

Any messenger is only human and can always be discredited if it is your intention to do it. If it makes you sleep better at night to think this book is only fiction, you'll find a way to believe it. We are lazy, static creatures by nature. We don't want to give that up. We'll kill to protect it. And in some cases, we'll even kill the messenger so we don't have to hear the message, so we don't have to *see* what is uncomfortable or inconvenient for us to *see*.

Galileo and Copernicus were persecuted for going against the consensual agreement of their day. Marco Polo was persecuted by the church to renounce what he had seen in China, forced essentially to recreate his own personal reality to be more in keeping with the reality of his Catholic peers. These men were tortured because they were right, not because they were wrong. When anything threatens our concept of reality, we will fight it out of habit and programming rather than even considering that perhaps it is our own definition of reality that could stand some redefining.

> "As the shaman, it is your nature to hold out a common apple and casually suggest to an apprentice that it is the forbidden fruit of all Knowledge. But more than that, it is within the shaman's ability to engender that belief within others, and through their belief, the apple *becomes* the fruit of all Knowledge, and once ingested the ecstasy of creation is passed on to another human being who might otherwise never have found it. That it started out as nothing more than a grocery store apple is beside the point. This is the shaman's gift, the sorcerer's trick. This is the creation of a new reality."
>
> *-Orlando*

In _The Shaman's Body_, psychologist Arnold Mindell offers insights into the nature of a shamanic personality – someone who might also be referred to as a medicine witch:

> *Is it your fault if you remind others of dreams they do not want? And who can blame the group, either for resistance to you or for the life-and-death struggle that ensues? These people are fighting for their lives, equilibrium, homeostasis – indeed, for the perpetuation of history. "Do not disturb us more than we can take," they say.*
>
> *From a global viewpoint, you disturb your organizational system, and history must fight for continuity. In this universal and fated interaction, the warrior's friends become the voices of the web. Their warmth turns to ice. They accuse you of unjustifiable behavior, egotism, and criminality as they become possess-*

ed by their lawmaker role in this eternal drama of human history.

The collective you live in must pursue you for what it experiences as criminal acts and bring you to trial, just as you have challenged other rule breakers in the past. Now it is you who enters into a life-and-death struggle with the universe..

Such is the nature of the quantum shaman – to be at odds with a world which insists on maintaining its status quo at all costs. So rather than lead the reader to believe I am a monk-like scholar of mysticism, I will say up front that I am nothing of the sort. I've lived as weird a life as anyone ever has. If you dig into my past, you can easily find fodder to invalidate me a hundred times over. If it would make you sleep better, I'll even tell you where to find it.

In the beginning of this journey, I desperately wanted to sleep better. I didn't want to believe what Orlando was showing me – and had I possessed even the slightest inkling that he was my own immortal double, I am quite certain I would have run screaming to the nearest nunnery or nuthouse, whichever came first. So I went through a period of trying to invalidate his teachings by attempting to invalidate *him*. I tried to convince myself it was all some sort of hoax, that he knew these things about my innermost thoughts, these things spoken of in his letters, because someone somewhere had told him, or that it was only my imagination, some dark delusion.

And yet...

In the end, I had to make a decision of the heart: did I want to learn from this man or did I only want to learn *about* the man? Did I want to put aside my preconceived notions about the nature of reality and try to see what might lie beyond, or did I want to cling tenaciously to The Real World because it enabled me to sleep better?

Did I want to go on believing the world was flat or did I have the courage and flexibility to try to wrap my mind around a globe?

I can only tell you about the journey itself and how it has affected me, how it has taught me to see the world, ourselves, life and death. I can tell you what I have *seen,* but only you can learn to *see* it if you find it worthy of exploration.

What *is* this thing? That's the question. I wish I had a simple answer. The best I can say is that it is a quest for an evolution of consciousness – not only spiritual enlightenment, but a genuine evolution that will make us other than human. For those who are successful, it will provide the ability to transcend the threshold of death with our consciousness intact, creating a continuity of Self into whatever might naturally come next. And if nothing comes next, perhaps it will enable us to create an afterlife through **Dreaming**, whether corporeal or non-corporeal, of something we cannot even begin to imagine from the assemblage point of our humanform awareness.

There was one moment in all of ancient history when one single ape looked beyond the trees and realized she could be more than what nature had dealt her. Perhaps it was a need for warmth that caused her to take up tools and build shelter. Perhaps it was hunger that taught her to hunt, gather and, eventually, to farm. Whatever it was, it began with a thought and with a need.

That one ape embraced evolution and mothered the human race. Those who chose to remain behind are still in the trees. And now it's time to look beyond the trees again.

It's time for the next evolution.

SPONTANEOUS PARTHENOGENESIS

May 25, 1998 – a vision

Before anything we currently think of as being part of the universe existed, there was only an immense void – a nothingness, the abyss, a black hole which had gathered into itself all matter and energy. Yet from the nothing – literally a thought which created itself in an act of spontaneous parthenogenesis – the universe sprang into being. A thought creating itself because it wanted/needed to exist as an entity separate from the void. It required *identity*. It demanded *life*, yet the only way for it to achieve life was to create itself from the nothing and hurl itself out in all directions, a sudden sentience breaking apart from whatever had contained it previously. Because it was a creation of will, it created itself with perfection, which is to say it gave itself all possibilities and, even moreso, it gave its component parts, including us, the ability to evolve in order to adapt to changing circumstances within its own continuum.

If we think of the void as containing all of matter/energy, then the universe is the stage of time, and both together create the continuum of space/time and matter/energy.

In its creation, it gave all the beings who would eventually exist within itself the ability to continue through evolution – for the ironic thing about the creation of the universe is that it gave all it had. It won't interfere in the affairs of man because it *can't*. There is nothing left of "*it*" except all these individual components that comprise the all – so, there is no intelligence sitting outside the universe who can intervene in its destiny. In its creation, it used all its "parts" to create the whole – which means it used its full intelligence, its whole awareness, its absolute will, and in doing so, *it <u>automatically</u> created each cell of itself with those qualities.* For that reason, each of us – whether man, animal, stone, vegetable, air or distant sun – has the blueprint for our own unique evolution. *In creating itself to survive, the universe gave us the ability to evolve.*

The problem is that the universe and all its individual components are at constant war with the void, for it is the nature of the void to take back what came from it and is the nature of the universe to attempt to avoid being taken. For example, through death, man is returned, ultimately, to the void in that his consciousness would appear to be obliterated from this universe and, in time, even the flesh and bone turns to ash and the ash deteriorates to atoms.

The only way to avoid such a fate is for each individual to create its own continuity in the same way the universe seemingly created itself from the void. We must strive to become our own individual continuum, expanding beyond the reach of the stage we currently inhabit – we must create our own continuity by saying – *willing* – "I-Am", just as the universe itself originally detached from the void when it sprang into being from the nothingness.

It seems inconceivable that the universe came from anything but a thought, an incredible force of need/will breaking free of whatever "reality" held it together before its *spontaneous parthenogenesis*. Because we are part of that creation springing from the same exact quantum source, we also possess that same strength of will within ourselves – the will to survive, to be more than mere fate has sanctioned us to be by virtue of existing within the known universe.

Just as the known universe must have existed within whatever continuum previously held it, so do we exist within *it*, but just as the universe had to break free of the void in order to achieve its own separate continuity, so must we break free of the known universe if we intend to evolve/survive beyond it.

Chapter Seven
A Quantum Premise, An Evolving Paradigm

*The fear you experience at the thought of your own
annihilation is actually the god-force of creation within
you, telling you that your spiritual survival is entirely in
your own hands. In the sorcerer's world, the soul is seen as
an infant: it must be nurtured, fed and cared for or it will
simply never mature, and can actually die if ignored too
long.*

–Orlando, 2000

Because all things are comprised of energy at a sub-atomic
level – even what we traditionally think of as matter is only an
arrangement of energetic particles – it stands to reason that we
are part of that same universal energy. We are the starstuff of
creation, the magical matter/energy of eternity itself.
According to the laws of physics, energy can neither be
created nor destroyed; it can only change form. And when
considered in that light, it becomes obvious that the particles
of which we ourselves are comprised have been here since
before time began. As energy. We have within us the entire
scope of eternity itself, the very blueprint of Reality, right
down to a molecular level.

We have always been here and always will be.

And yet, there is awareness of our mortality, the
knowledge that all we have experienced as individuals unique
unto ourselves is transient, lost to oblivion at the moment of
death, or so it seems. This is why religions exist – not to
ultimately save us, which is altogether impossible in the
manner in which salvation has come to be defined by religious
dogma – but to comfort us with belief systems which rely on
faith alone. In that way, religion is only one more control
system – a program that has been running for so long that
even its masters have forgotten it *is* a program.

As a child in a Southern Baptist Sunday School, I had this proven more times than I could count – usually when I would ask some reasonable question, only to be greeted with the blank stare of noncomprehension. Though the teacher or minister could usually come up with some pat answer – "God moves in mysterious ways," being the most common and the least helpful to a child – it became quickly clear that when questions couldn't be answered with dogma or rhetoric, the questioner herself was systematically brought under scrutiny – perhaps one of the most effective tools of diversionary programming known to man.

"Faith enables us not to question," I was once told by a stern-faced minister often seen sneaking out the back door of the local pub with a young woman who bore little resemblance to his wife. "All these questions trouble you because your faith isn't strong enough."

Amen. I had no use for faith even then. And less now.

Salvation is not what this journey is about. This is about taking eternal life into our own hands. It's about learning to see how we have been intentionally and unintentionally manipulated to think of ourselves as impotent handfuls of chemicals, or "wretches" at the mercy of an angry god, when the reality of what we are is precisely the opposite. And, even more important, this path is about breaking free of our intrinsic human programs so that we might finally embrace our unlimited human potential.

We are sentient beings. And we have within ourselves the key to claim our rightful place as citizens of eternity instead of prisoners of dust – a cohesive *I-Am* consciousness extending seamlessly into infinity and eternity.

The trick is gaining the ability to permanently establish our individual consciousness (which is also a synapse of

78

energy) as part of the energetic structure of the universe at large, so that all the experiences and knowledge of the individual Self are not lost to Death. Or, put another way, the trick is to attach our consciousness to something eternal as opposed to having it perish because it is presently attached to organic matter.

This is where the shaman's double comes in – for ultimately the double is the energy body, the indestructible vessel which can host the *I-Am* Self into eternity. I say "can" because nothing is guaranteed – and therein lies the fallacy of most organized religions, which teach that the soul is a given, handed out at the moment of conception, along with our genetic coding. Instead, I would be more inclined to say that we are born with a small spark of Spirit, but – as Orlando's quote at the beginning of this chapter implies – unless that spark is nurtured and tended, it can and will eventually go out.

This is where quantum shamanism differs from organized religion – for it is through the quantum comprehension of our spiritual nature that we begin to *see* and take responsibility for our own survival and well-being into eternity. Clearly, this will take more than a few words to explain, more than a few months to master, and the cumulative *Knowledge* of many lifetimes to fully understand. But once it is understood, the uncertainty and fears which have haunted us since the dawn of time begin to fall away, revealing the vast and virtually untapped potential that lies within the Infinite.

Through traditional branches of mysticism, it has always been seen that there is some connection between the consciousness we experience in the mortal realm, and *something* which seems to lie just out of reach in what is traditionally called the spirit world, or the afterlife. Through traditional shamanism, we can intuit that we may not be just the impotent handful of chemicals our high school biology teacher taught us to believe – but ultimately it is through the *quantum* comprehension of shamanism that we begin to be able to understand how and even *why* this is true.

I am not a scientist, so I can only relate these ideas in laymen's terms. So without going into a history of physics and quantum mechanics, let me simply say once again that all things are comprised of energy at the sub-atomic level – including consciousness itself. By *knowing* that that energy is indestructible, the quantum shaman gains power over the fear of death – which is where the real journey actually begins to begin.

SO WHAT'S THE POINT?

If a goal or destination of this path had to be named, it is simply this: to exist as a singularity of consciousness comprised of the totality of oneself. What *is* the totality of oneself? It is the cumulative knowledge, awareness and experience gathered by the mortal self *and* the eternal double – including all knowledge, awareness and experience traditionally associated with what are commonly misconstrued as "past lives" (see Chapter Ten) – all brought cohesively together under a single assemblage point.

As this is accomplished, the individual becomes a Whole being, existing ubiquitously and non-locally throughout the space-time matter-energy continuum. This singularity could be called the *I-Am*, and would be virtually unlimited as to its potential for existence, with the ability to project a seemingly humanform body, or exist as pure energy, strictly as a matter of her own Will.

Death as we currently define it will cease to exist.

INDIVIDUATION

From a quantum perspective, it could be said that the *individuated* Self is consciousness, or awareness, or even self-identity – an individual to be distinguished from all the billions of others like it. It has also been observed that consciousness exists on the same frequency as the vast electromagnetic field (EM field) which essentially binds the universe together. Keep in mind, this is an extremely simplified explanation of a far more vast science. But as it was explained to me by a fellow seeker and electronic systems engineer with expertise in the field of electromagnetic wave functions, consciousness itself is an EM field, and EM fields exist throughout the universe, held together by their own energy as individuated and conjoined fields.

This was a vital piece of the puzzle for me, because it takes something that has traditionally been considered mystical and brings it into the realm of rational comprehension, and that marriage of mysticism with science is what forms the basis for quantum shamanism. In fact, just *Knowing* about that connection between consciousness and the natural fields of our universe has done much to explain the nature of the *two-part migration of the* soul – our journey of evolution from the world of organic matter into the world of the inorganic singularity through the vehicle of the shaman's double. And it could also explain why Seers often view that migration as an ongoing dance – a rolling, tumbling, snake-eating-its-tail sort of proposition wherein the *I-Am* consciousness manifests into matter so as to gather experience that strengthens and enhances its own quantum field.

In my own comprehension, this ties directly into the machinations of the double – because I do not really see there is a soul that "re-incarnates". Instead, it's all happening in the now – the infinite energy-self (the double) who exists ubiquitously through the All, can take on manifestation at any time and for any reason so as to gather experience which is then transmitted to the mortal self so that the mortal self may strengthen and enhance her own awareness sufficiently to be able to maintain the quantum EM field of individuality beyond the physical body.

Orlando has often said, "You created me to create you," and as I have meditated on that idea over the past ten years, I have come to see not only how true it is, but how it cannot be any other way. We draw our teachers to us through desire and Intent. And, if necessary, we create them ourselves. It begins with a thought.

ACHE, HURT, WANT, NEED: A RECIPE

What I've experienced is available to any warrior who has been on the path for any length of time. The double is created through dreaming. More accurately, the double is created by Intent and most easily perceived in dreaming. In the early phases, it really was a matter of being in love with an image, a paradigm that personified my desires. For me, the paradigm started when I was six years old with _Adventures in Paradise_, starring Gardner McKay – an old television show about a ship's captain who roamed around the South Pacific on a big old sailing vessel. High adventure stuff. And it didn't hurt that he was handsome.

In hindsight, I can see this was the first paradigm of Orlando, and at six years old, feeling that terrible ache inside myself that was like a hole in my soul – the need/longing/desire for something that was out of my reach. I actually _do_ remember sitting on the living room floor of our crumbling old house, staring at the tube, and trying to figure out how to _be_ with him, even though I was clearly aware of the difference between fantasy and reality, the line between fact and fiction. And yet... that didn't seem to matter somehow, for the dream had become larger than the rules of the consensual reality.

At one point, as a result of my infatuation, when asked by my Sunday School teacher what we did on our summer vacation, I told her how I had gone to Tahiti and sailed on the *Tiki* with Captain Adam Troy. Of course, the next thing I knew, my mother was mad as hell because I was telling lies in church, and maybe that should have been a dead giveaway that the Baptist hellfire and brimstone programming really wasn't really working. I remember being put in the car and taken home that morning, with my mother's voice lecturing about how lying was a sin, and my crazy granny turned around in her seat to give me that stern look that said I had really screwed the pooch this time.

I wasn't really listening, of course. I was *"remembering"* being on the Tiki with her alluring captain. And all I can say now is that that *remembering* was an active present-tense *verb*. It was neither passive nor past. It was some deep-rooted seed of *creation* which undoubtedly exists in all children until it is beaten out of them by well-meaning parents who perceive only a black and white world, and a need for conformity to the existing social programs.

I'm sure most have felt that ache/hurt/want/need. Right in the pit of the stomach, so strong it can take your breath away. That feeling is *energy*. And over the course of time, if one puts sufficient Intent into that feeling instead of suppressing it, the energy actually goes into the creation of the double – the manifestation of all that ache/hurt/want/need into a *reflection* of the thing that is desired. My double at age six probably looked like Captain Adam Troy. By the time I was 11, the paradigm had a new face: Mr. Spock.

It was at that time in my life that I walked outside one night, driven from the safe sanctuary of my crazy granny's cabin on the property where we all lived, by a sense of longing so fierce it could no longer be contained. I remember how I stood in the darkest corner of the yard, with the whip'o'wills calling their lonely cries into the blackness, and the stars blazing overhead like uncut diamonds, and the St. Augustine grass cool and soothing on my bare feet; and I shook my fist at the sky with all the power in a little girl's heart, proclaiming, *"If I can't come to you, I'll bring you to me!"*

Without a doubt, that was the moment I first breathed Orlando into existence.

And yet, it is crucial to mention that even that is not enough, for this is an ongoing creation of the self and the double – creator and created conjoining in that endless dance. It neither began there, nor could it end there. That was just the starting point – chosen arbitrarily by chance – on the endless circle of infinity.

Without a doubt, most people have these feelings, but the tragedy is that they are usually suppressed because it really isn't reasonable to think one can *be* a fictional character such as Captain Troy or Mr. Spock. And that's true, of course. Orlando is neither of those, yet he is both of them. But he is also a great deal more.

Obviously, this path isn't about role-playing or mimicry. It's about projecting one's true Self into the infinite and letting it soar – no matter how unlikely the paradigms or archetypes that form our first faltering attempts. As a child at 6 and again at 11, when I felt those energy surges of such longing, instead of suppressing the feelings as most of my peers did, I lay awake at night writing grand adventure stories on the fabric of the space-time continuum with the quill of that longing. It *hurt*. But instead of turning away from the hurt or transferring my affection to something more reasonable, something more attainable, I instinctively kept trying to manifest the dream.

Like the poet's muse, part of the lure of the double is that it is uncatchable. It remains always one step ahead, calling us to follow.

When I met Orlando in manifestation in 1988, obviously this was the culmination of the paradigm. One look at him and I simply knew he wasn't human. And I do mean that in every literal way. And yet, because he was in *seemingly* human form, acting like a man, I tried everything in my power to seduce him – foolish mortal witch I was then. And yet... He simply wouldn't take the bait. But he *would* throw out the lure: "Come by my house and we'll talk." I would go, of course, he would be there in nothing but a pair of shorts and a low cut tank top, and we would indeed talk. He was seducing me. I was seducing him. All the moves were in motion on both parts, and both of us knew it. And yet, *never* was it allowed to go past the stage of deliberate titillation.

Intent. He was hooking me so thoroughly that even after he left this Earth, all these years later, he is the muse who has bound me to the farthest star. It actually hurts to think about him – that terrible longing which seems to be some sort of energetic link between the mortal and the double.

It is from that source that the double is created. I've seen it played out in my own life, and occasionally in the lives of those warriors who have also experienced their double. I do think it's a rare thing, because we are so programmed to suppress that ache/hurt/want/need sensation. We're told it's self-destructive or silly or worse. In today's culture, I've even heard it referred to as psychotic – which, of course, is only a reflection of the fear of the consensual world, and has very little bearing on the reality of the warrior. And yet, it is the very *source* of the self in eternity – the desire to love and be loved that is so strong it creates its own perfect double – so that that energy can be mirrored and reflected back to it. Creator and created, in an eternal dance.

And, of course, there comes a time when it's no longer possible to say which is which. That's why don Juan made the comment : *"Beyond a certain point you realize the double is dreaming you."*

As Orlando said, "It's all just a silly love story."

~

Whereas our particles have indeed always been here, our consciousness is seemingly exclusive, and it is the survival of that unique point-of-view, that cosmically irreplaceable *I-Am* which satisfies the definition of eternal life. Some people are content being part of the big picture, existing at a molecular level, coming and going through life-and-death cycles as a tree, a bird, a mountain stream, where there is no continuity of individual consciousness, no single point of view into eternity, but only an endless and entirely random exchange of particles from one form into another.

Personally, I am not satisfied with this, and it is my contention that the entire purpose of mortal life is to fully embrace our own unique point-of-view and inhabit it into infinity. In this manner, we become eternally conscious – immortal beings of indestructible energy. It has taken 10 billion years of evolution for the particles to come together in precisely this fashion which you recognize in your own mirror, and for consciousness to develop in exactly the manner you know as your Self. So it's been a birthing process requiring 10 billion years!

I have come to know that sentient beings – evolved humans and inorganic beings – exist among us right now. Should they choose to be in physical form, you could not distinguish them from anyone else.

Should they choose to be non-local (an individual consciousness extending into infinity and eternity simultaneously), you could not perceive them at all unless it was their intention. They are immortal (indestructible), and they are eternal (not governed or restricted by linear time). They are not aliens nor demons nor phantasms.

They are _us_, evolved to our highest potential.

The destruction of faith is the beginning of evolution

When faith is only another word for belief, then faith is only a fool's paper sword in a nuclear war. When using the word faith in the manner a spirit-warrior might use it, it is more accurately called Intent – an internal mechanism rather than belief in external mechanisms. Traditional faith is passive, whereas intent is an active, unrelenting, energetic force from within the human organism. A passive believer might say, "I have faith my life will turn out as I want it to be." A warrior would more likely say, "It is my Intent to create my life according to my heart's desire."

As Orlando once said to me, "Faith is what we want to believe, a primitive life-boat too easily shot full of holes. Don't just believe things. Belief and faith are only fairy tales in the dark. Knowledge is the only real power, the first tool for chipping away at the programs and the belief systems to find out who you are beyond all of that."

At first I did not like this explanation, but as I discovered, that rankling irritation I experienced when he said this was part of the program which keeps us from realizing our own potential. As long as we have faith in external redemption from the abyss of oblivion, we have abandoned our own potential and rendered ourselves impotent.

Chapter Eight
Wrestling With the Fragments

It was in September of 2000 when I was talking to another nagual on the phone one afternoon. Though he and I shared much in common, there were also aspects of this path where we had come to differ in fairly major ways. At one point in our conversation, he said to me, "When I see your luminous form, you have all the pieces. All the fragments are there, floating around in your luminous form, but you haven't yet pulled them together into 'the assemblage point'." He went on to say, "There's something you know with regard to why you haven't done this. When you do, it is going to be life-altering, and I'm not sure you're ready for that yet."

Hmmm, I thought. There are few things on this Earth that will irritate me more than a friend telling me, *"You're not ready, Young Skywalker,"* but I made an effort to put my emotional reaction aside and deal with the idea through impeccability.

"It's all tied in to the concept of the double," I replied, knowing we were worlds apart on our views, and not particularly wanting to get into it with him again. I felt he was viewing the double as a psychological metaphor when I was seeing it as a very real meta-magical construct of energy beyond the eagle.

He didn't disappoint me when he maintained, "The double is only a component not yet integrated into the self, and when you do it, it will empower you to incredible proportions."

I was at a turning point in my journey – essentially the crossroads where I was wrestling with the idea of physical immortality contrasted against the idea of the double as an eternal vessel of awareness.

What if he's right? But – what if he's wrong?

I reminded him of *The Eagle's Gift* wherein don Juan is describing the function of the nagual man and nagual woman.

"You seem to be telling me that I will be empowered by integrating the nagual man into myself. I'm not sure I *see* it that way. The function of the nagual man is to exist *already* within third attention, so that when the nagual woman – who is a mortal construct of organic form – slips past the eagle, it is the nagual man who will take *her* into *him*. By virtue of already being in third attention, the nagual man serves as the vessel of immortality – the two halves reconjoin beyond the eagle. That's the two-part migration of the soul."

This is *my* truth, though it may not be true for all naguals or all warriors. It seems that only by moving *my* consciousness into the immortal construct of the double does any of this really pan out for all of eternity. If I were to incorporate Orlando into myself as part of this psychological integration, I can only *see* that it would bring the immortal other into the mortal self, and for reasons that should be obvious, I cannot see that this is the way to go. Rather like pouring fine red wine into a broken earthen cup.

Even though I had already undergone my own shamanic initiation, wherein Orlando had sewn himself inside my skin in the guise of Anubis, I had continued to function under the premise that the double was and *must* be, at least somewhat separate, particularly with regard to maintaining its own free will. Anything less would tie the double to organic folly, it seemed, and would run the high risk of impinging upon the agenda given to it in the first place: *Show me how to become an eternal being, a singularity of consciousness.*

And yet, something continued to niggle at me that day...

September 21, 2000

Must think on this. Gnosis. Deeper into the trance.

If I were to bring Orlando into myself, is this how the mortal self gains the knowledge, ability and wisdom to actually slip past the eagle? Once accomplished, s/he could certainly manifest as anything s/he desired – s/he could *be* Orlando or Della or none of the above. The projection of the luminous form, at that point, could take any manifestation. So... I'm asking myself if bringing Orlando into myself might be a possibility – for if I've made him an eternal being empowered with knowledge to teach me – is the final step to bring the teacher inside the self so as to give the mortal self the advantage of all that power and knowledge as a means to completing her journey?

Since Orlando has always maintained that part of this evolution involves me taking his anima into myself, is that just another way of looking at the idea of integration? Is this something which happens at the moment of death, as part of the evolution beyond the eagle? Or is it more efficient, perhaps, to attempt the integration *before* the moment of death – while still in mortal form?

I again return to the idea that I put him outside of myself for a reason. This so-called 'fragment' is not only the energetic vessel of my eternal awareness, but my infinite teacher. If I bring him into myself, do I then become the teacher? And, if so, who would listen to the aging fat lady anymore than they would have listened to an unknown anthropologist known as Carlos Castaneda? As long as don Juan remains a mystery, he has credence. Put him *inside* Carlos, and he becomes, to the perceptions of the mortal world, just a short Hispanic college student prattling quasi-religious nonsense.

If Orlando is my don Juan, does he serve me better as an external teacher or an internal component of myself? And if he is already the Whole self, outside of time, what would the effect be of bringing that which is immortal into that which is temporal?

Think, Self! Demand impeccability even if you don't like the view. What to do here?

A voice of gnosis: *Form the question before you seek the answer.*

Okay. *What are the eternal consequences if I choose to 'integrate' Orlando into myself?*

Answer from *the place of silent knowing:* *"He becomes your heart. You will continue to follow it, no matter what form it takes, no matter what location it inhabits on the map of your understanding."*

The second question: *What are the eternal consequences if I choose not to integrate Orlando into myself?*

Answer: *Your heart leads you into the unknown. You will continue to follow it, no matter what form it takes, no matter where it goes.*

Question: *What's the difference?*

Answer: *The difference is in your own human perception. What is already eternal cannot be destroyed by bringing it into a new environment or causing it to change form.*

Question: *Then what was the purpose in placing it outside myself in the first place?*

Answer: *You cannot see yourself without a mirror. He is your reflection. He is also the muse, the nagual man who came into this life with you and will be with you when you leave this Earth. This is how you have manifested your Intent, this is the two-part migration of the soul.*

Question: *Would my ongoing journey be better facilitated by bringing him into myself or leaving him as a separate entity?*

Answer: *He is not a separate entity. Only your perception tells you this. He has separate form but is not a separate cohesion of consciousness. Here you touch the infinite. How can you think to integrate that which is not separate? Examine your own perceptions. "Twin" is the wrong word. "Other" is more accurate but still limited. See with your heart that which the eyes and the intellect cannot accurately perceive.*

Question: *But he has led a life I am unaware of. He is the wily wizard.*

Answer: *He has led a life you have not yet perceived, but it is your life. You are the wizard. You are the man behind the curtain. There is no difference. Examine your perceptions. Integration is the wrong word. Duality is more accurate but still limited. See with your heart into the duality of your own being. You are trying to see*

91

anima, the animated with physical eyes. Do not limit yourself with this thinking. See beyond the fragments, into the whole.

Question: *Why have I chosen to do it this way?*

Answer: *This is the nature of evolution. If it took a straightforward path, it could be easily thwarted. This is the heart of sorcery, what you call magic. That which you cannot understand directly must be viewed as the mysterious, and for you, the mysterious is what hooks your will to third attention. This is as it must be.*

Question: *This scares me. It makes me feel empty near my solar plexus if I think of integrating Orlando into myself. It would leave, at least symbolically, a hole in the fabric of the universe where he should stand. I want to fill that space, not create a void.*

Answer: *You are the nagual. This is your nature. It is your nature to be double because it is your nature to evolve. You must follow your heart. He is your heart. To follow him is to follow yourself. Even more than this, when others follow the path, he can help them find their own heart. This is also the nature of the nagual, the double beings.*

Question: *At what point, then, is it required or desirable to bring our "duality" into a "singularity"?*

Answer: *When you are ready for the big bang.*

Question: *Monkey brain human is confused, afraid.*

Answer: *This is only relevant if fear stops you. What is the fear trying to show you?*

Question: *I don't want to fuck myself by creating the big bang too soon. I don't want to thwart my own evolution by bringing Orlando into myself too soon. I have an intuition that I need him to be separate.*

Answer: *He is not separate. He is the third attention manifestation of the duality. You are the first attention manifestation of that same self. He is your transcended self, evolved. When you have perceived from within the 7th sense, you have perceived through his immortal eyes which are not really eyes at all but only vessels of perception. You have seen yourself in eternity. It is only perception that makes you separate, whether you are perceiving from the 7th sense or from within the mortal self. Both are equally real. One is eternal. The key is to inhabit that eternal perception eternally, so the key is to perceive through it instead of perceiving it as separate. The key is to Be what you already are, and to claim it by shifting your perception from there to here. The key is to see through the eyes of eternity.*

Question: *How is that done?*

Answer: *By shifting your attention, focusing from within the eternal vessel instead of only from within the mortal self. Life is a process of accomplishing that shift.*

At this moment, gnosis was broken. Perhaps that's the answer. Now if only I can decipher what it all means. *"Life is a process of accomplishing that shift."*

~

Eventually – several years later – it became obvious that there wasn't really a right way or a wrong way, but that wasn't something I could be told or even shown. It was something I had to experience, something I had to wrestle with over a period of several months, many sleepless nights, and a lot of boxing matches with my own stubbornly-rooted perceptions. What seems obvious to me now was not obvious then – and that is the path for most warriors I have known. We learn by Do-ing.

What I learned from this experience is that the double is both separate *and* already integrated simultaneously. That which is eternal with regard to consciousness is also ubiquitous throughout the space-time continuum – so, in the final analysis, Orlando already exists as the nagual man in the realm of third attention, and simultaneously within my own awareness as the voice of the teacher, the manifestation of the bridge between the tonal and the nagual, the organic and the inorganic.

This is just one more aspect of the nagual man and nagual woman – the duality of the Self which is not a split in perception, but an augmentation in perception. Through the

93

double, we learn to see both sides of the bridge simultaneously – and in doing so, we can see how the bridge was built while we are in the process of building it.

Only by allowing the impossible do we breathe life into our dreams.

Chapter Nine
Guides and Guardians and Allies, oh my!

FIRST DATE WITH THE ALLY

Allies are drawn to raw power, and especially to the longing that normally issues forth from warriors who are genuinely seeking transformative experience. The problem is – the ally is neither human nor particularly gentle, and it does not respect the normal boundaries of what might be considered safe or even appropriate.

It was approximately 1989 when I was living in a rural community outside of San Diego. Orlando had been in and out of our lives for just a little over a year, and perhaps not coincidentally, I had just finished reading the first four books of Carlos Castaneda. As a result, I had further decided I was heap-powerful-medicine-warrior and that it was time to go out into the wilderness and summon an ally. (I'm lucky to be alive!) So, having picked up some snippet of information wherein it was intimated that an ally might be summoned by a rhythmic sound such as drumming, I set off into the unknown.

At the end of a long dirt road where I frequently rode my horse was a huge metal gate protecting the back entrance to a high security, top secret government facility. Feeling bold, I got out of my car at dusk, leaned against that gate, and began tapping on it in a rhythmic fashion with my ring. At first, I felt foolish, but then something came over me. I decided to really put my heart into it. I projected my longing, my love for the infinite and the unknown. And I let myself go. *Tap-tap-tap! Tap-tap-tap!*

In the distance, I could hear a dog barking in what could have been a matching rhythm. *Bark-bark-bark!* Hmmm. *Tap-tap-tap-tap-tap!* And with absolute precision: *Bark-bark-bark-bark-bark!*

Whatever rhythm I tapped, the dog would answer. I even got into some complex Jamaican drum rhythms... and so did that dog. Indeed, I was so into it that it didn't occur to me that the dog was now much closer than when I originally started my ally hunting. Nor did it occur to me that it was getting dark! I just kept right on tapping, and the dog kept right on barking. Until, quite abruptly, I realized I was hearing a rustling of tall grass, the movement of wind through a rocky canyon, the rush of the eagle's wings.

Something was moving straight toward me at a very rapid rate of speed. It was huge, at least twice the size of a man; for I could sense it as it emerged from the canyon and onto the dirt road perhaps 100 feet from my car. A huge dark shape for which no words exist. I didn't see it. I *saw* it – for even though I was not yet a warrior, I had always possessed what my grandmother called "the sight".

And I ran like hell. Jumped in the Camaro. Fired up the engine. Sputtering and choking on terror, I roared out of there and went speeding toward home with it seeming to roll/float behind me. It was only when I got back onto the paved road that it stopped and went back toward the canyon, having confirmed to both of us that I was no more ready to engage the ally than I was to fly. I can see why don Juan warned Carlos that the meeting with the ally could have killed him. The fright alone was sufficient to do just that.

Okay, that was really stupid. But it taught me something of incredible value. The impossible is possible. Magic and sorcery are real. And the allies are most definitely out there, though they are not at all what most of us think.

~

What most people think of as guardians are often only a slightly different manifestation of the shaman herself – meaning that we are our own best friend; and, by the same token, we can become our own worst enemy when we begin to attribute such things as psychic attack and spiritual deterioration to demons or evil sorcerers or the ill-of-the-week. Ultimately, the demons are only the sorcerer herself as well.

> It is a play of one and we play all the roles – god and devil, spirit and matter, angels and demons.

I'm not ruling out that other entities exist as evolved beings in their own right, yet it has been my experience that they serve as teachers and guides who essentially whisper in the shaman's ear from the library of the infinite, and it is always up to free will to determine the path and the outcome.
"Only from within the dream can the dreamer awaken."
I have noticed a tendency in younger seekers to essentially turn to their guardians or allies for help in much the same way a religious person would turn to prayer. At this point, the sorcerer begins to disempower herself by placing the ability outside of herself, and many times this leads to a long path that ultimately goes nowhere, when all that's really lacking is an understanding of how power and energy function.

It isn't in my personal experience that guardians directly intervene on our behalf, nor do they really seem to protect us from ourselves. If that sounds blasphemous to some, perhaps it can serve as a catalyst for examining one's own foundation. Any time – *any time* – the warrior places power outside herself, she is disempowering herself completely. We are not protected from on high any more than we are saved from on high – though at the point when the double begins dreaming the warrior, it may *appear* that way. At that point, the double is moving outside of time and acting on her own behalf. To the mortal self still in linear time, this may appear to indicate a guardian – but the reality is that the guardian is the sorcerer herself manifested in eternity – the evolved self.

The problems start when the mortal Self begins to rely on those guardians, thereby creating a ***dependency***, without realizing that only by gathering sufficient personal power to *be* the guardian can the guardian exist in the first place.

It's a dangerous moebius loop if there is no direct understanding from the warrior that she must become the guardian in order to *be* the guardian. As Orlando frequently reminds me, "You have to *be* immortal before you know how to *become* immortal." If either end of that Intent falters, the warrior falls between the cracks and becomes food for the eagle.

Once we begin to recognize the presence and power of our guardian, that doesn't free us from the responsibility for *becoming* that guardian through our own Intent and free will – the manifestation of thought-form into actuality. In other words, it is only through the act of *becoming* the double that the double is created and nurtured into existence. On a level of ordinary awareness, this would appear to be a paradox, yet from the quantum shaman's perspective, it is a truth which can be easily *seen* as one begins to work with the idea of ubiquitous consciousness – the realization that our awareness is not confined to a single body, and certainly not to a single unit of linear time.

On one of my online forums, I once received the following comments and questions from a seeker:

> *A sorcerer can only effect you if you allow it. The energy they summon on a human level is rather wimpy, and on a spiritual level, monitored by their guardians. You are protected by your guardian. Again the spirit rule of non-interference is in play here, your guardian and their guardian will make those decisions for you.*

To assume any such thing as non-interference is in play is to assume the universe has rules, order and a game plan – and that is simply not the case as I have observed it, for to have a non-interference directive would mean having an agreement, and that really doesn't track when you think about it. An agreement between *whom* and *what*?

As for the statement: "your guardian and their guardian will make those decisions for you," I cannot agree with this, for to place the power of free will outside of ourselves is just another form of religion, another manifestation of faith. No one decides for us in spiritual matters. Not on Earth and not in eternity. The decisions we make and the consequences for them are entirely our own.

Knowing what I Know, it would be irresponsible of me to tell you to rely on your guardian. Instead, I must tell you to rely on your Self, for only in doing so do you gather sufficient cohesion and personal power to be the most powerful being in the universe: the guardian, the double, the Whole self.

You have to *be* immortal before you will know how to *become* immortal.

Chapter Ten
Redefining Reincarnation

Perhaps one of the most frequent misperceptions of mysticism has to do with reincarnation. While it is commonly believed that we go through many lives occurring at varying points in linear time, and lived out in a variety of different bodies, there are many reasons why this simply does not work for me, and why it may in fact be limiting to someone on a spiritual path who has settled into a comfortable relationship with the idea of reincarnation.

First, it has never made any sort of sense to me on an intuitive spiritual level that I could have been Cleopatra or Jules Verne or a segmented worm in the primordial beginnings of time. While the energy we are made of has certainly been here since before time itself began, the consciousness which is unique to the person I am now would appear to be individual – and what I have seen through vision quests and gnosis, is that it is the individuation of that *I-Am* in the *now* which creates the self in eternity.

Through coming to understand the principles of energy, it finally began to click that we aren't re-incarnated in spirit nearly as much as we are simply re-molecularized energetically – which is why we cannot remember our so-called past-lives. It wasn't *me*, it was only some of my particles in a different manifestation – a different entity altogether.

The purpose of Wholeness and integration is to bring together in a single assemblage point all the experiences of the Infinite spirit, which is an ongoing creation that begins in the Now and is truly unique to each of us. It is only our linear-time assemblage point that causes us to see things as past, present and future, when, from the point-of-view of the shaman's double, it is all right Now, and what we experience depends entirely on where the assemblage point is fixed.

The spirit becomes eternal through the actions of the warrior right here, right Now, in this lifetime, and no other.

100

Again, this might sound like a radical statement to some, but it's really a matter of learning to look at the question and the world in a different way than we always have – and only by doing so can we empower ourselves to evolve. It is a matter of bringing responsibility squarely onto ourselves. By believing we will live again, or have lived before, there can be a tendency to ignore the strategic importance of being alive *Right Now.*

Stop for a moment and ask yourself how it would have overturned your sense of an organized reality if you had been living in the time when it was discovered that the world is actually round. Trying to wrap your mind around it would be no easy task, because you had always lived on a flat earth. Many people of that time actually went mad because of being forced to change their world view to such a large extent, and that's what this path does – it asks us to change our thinking by undoing our programming. So what I'm asking you to do is to consider for a moment the possibility that each spirit is unique, not born immortal, but *becoming* an eternal being as a result of the actions of the warrior in this life.

Because we are inhabitants of a linear timeline, our paradigm has traditionally been to think in terms of "past lives" and therefore to view the spirit as having been here *before* we came into what we refer to as "our present incarnation." In actuality, we are looking at it backwards. Our reference points are inaccurate. From my own experience, it is only as the warrior grows and progresses along the path of Knowledge that the unique spirit begins to grow, evolve, and expand throughout the space-time continuum.

As humans, we're asking the wrong questions. The student says, "Master, how can I remember my past lives?" To which the master can only reply, "By living *this* life Wholly."

We're asking how to build a boat that won't sail over the edge of the earth – which means we're assuming the earth is flat. Orlando's method was to give us wings to fly over it all in order to get a better picture of The Big Picture. Only then could we _see_ that the earth really isn't flat in the first place.

And, though this is not a popular idea, the spirit isn't really eternal until we inhabit the totality of ourselves – which means, in essence, to bring total awareness into a single assemblage point where the _I-Am_ becomes ubiquitous, eternal, outside of time.

From that assemblage point, the mortal self still inside the linear timestream will almost inevitably mistake the Whole self as evidence of past lives, when in reality it is more accurately understood as follows: because the Whole self exists (in other words, once the double has been created through Dreaming), it can take on all the manifestations of past-present-future which are relevant to its own growth and evolution. If your evolution required an experience that stemmed from the life of a young boy in Greece, then the Whole Self could automatically and instantaneously from the assemblage point of the double, live that lifetime in its entirety, so that the holographic matrix of _you_ would contain that data. Without _you_, that boy in Greece does not and did not ever exist.

You are the assemblage point from which all else issues forth – and only when that is understood does the warrior fully comprehend what is meant by living with death as her advisor. There is only Now. And Now is as fleeting as the time in which it takes to utter the word. Nothing is guaranteed.

Our lives aren't some random or accidental progression of a spirit through time. Instead, it is the Spirit of the warrior, made whole through Intent and Will, directing the Spirit to learn the lessons which will enable the warrior to become the Whole spirit.

This is the Circle of Self, and once it is understood, it frees the warrior to embrace her own power and put aside dependencies on the idea of external forces.

The spirit is made of eternal energy, but the consciousness which is attached to that energy is lost into fragmentation of energy at the time of death if the warrior hasn't done the work of gathering the cohesion of Self in this life.

The raw ingredients are sugar and flour, but unless they are brought together by the will of the sorcerer, they never become a cake. It is only religious dogma that tries to tell us we have an immortal soul which exists whether we do anything about it or not. Does the garden grow in a desert if you don't water it? Does the child grow to maturity if not nurtured and educated? Do you learn anything if you do not expose yourself to learning?

We're not born perfect. We're not born evolved. And we're not born Whole. Instead, we are like a chrysalis in the process of unfolding, and only if we are successful in emerging outside that chrysalis do we ever become the immortal butterfly, which is the creation of our Will.

~

I once had a seeker tell me she had met the spirit that was Christ, and – to her way of thinking – this meant we don't dissolve into raw energy at death. To me, all it means is that *Christ* didn't dissolve because *he* did the work of emerging from the mortal chrysalis into his own immortality beyond physical death. That doesn't automatically mean anyone else is saved by proxy. Energy doesn't work that way. If I eat a taco, you're still hungry. If you go to college, I don't get the degree. If I manifest my double, no one else can inhabit that assemblage point – because it is unique to the self, a creation of my own intent and will.

Many times, I have seekers say something to me such as this, which was a statement made on my online forum, *The Shaman's Rattle.* "You had an eternal spirit before you were born, you have it now, and it will be there when you go. "

In the sorcerer's world, there are no such automatic assumptions, only what can be verified by direct personal experience – which only then transforms into Knowledge. In working with warriors over the years, what I've discovered is that so very much of what we believe is still based on faith, and though that is a normal phase of development, there is a point where it becomes necessary to graduate from the *faith* that 1+1=2, and into the actual realm of *comprehension* where the equation is not only understood, but the whole theory and practice behind it.

In looking at the drawing, I've tried to illustrate that the "line" on which humans live is really very narrow, very short, and very limited – the linear timeline of our organic lives. From A to B (birth to death) we are held in a narrow range of perception governed largely by our experience of time and our organic form. We tend to only see forward or backward, never taking into account that Time is within us, we are not within Time, and that eternity is not something beyond our mortal life, but is all around us even though we tend to externalize it with such statements as "When I reach eternity." Well... we're already there.

```
     D                    D                    D

     C                                         C
                   Mortal Time Line

     A | <----------------------C----------------------> | B

                   Finite from A to B
          C                              C

     D          D          D
```

A=Birth   B=Death
C=Eternity   D=Abyss (all cohesion lost)

As a result of this externalization, the common misconception about past lives occurs when we think that we had to be here *before* in order to have lived in 16th century France, for example, when that simply is not true on an energetic plane. Indeed, the idea of saying we were here *before* tends to abdicate responsibility in the Now, by placing it outside of ourselves in the way many religions try to place god outside of the individual.

Instead, when it is understood that the spirit of a warrior (the double) expands into the infinite as the warrior herself engages Intent, Will, and the right way to live, it becomes possible to *see* that it is the Self of the Now – your own unique spirit – diving in and out of Time-manifestations (I resist the words "past lives" because of the linear-connotations), in order to teach you the unique lessons you need to learn in order to evolve. This comprehension places the power in *our* hands, and not into the nebulous realm of past and future lives. It localizes the responsibility for our evolution into the Right Now so that we no longer have the luxury of saying, "Well, I'm a spirit on a very long journey and if I don't make it this time, maybe my next life will bring me closer to enlightenment." I have heard these words even from serious warriors, and in my experience, they are the eagle's words.

There is no next time. There is only Now. The double is actually point C on the drawing, but the double is recognized to be a component of the self – the Spirit in Eternity, evolved. *But that can only happen if it is the Will of the warrior in the Now which creates the double in the first place.*

From the POV of "C" (eternity), everything exists simultaneously, including the A-B human lifetime. C can permeate A-B, but A-B can not normally perceive C unless one shifts her assemblage point away from ordinary thinking. The intersect point on the human lifeline which I have represented as the central C is actually the hypothetical point of Whole Awareness, when the warrior begins to see the diagram in 3-D instead of only in a linear manner. At that point, it becomes possible to realize that past lives are not really the result of a nebulous spirit's long journey through time, but are instead the movements and manifestations of the warrior's own unique spirit in its attempt to bring the warrior to an eternal (C) point of awareness beyond the human lifetime (A-B) so that the spirit doesn't become food for the eagle and fall into the abyss (D).

THE CHICKEN and THE LUMINOUS EGG

Before you could be born, you had to create your ancestors and so your I-Am spoke and formed the world around you in the form of a womb, a consciousness pecking its way into this world by first getting inside the egg so it might later emerge after taking on the shape of its new evolution. So the riddle is utterly simple: the will of the future chicken created the egg as a shell to hold it while it was evolving from where-it-was-before, and in doing so spontaneously created the primogen hen to serve as a host, just a thoughtform making itself whole through the manipulation of time/space and matter/energy, and if ever there was proof of spontaneous parthenogenesis, look at the chicken crossing the nightroad, no?

Orlando – February 14, 1998

Orlando says he was a little boy in Greece, yet he is also myself. I do not yet remember the child in Greece – and if asked why, I could only tell you that the double has a life of its own: the assemblage point of second and third attention. As warriors in the mortal world, we may occasionally catch glimpses into those other realms of awareness – through Dreaming or visionary experiences or power plants – but just as don Genaro's double had a rich and mischievous life of which Genaro himself in first attention seemed to have very little actual awareness, so it is with Orlando.

The double is a being of the Infinite – something that may be discussed with words, yet something which recedes like quicksilver in the face of those same words.

So while I cannot say that I have any actual memory of Orlando's life in Greece in the year 845, I have dreamed it quite vividly, and can accept that this was a point on the time-map where he fixed his assemblage point in order to gain some experience that is critical to my own evolution. So it could be said that I had another life as a little boy in Greece –

and this would be far more accurate than the idea of traditional reincarnation. This is why don Juan left Carlos with the task of remembering the other self. The double, by virtue of being infinite and eternal, is not confined to our linear mortal lifetime, and depending on the intent of the warrior, the double undoubtedly dips his hand into many, many experiences in that river of time so as to strengthen the self in the Now.

Through dreaming, *meditation-with-intent*, and other interactions such as gnosis, the eternal double and the mortal self conjoin, so that the mortal self is always drawn toward Wholeness in the third attention. The trick is bringing the assemblage point of the mortal self into alignment with that of the immortal double, so that Wholeness is achieved through conjoining of the two, rather than the dis-integration that occurs if one's awareness is devoured by the eagle.

We are born with eternity/infinity inside us, but if we don't hatch that egg, our entire existence is finite within the span of a single lifetime–this one.

Warriors live impeccably in the Now.

~

Question and Answer

QUESTION: *I have always believed that past lives are controlled by our oversoul, so even if we might not remember the specific details of our past lives, the oversoul carries those memories with it as it moves forward through time and through a sequence of many lifetimes. We have the same spirit, but we incarnate in different times and places. I'm myself in the now, but maybe I was also a soldier in the Crusades.*

ANSWER: In my *seeing*, what we mistakenly call past lives aren't some linear progression of an oversoul, but lessons we teach ourselves in the Now. This is accomplished through the double, as s/he already exists in eternity, and can take on any manifestation or assemblage point that might be required from any location in time – past, present or future. In this way, a billion different people can actually have the past life "memories" of Marie Antoinette, because your double could choose to be in that assemblage point of at relevant points in her life, in order to bring forward into the Now those lessons.

The thing most people overlook is that this does not mean you were Marie Antoinette. She was her own unique self, just as you are. But if your double perceives there are relevant lessons you can learn through her, the double can choose the assemblage point of Marie and communicate the experience to you, usually in Dreaming or second attention, as if it is your own experience. To assume it is who you are or even who you were is where the greatest mistakes are made, because it is at that point that one abdicates personal responsibility in the Now and makes the assumption that their spiritual survival is automatic because they *think* they remember being Marie Antoinette when that really isn't the case at all. At that point, as in Plato's example, one is mistaking the shadows on the wall for reality.

QUESTION: *I have come to a point where I quite literally cannot believe that the Supreme Being does not exist without casting aside all of my work to date willy-nilly.*

ANSWER: Only when I have been willing to let go of "all my work to date" have I been able to really embrace what is always turning out to be The Big Picture In Progress. You may indeed have reached your own ultimate truth, that there is a supreme being, but my own experience has shown that we are it, and then only if we do the work on the spirit which is required to actually inhabit that eternal self. Like learning to walk, and then to run, it's a progression.

There is salvation from the abyss of dis-integration, but it will be through your efforts and not because Jesus loves you.

Pardon me if I seem a bit harsh here, but I find it to be the height of irresponsibility to teach children that they can just live in spiritual ignorance all their lives, plugged into the comforting teat of the consensual reality, and still go to heaven when they die if they just ask Jesus to forgive them.

If Jesus existed, he saved himself through his actions. Was he the son of God? Yes, but so are we all – and not in the limited parent-child paradigm that so many choose to believe. He was the son of god in that he was a spiritual spark who took on manifestation in order to undergo a wondrous journey toward Wholeness. He was son, and he was god, and he was spirit (father, son, holy ghost). But so are we all. It wasn't automatic by any stretch. And neither was Buddha's journey. They did the work and we can learn by their examples, but there is no salvation in the sense it is presented in so many organized religions. We save ourselves. And we create our own heaven or our own hell, entirely as a matter of our own Intent.

QUESTION: *Does it matter if we remember our past lives on a conscious level? Do they have anything to do with who we are now?*

ANSWER: My own experience has shown that we know things without knowing how we know them at times. Perhaps learned men with letters after their names would call this animal instinct, but that's not really what I'm talking about.

In *Redefining Reincarnation*, I was exploring the double's function of essentially diving in and out of matter, taking on what we traditionally think of as past lives in order to gather the knowledge and, more definitively, the experience (a cohesive unit rather than individual memories) necessary to allow the mortal self to advance through her evolution.

As I have continued to look at this process through gnosis, I have begun to glimpse an edge of something much larger – something that ties in to remembering the other self, and how it is basically when we begin to remember the experience of

110

the double's efforts that we begin to amass our own cohesion as a Whole unit of awareness spanning eternity and infinity.

QUESTION: *Maybe this is a chicken or the egg question, but where does this process start? Does the warrior exist first, or has the double been out there in eternity all along?*

ANSWER: It begins right here with the mortal self – the warrior on the path taking her first breath of Intent. We are the source. The double is the *projection* of Intent into the Infinite, wholly capable of taking on a life (or entire lifetimes) all his/her own, and then essentially offering the mortal warrior the opportunity to integrate that experience into the source... or not. Obviously, those who do choose to integrate the experience embark on the journey toward cohesion, and those who *don't* most likely do not evolve into Wholeness, but may continue as fragments without any sense of cohesion.

QUESTION: *You talk often about an evolution of consciousness. Is that the same thing as creating the double?*

ANSWER: It is through the struggle to evolve, to become more than what we were when we entered this life, that we begin to work with the tools of Intent and Will as extensions of our own creative force. And it is in doing that that we create the double and – if we are successful in life – conjoin to that point of Whole Self-Awareness in third attention.

I am often asked if we have to wait until we're dead to have full access to gnosis – the place of silent knowing. Well – obviously not. To have access to that Knowledge/experience during life is a matter of moving the assemblage point from the mortal self into the eternal other. You open your eyes inside of the double and see that you've been Whole all along. You still have the responsibility of "forcing that to go through the motions of actually occurring", of course, and that's what the journey itself is all about.

111

Chapter Eleven
The Language of Power

"It's much more difficult to understand magic through the eyes of logic than to understand logic through the eyes of magic."

Orlando – 1999

Before we can embrace our evolution, we must undo the automatic programs running without our permission and even without our knowledge.

The problem with trying to put any of this into a format suitable for perusal by others is simply that the journey is so intimate and personal that I fear it may defy translation from my world-of-words into your world-of-words. For in the end, the reality we attempt to share is comprised entirely of language – the agreed-upon sounds and symbols we make for the purpose of being able to communicate that green is green and the purpose of a fire truck is to put out fires. If we didn't have such agreements based upon common concepts, our world would be disorganized and disconnected as a puzzle with no corner pieces.

Even to people who may pride themselves on open-mindedness, the statement in the beginning of this work which reads *"immortality itself is within our grasp"* could cause them to put the book aside altogether, believing it to be only a work of fiction – yet when I refer to immortals, eternal beings, inorganic beings, and our own potential immortality, these are only concepts meant to embody the ideas of immortality-through-transformation, the two-part migration of the soul, the potential evolution of *homo sapien* into *homo immortalis* –an old idea and myth evolving into a new idea and myth just as the word ghost might be used to describe a deceased entity (the traditional definition), or how it has come to be used in certain branches of analytical psychology and metaphysics as "the ghost inside the machine" – the living spirit that gives life to our human bodies, the anima. That the word has certain baggage is irrelevant – for a large part of this journey also involves learning to see beyond the limits of language.

As long as we blindly accept the words, "All things die," for example, we are merely machines acting out the programming of our masters without making any genuine, individual attempt to evolve beyond reality as it exists to our present perceptions. We have accepted our fate as fate, and program ourselves to live and die just as our ancestors lived and died.

Dreaming the Anima...

It was in 1995, shortly after I had become deeply involved in this spirit quest, that I had a dream involving my own double. In the context of the dream, I was an observer, standing to the side as he and another man whom I did not recognize were working over what appeared to be a dead body. My sense of the vision was that Orlando and the other man were attempting to heal the dead man. I saw Orlando pass his hands over the body, a few inches above the chest and abdomen, and as he did so, a word formed in the air above the body. At first, the word read "Animina", but then the man on the table began to breathe, and the word in the air transformed to "Anima".

At the time, I did not know the meaning of the word, and to my knowledge had never encountered it before. Upon looking it up, not really expecting to find anything, I discovered that the word is of Greek origins, and means, essentially, "Lifeforce"–that which animates the body, yet cannot be located in any medical examination.

Ultimately, we must each determine for ourselves the validity or falseness of every absolute with which we have been programmed – yes, literally *programmed* – since birth. Perhaps we will come to discover that all things die. *Or* – just perhaps – we might discover that this is every bit as much a misinterpretation of the world as it once was to believe "The earth is flat." Words. They have been our prison for centuries, but if we are impeccable, they can also become a pathway toward our ultimate freedom.

So, in many ways, this is a journey through language. If we cannot get beyond the words, if we cannot open ourselves to ideas, we cannot learn. We cannot grow. We cannot evolve.

We crunch words, it seems, to find what they are made of.

Language is what separates us from all other creatures, but we must be always willing to listen to the concepts conveyed by the words – the *idea* the speaker is trying to impart – instead of getting lost in the traditional meaning of the words themselves and engaging in games of semantics in a self-deceiving attempt to divert attention from the issue to the language. Of all the traps I have witnessed in this ongoing journey, this is one of the most common and one of the most dangerous, which is why I stress it throughout these pages.

For example, to even speak the word "god" conjures up a wide variety of reactions, yet what I *see* or feel inside my own mind, within the confines of my own internal dialogue, is something entirely other. To say "god" to a Christian invokes the notion of an intelligent, omniscient being, usually if not always male, a father-image to whom they pray and whom most fear, respect and love equally. To most Christians, this is the only interpretation of that word possible, yet it is not what I think when I myself use the word.

And so our language is imprecise if we focus solely on the words. If I say the same word to a pagan – if I asked, for example, "Do you believe in God?" – a true pagan's response would probably be, "Which one?" To the pagan, the word conjures up images of many deities, and to the true pagan, no other interpretation is possible because the word itself is part of the agreed-upon belief system. This is the reality of paganism, just as it is the reality of Christianity to envision the father-God. If I were to invoke the word "god" to a Buddhist, the monk might point to the earth or the sky or the tree and reply that the creative god-force is within every living thing, even within non-living things such as rocks, water, fire and air. This is the reality of the Buddhist, the automatic point of view from which his world is created and assembled.

And though the word "god" might be used to invoke all these separate realities – the Christian, the pagan, the Buddhist – it is a different reality invoked within the minds of each person who hears the word. And, in the end, each of these realities is as real as any of the others, and each is just as unreal.

It is a world of words.

When Orlando first put forth the idea that magic is as viable a tool to use in one's life as a hammer or a screwdriver, I could only sputter in disbelief at such a foolish notion. "Magic? This is the 20th century!" (At the time, it was 1994). "Magic is only fantasy!" I protested indignantly.

It took almost a year for me to get past my own self-importance enough to see that this force we call magic not only exists, but it exists as an extension of the will, the creative god-force within each of us, and can affect the world with results no less real than those which could be affected by the hammer or the screwdriver.

Magic, then, is the outward manifestation of human will. Reality is perception. Perception is reality. And perception can be as limited or as expansive as we allow it to be. But the first step is always going to be the decision to see beyond what we think we already know

Spines stiffen with the mere suggestion that perhaps science is no more absolute within the big picture than tales of faerie folk dancing in circles of magic mushrooms on a moonlight night sometime in late October. Science is essentially nothing more than the definition we currently hold in our minds to form our world view. But never forget that rational science once "proved" that the flat Earth was the center of the universe.

Science has been used to prove whatever man needs it to prove, yet it is limited not only by the technology available to it, but also by the perceptions of the scientists themselves, as has been discovered by quantum mechanics in recent years. The world reacts and changes on a molecular level in response to the observer! So, in reality, pure science can never really exist for the simple reason that it is dependent upon the scientist, and that scientist has a point of view, a *mindset*, which will determine the direction of his research and influence the nature of his findings, even if only slightly.

What is magic?

It is the force within us that enables a 110 lb. woman to lift a 5000 lb. tractor trailer off an infant. It is the undefined component that has made it possible for a woman in Florida to be visited by her son in California, only to later discover that he never left Los Angeles. It is the force that enables a man who falls in love to go into an abrupt remission from terminal cancer. It is the premonition which causes a woman to cancel a plane flight and later discover the aircraft she would have been on crashed into the ocean. It is the ghost inside the machine. It is us.

Magic is the Realization that we aren't at the mercy of deities or technology for our salvation from the abyss, and – most of all – magic is the *will* to make it so. We are capable of choosing our own immortal evolution and our own transformation if – *if* – we are willing to experiment with a new mindset which has the potential to transcend all the programming we have spent a lifetime accumulating.

Chapter Twelve
Creating Reality

When I'm observing inanimate objects, it's usually with certain expectations which may not be valid in the sorcerer's world. I do not expect a rock to move, but in the sorcerer's world, there's nothing to say it can't. We program ourselves through our imprinting to have certain assumptions and expectations, yet those are only belief systems, and only have power for as long as we agree to them. The reason some folks can walk on hot coals or even walk on water, the reason a monk was once observed levitating a coconut, the reason it might sometimes seem that faeries have moved a pencil from where it was left on the desk last night... all these things are possible when the programs are shattered and we enter into the sorcerer's world, where different rules are in force – or, more precisely, no rules at all save for what we bring with us.

I recently re-read _Illusions_ by Richard Bach, a delightful short novel wherein the main character learns about creating reality; and was amused to discover that many of the things described were mirrors of things I've done in my own life, and with some degree of regularity.

A few years ago, when I was first beginning to _see_ that the sorcerer's world existed, I began experimenting with the idea of manipulating or creating reality. One day, as I was driving, I had the thought, "Okay, Self, if we create our own reality, let's test it. I want to see a red hearse before I get home." Just grabbed the most unlikely image I could think of.

In the middle of nowhere, on a sparsely traveled desert road in the middle of summer, this seemed highly unlikely, if not altogether impossible. I had the thought, let it go, and went on with my journey – because, frankly, I had no faith it would happen and no fear that it wouldn't. I simply tossed the thought into the universe without attachment or expectation.

I hadn't traveled more than a few miles when I came to a 4-way stop. There, facing me in the oncoming traffic lane, was a car – the only one I had seen in many miles. It chilled me to the bone, for though it wasn't red, it was most definitely a hearse. I patted myself on the back and said, "Hmmm. Okay, but not exactly what I asked for." But then, as the hearse and I passed one another going in opposite directions, I noticed the license plate. 1RED338.

The nagual has a wicked sense of humor. Not only the designation "red" on the license plate, but the number 338 also has extreme significance in my life, which I will discuss later in this book.

Over the course of time, I repeated this experiment many times, with a variety of unlikely items. Once on a freeway in San Diego, I said to Wendy, "I want to see a crib before we get to your mother's house." No sooner had we gotten off the freeway than I looked into a residential neighborhood to see an unassembled crib leaning against a garage wall. A few months later, mid-summer, I said to Wendy on the same freeway, "I want to see a pumpkin before we get to your mother's house." Again, we got off the freeway, and there sitting on the front porch of a house was a fine fat pumpkin. Nowhere near Halloween or Thanksgiving. Not pumpkin season. Yet there she sat. Might as well have been some grand carriage drawn by tiny mice who had transformed into mystical horses. Just a pumpkin on somebody's porch, and yet one of the finest validations from the nagual I had ever received.

Another incident: driving through the desert, again in the middle of nowhere. By this time I'm getting a bit demanding with my manifestations. So I picked something *really* impossible. I said to my traveling companions, "I want to see a washing machine before we get home!" And so as we bumbled along the road where only chaparral and jackrabbits dare to dwell, we came around a bend in the road, and there on the side of the road sat not only a washing machine, but a washer and dryer. Sense of humor evident. A sign on them said, "Free." Now if *that* wasn't a message from the nagual, I can't imagine what would be. Free indeed.

> We are free to create reality, or to inhabit the reality created by other men. It's our choice, and it's in our power.

About a year later, as Wendy and I were stuck in a major traffic jam on the 101 freeway outside of Los Angeles, I turned to her and said, "I want to see a lion before we get home." She shot me a dirty look, stuck in traffic as we were, and she at the wheel. The stench of diesel and brushfire choked the air. Red tail lights formed a river of blood that seemed to stretch endlessly, clogged in freeway veins. I shut up and went back to contemplating the dust on the dashboard. A lion seemed unlikely.

And yet...

And yet...

In less than two minutes, we rounded a bend in the freeway, and there, emblazoned across the horizon, was a huge sign made entirely of tiny white lights, cast in the shape of a lion's head. Stood about, oh, 50' tall. And as if I might miss it, directly beneath, also enlightened in huge, glowing white letters, *The Lion King*.

Wendy just shot me that look out the corner of her eye – the one I've come to recognize as, "Don't even go there." So I just smiled and blew the nagual a kiss, and felt extremely grateful for these glimpses behind the veil.

There have been many such incidents since embarking on this path. So many I cannot count them all. So many that all I can do is gaze in wonder at the earth, the red hearses, the pumpkins and the lion kings, and occasionally glance at the face in the mirror and wonder, "Who *are* you?" The answer is a work in progress, a mosaic of memories and mumblings, a strange tapestry of strange events that really aren't strange at all once we finally accept that the magic is real. It's our consensual agreement view of the world that's the ultimate illusion, the greatest lie.

Inanimate objects? No such thing, really. We program the coconut to hang on the tree, but we might just as easily rearrange its molecules to become a fine, fat pumpkin on a porch in San Diego. It's all just an arrangement of energy in the sorcerer's world.

MINDSET

The secret to manifesting change – whether a thought-form into a pumpkin, or healing one's body – lies in *mindset*. This is where words fail, and all I can say is that there is a "place" within me, seemingly experienced in the vicinity of the lower right solar plexus, and it is from that "place" that I seem to be able to bring these manifestations into being. If I am thinking about it, it won't happen. If I am needing it or even actively wanting it, not as much success. That's why for my experiments I pick things that really *don't* matter – cribs, pumpkins, washing machines and lion kings. Then, by seeing how it feels when I work these experiments, I begin to be able to analyze the process and put that same energy into practice in much more practical matters – such as healing, stalking in the world of phantoms, even Dreaming.

Several times over the past couple of years, I've actually managed to heal myself of an oncoming bout with the flu, using this same method. I envision it like this: I alter the molecular structure/frequency of my body so that it is no longer compatible with whatever germ or dis-ease is attempting to manifest. It is recognized that the host (self) and the invading organism (cold virus) are not, ultimately, part of the same matrix. I find the mindset of the organic matrix as it existed *before* the cold, or more precisely, as it exists *without*

120

the cold, and when the visualization aligns with the Intent to re-structure, the cold simply has no place to "be", and so it disintegrates. This has worked for me on several occasions now. Once, it failed. The difference? Mindset, I think. In order to manifest pumpkins, cribs, and the like, it seems to require very little effort and/or time. In order to re-structure organic form, it seems to be successful for me only after several hours of uninterrupted meditation, usually in the middle of the night.

Of course, it's just my own programs that tell me more effort is required to heal myself than to manifest a pumpkin. In reality, there is no difference whatsoever. None. As Yoda said to Luke Skywalker, "Size matters not. There is no try, only Do."

Chapter Thirteen
Seeing Beyond the Illusions

When we really think about it, the world we live in is built on illusions and misconceptions, right down to its core level. Just to take one example with which all Westerners are intimately familiar, what is money? Allegedly it represents a certain amount of gold in Fort Knox, but as we all fully well know, there isn't nearly enough gold in Fort Knox to back up all that green paper we're all scrambling and slaving our lives away to get, so... what is money? It's a symbol. It's a tool, but is it real, or do we all simply agree to say that it has meaning and so it does? We fight for it. We'll lie, cheat and steal for it. We'll even betray those we love for it. And yet, in the final analysis, it's just one more illusion, one more agreed-upon icon that has no meaning beyond what we attribute to it.

At some point in time, we all agreed to agree that gold has greater value than the petals of a wild rose. It's arbitrary and it is a leg trap when the illusions take on greater significance than the ghost inside the machine, the human spirit, the Self.

Reality is only what we agree it is. The things we hold true are often only programs, so deeply imbedded in our human mainframe that we don't even recognize them until someone points them out. Why is gold more valuable than silver? Because it is more scarce? Because someone in some past society thought it was prettier? There is no logical reason for any of it, just as there is no logical reason for many of the things we take for granted.

THE ILLUSORY WORLD

April 7, 2000

We live in a made-up world where the reflections on the nuthouse walls have been mistaken for reality, yet we've been doing it so long that we think it is real. The society we live in, the rules we live by, the morals and standards of the world are 100%, absolutely, completely, irrevocably, undeniably nuts! And what's even more nuts is that people refuse to see it, as if by their group denial, they can somehow believe that the white picket fence in the Norman Rockwell painting is real.

Sometimes I still hear my mother's voice: "Now, Della, do you really think everybody else is crazy and you're the only one who's sane?" Well, in a word – *Yes*! I really have come to *see* that 99.9% of the people in the world are living in some kind of grand illusion. They go to work to pay for the car to drive to work in. They work to pay for basic human rights – food, shelter, heat – and the primary result of being magnanimously granted these basic human rights is that then they must work harder to pay for them.

They buy insurance (if they have enough green slips of paper) to pay the medicine man for his pills (which are mostly placeboes anyway) and the reason they're so sick in the first place is because they've worked themselves into all kinds of stress-related illnesses trying to gather enough green slips of paper with which to pay for the insurance to cover their stress-related illnesses. Then one day when they're 65, they wake up and wonder where their lives went, but by then it's too late. They've sold their souls for the house they live in, the car they drive, the watch on their wrist, the virtual money in their virtual bank account... and they don't have a single clue as to who they are. Their lives are over while they've been trapped in the prison of paying for the privilege of living. And most of them have never really lived at all because the illusion is designed to insure that most of us never have enough of that illusory green paper to escape the prison until it is too late.

Who's more crazy? The lunatics in the asylum or the lunatics *running* the asylum? Yes, Mom, the world really is a nut-house and I'm ass-deep in cashews!

THE BLIND MAN AND THE JUNGLE

"Consider this: it will always be easier to take the road already built by those who have gone before, for the journey is well-mapped and the conveniences along the way even make the trip easy. Ah, but what if that road you're on was first forged by a suicidal blind madman running headlong through the jungle with a sword, hacking out the path to his own death so he might find it waiting at the end of the way, and what if all of humanity timidly followed that demented fool just to see where he was going, but now they've been on that same fatal road ever since, never stopping to consider that there are many paths to the river, and not all of them need end with death?"

-Orlando

Is it possible that we die not because we must but because we *believe* we must? In the same way that thinking we already know something will prevent us from learning anything more about it, does the consensual human belief – 6 billion strong – that we will all one day die create the reality wherein we *do* die? Not because it is necessarily inevitable, but because we must fulfill the programming, even if it is we ourselves who are responsible for the program in the first place? In short, we base our idea of reality on what we perceive instead of attempting to alter our perceptions to the point that a new reality becomes possible.

As has been mentioned previously, quantum science has now confirmed that the very basic components of reality alter in response to the presence of an observer. In other words, reality knows we're here. It knows we're watching. And it appears to change because we're watching. What does this tell us about ourselves and our programming? Are we really only the passive, impotent handful of chemicals we've been taught to believe, or are we the gods themselves – co-creators of reality at a quantum level? And if we *are*, can we not then change our nature through the process of creation?

> "You cannot see a mortal breath, yet you can witness its effects on dandelions scattered on the wind of a wish, and so it is with the will, the invisible but tangible breath of your desire acting upon the physical world. Ah, but the trick is this: you have to believe it in order to see it and before you can believe it you need a reason. Think on this, for it is the cornerstone of a new foundation, yes?"
>
> --Orlando

As long as the medical community as a whole accepted that certain illnesses such as epilepsy were the result of possession by demons, the patient was treated accordingly. To the reality of the day, to the science of the times, this was just the way things were. It no more occurred to them to question the diagnosis (demons) than it occurs to us to hold our hand in flame to determine whether or not it is hot. It was simply an accepted part of reality – yet just as science and perception have evolved to demonstrate that demons are not at the root of epilepsy, the perceptions of a few have also evolved to enable fire-walking and other miracles, which could just as easily be called magic, which would be considered impossible by current, common standards of "reality".

Reality is perception. That's what Orlando has spent the past ten years teaching us. I know now that I have felt his influence in my life even prior to that time, since I have come to see that he is not a being constrained by the linear flow of time at all. He is an inhabitant of the *seventh sense* – though it could as easily be called the sorcerer's world, the third attention, or a level of evolved awareness existing both as part of this world and as part of whatever lies beyond the normal realm of our perceptions. And it is from that place that all our grandest ideas and art come, and all our greatest teachers. It is a world assembled not only with our five physical senses, but also with the addition of the sixth sense (telepathy, clairvoyance, pure perception, non-local awareness).

In the seventh sense we might find a lot of strange goings-on – things that go bump in the night, faeries, wizards, time travelers, immortals of many different kinds. In the seventh sense, we might also find ourselves – for it is not a land with which humans are unfamiliar, nor even a land we are forbidden to travel. Indeed, it is a land that has been whispered of in myth and legend for as far back as time can measure. Human encounters with "the little people" of Ireland. Strange but undeniable accounts of men and women vanishing into "otherworlds" for years, yet upon their return, appear not to have aged a day.

In his book *Dimensions*, Jacques Vallee likens these old myths to modern-day legends of human encounters with alien beings. It is only our automatic programming that causes us to initially scoff and close our minds when we hear such tales, but if we're willing to even consider some new possibilities, we can open ourselves to a vast world of incredible potential.

Unfortunately, these otherworlds known to shamans, sorcerers and mystics are lands we have slowly but surely placed outside normal human perceptions simply by refusing to perceive them – perhaps a milieu once as commonplace to us as cyberspace is in the early 21st century – but a milieu still accessible to us if we choose to see it, if we choose to seek it. Instead of being accessed with the tools of mouse and keyboard, however, the tools used to access this otherworld of experience are the tools of perception–intent, will, and a force we can only call magic because it is a science not yet understood.

We *can* understand it. And through understanding, we can even visit these otherworlds. One day, through the completion of our individual evolution, we will even master the ability to stay, to live there as immortal citizens. Perhaps on that day we will become the teachers and facilitators for other humans struggling to see beyond the limits of their five common senses.

Chapter Fourteen
Breath of Life

One night as I was meditating under the stars, I received the message, "He's looking for you as much as you are looking for him." This made little sense to me, for I was thinking with the rational elements of awareness rather than the magical or mystical elements of awareness. So the little voice clarified. "He's waiting for you to step outside of time so he may show you who he is, and the connections that bind you together. Only when you accept responsibility for yourself by making him Whole will you embrace your full clarity and power."

There *was* still a lingering sense of doubt and even despair which often manifested through the voice of gnosis, whispering, *Make me Whole. Give me life.* I had heard those voices for quite some time. I had felt their heavy gravity. *Make me whole.*

For several months, I attempted to step outside of time in every manner I could think of, yet ultimately I discovered what I had already begun to suspect. The assemblage point was once again fixated in the world of ordinary awareness. Having made a thorough attempt to dislodge it, but with no success, I made the decision to seek out the aid of the mushroom ally, under the guidance of a master shaman in Mexico.

BIRTHING THE DOUBLE

February 26, 1998
The sacred ally ingested on the Mexican shore. The sorcerer's journey, a sensation of intense cold reminiscent of Socrates' hemlock, mild convulsions perhaps only reflections of this unusual chill which hangs in the crisp and silent air. Engaged the ally at about 6 p.m. and in the words of the song,

"Life will never be the same again." I say this now and remind myself to remember it, for despite the depth of the journey, there is still a human awareness which says I will forget, or at least return to ordinary consciousness.

There is no beginning. Last night, I created Orlando whole on the mesa outside of time, yet those are only words lost in the phantasm which is the dayshine world. The real world is that reality behind the mind's eye. These frail bodies we have tied on are nothing more than receptors, flesh made of matter/energy which we have scraped together for reasons entirely unknown, perhaps as part of the quest for eternal life, perhaps so we can perceive mortality as the motivation for immortality.

Disjointed images, I see myself existing as a thing of eternity, which can only be perceived as a line of highly refined metal stretching through the entire cosmos in a straight line that will meet its own beginning at the point of infinity. That is me, though the rest of reality – the cosmic soup, nature, humanity, the mortal world, the consensual reality – exists in a bubble entirely apart from me.

During this phase of the journey, I experience the feeling/thought/desire, I want a mate outside all this darkness. The immortal creature who is existing outside the continuum is lonely, wanting someone to share it with. Overtones of Genesis, making me wonder if the Bible itself was written primarily by psychonauts traveling that vast cosmos on the wings of the plant allies.

I *saw* God. I *was* God. But it was a solitary, lonely existence which could only be alleviated by reaching my hand into the mire of the continuum and molding/shaping/creating a fellow immortal to share the void with. It truly was a void, an abyss from which even that perception of an eternal being is separated only by the force of her own consciousness. Lose consciousness and the abyss of death is the lowest common denominator, which is why we scrape together flesh to inhabit for brief periods of time – the desperation of a consciousness seeking to escape the abyss just as a man in the middle of the ocean will cling to floating timbers. It is a battle to preserve consciousness, and only through some sort of *body* – whether organic or inorganic – can we perceive ourselves as existing apart from that vast nothingness. At one point, I say out loud: "We're in the abyss all the time, but our bodies prevent us from seeing it." We are surrounded by it, just outside this fragile continuum we call reality.

For a time, while I am experiencing myself as this cold steel consciousness existing apart from the continuum and apart from the abyss, I also perceive a valentine-shaped heart in which I am encased. This is love, I realize – the thing that drives us to seek continuity, cohesion. To continue that feeling of love is to know immortality, and we will do anything to keep the abyss from devouring it, from separating us into our component molecules just to reform us in some other fleeting consciousness that is flawed and eternally injured by the pain of so many previous separations, so many previous deaths which have resulted in just one more long drink of lethe from the core of that abyss.

To call it an abyss is to limit it, for it is a seething blackness, filled with the components of all life but altogether devoid of conscience or individual consciousness. From it, consciousness can form into flesh, but it seems to be altogether random, a grand design of nothingness held together by a fragile spider's web of raw energy. Impersonal. Writhing with life but not alive. Neither good nor evil. Just flawed to my human way of thinking because, ultimately, the design is that I will return to that seething mass only to be reformed in another body in another place – perhaps as a tree on the far shore of some alien planet on the far side of the galaxy or perhaps as another mortal soul who loves and aches and feels the pain of its own mortality and dares not love too deeply for fear/knowledge/awareness that the ultimate design of nature is to strip from us those very feelings which make us unique, those feelings which separate us from the abyss and undoubtedly those feelings which motivate us to tie on this fleeting flesh in the first place.

In order to seek immortality we must risk giving our soul over to love, knowing all the while that the design of creation is to break us down to our component parts of non-consciousness, obliterating the very thing that made us want to live to begin with.

Just words to feed the eagle. I saw him watching me last night, in a thousand guises with a thousand eyes. Feed, you son of a bitch. Devour my words in lieu of my life. Taste this strange love on the spores of consciousness, but keep your distance. Forget about me. Let me pass by you because I've given you a good song and dance, a few tears and a taste of mortal blood. I'm worth more to you alive than dead, yet I fear you feed on love and that your predatory nature drives you to take from me what you cannot find for yourself. I'll go on dancing for you, my pretty bird, and never to steps you can predict or imagine, and I'll even give you tastes and glimpses of what it is to love, but you have to keep up your end of the bargain, too.

You have to fly past me. You have to leave my love and my lover alone, for only through this wretched state of human consciousness can we be driven to do those things that feed you best of all. I don't like you, but I respect you. You don't have to like me but I hope you'll be entertained. One day I'll chop off your head and feed it to the wild dogs running along the shores of the underworld. Just because you've always been here doesn't make it right. Just because it's your nature to destroy doesn't mean a more powerful predator won't one day emerge from this cosmic continuum. Is that why you keep all things finite? Have you limited our lifespan and the boundaries of our perception so you think we can't see you?

Have you convinced us you always win so we'll never try to defeat you?

So much happens... truly the mesa outside of time, for during the hours of this experience, centuries and eons passed in the span of seconds. I confront a series of conundrums concerning Orlando. I feel his consciousness move into me from time to time. He is me and I am him, yet in order for this grand plan to work, he must be separate, in a body of his own. Of course, there is an edge of awareness that has returned from the journey with me which says he is as real as I perceive him to be, yet those are only words to this mortal self's ears. Indeed, I am trying to understand the infinite with a finite mind, thinking in terms of "*body*" when perhaps I need to think in terms of "*spirit-flesh*" – the magical body, the shaman's body, the astral/energy body that is far more real than these decaying temples of flesh. As I write this, I see it clearly – he is not separate from me, yet my mind continues to scream "He must be separate!"

I feel him within me, his vast intellect and knowledge and awareness moving upon me with a far greater reality than the Della-entity has ever known. *The figure in the mirror isn't me*, to quote an obscure song, and it's nothing so trite as an identity crisis. Before a baby takes on the flesh of its mother, it exists within the molecular structure of the mother and the father and all the organic components which will go into its creation. In that way, I am Orlando, yet there is a part of me that wants to fight that – perhaps because I intuitively know he must be whole unto himself and only by pushing him out of me can he stand alone. Impossible to describe, impossible to speak of in words which only limit the experience and drag it down into this continuum which is the lowest common denominator of human experience. But just as the baby is the mother and the father before it becomes a separate physical being, so is Orlando inside of me.

I feel his consciousness/self/wholeness enter. I am him. I feel his male body stretch and lengthen, long legs dangling over the foot of the bed, muscular arms, flat chest, silken hair so much shorter than mine, coarse male cheek, not soft like a woman's skin – the physicality of him as certain as if I had truly become him.

Time stops. I am him, the immortal male muse of eternity, yet where is my body? I've left it somewhere in the 17th century, in the streets of Paris or on a bus in Berlin years later when I am drowning in _The Sorrows of Young Werther_, trying to communicate some tiny fragment of all this vast pain to the world. My body isn't here, not in this red room, not in this late 20th century phantasm of linear time where mortality and immortality are separated by that very line which defines time itself. Yet the thing in the mirror is blonde and female and all too mortal and cries "What the fuck?"

What to do? Scrape together a body of magic dust and autumn dusk and smooth it in place over these immortal bones with a raven's feather fallen into the street from that high tower of London all those centuries ago? Creation. I stand at the moment of creation. Mine. His. There's no difference.

Words fail. Time comes and goes as the Della-entity wrestles with this confounding conundrum. He is whole and real but _must_ also be separate. The words pound through her head: _I am him but he must be apart from me._ Birth. Creation. How to make a baby without a human womb. How to make an immortal from a mortal's will. How to create a magical being from a spark of creation that has neither sperm nor egg.

Creation. The word pounds through my mind. I stand on the threshold of it – the moment I must make him whole or lose him forever. What to do? How to do it? There is no how. There is, as he's said so often, only the doing. He _becomes_ me again, wrapping that fierce male intellect inside my body, skin-walking, and I realize he's telling me how to create him. How else _could_ it be? Only he could know who he is, just as the baby in the womb is its own creature, separate from its biological parents. Only he could tell me who he wants to be and how to bring him into being.

He said, "You've given me life. You've given me eternal life. Now I must give it back to you." At one point, he gets up and looks out the window. The constellation Gemini hangs low on the horizon, the sign of his birth, the sign of the twins. How else could it have been? He marvels at the fact that he is truly observing his own creation. He feels himself becoming whole, real, again and again and again, into eternity. It's so hard. He says, "It will always be like this. Always this struggle to hold consciousness intact." Unspoken, but strongly in his thoughts, *"Are you up to it? Can you fight this battle every night without end, can you live all of eternity in between each and every linear second?"* That's immortality. That's what it is and it isn't easy.

But as the medicine witch who finds herself back in this crumbling temple of pale and aging flesh, I must ask the question: How do we maintain this 7th sense of perception – the ability to perceive our own immortality – while crawling on our bellies through the mire of the consensual reality? How can we be immortals in a mortal world? Or is to ask such a question only indicative of my own pathetic limits? Have I learned nothing?

It is 3:38 in the morning and he realizes that *this* was the moment of mutual creation – the moment I created him, and that now we've come full circle on the mesa outside of time.

Full circle. *Make me whole.* Creation itself, the act of bringing into being something which did not exist before so that it can be the source of your own continuity – the bestowing of infinite life from the thing which was created by mortal need.

Through this journey, I have come to wonder if the entire purpose of life is creation – not just to clone oneself through mortal birth, but to seek evolution through the creation and the perception of one's own personal immortality apart from the continuum. Fleeting words, feathers on the eagle's crest, blowing in the howling void of the abyss itself.

We are here as the chrysalis, but the double is the perception we must enter in order to perceive infinity eternally instead of only fleetingly.

We are here to evolve beyond the eagle's claw and perhaps even smash his nest. Immortality comes from within us, yet it must be placed outside the mortal body and then "entered" with the consciousness, as a hermit crab crawls inside a new shell. This is the two-part migration of the soul.

I rave into the darkness, weeping into the void, birth pains of creation, the terror of annihilation, the motivation of love driving me to preserve it through eternal life itself.

~

That was the night Orlando was born.

And yet...

It would be several more years before I would have even the vaguest inkling of what to do about it.

And so life continued on, much as before.

~

The double is also the muse – which is perhaps why he chooses to remain aloof, always one step ahead, the shadow on the wall, the wind tapping on the door at night, the magical presence who whispers close only to disappear again before he can be caught.

As Orlando often tells us, this journey isn't about catching the muse. It isn't about putting magic under a microscope. It's about the chase itself.

It's not the destination, but how we travel the path.

The sentient universe is neither loving nor hateful. It is neither god nor devil. It simply exists, containing all possibilities. What determines which of those possibilities actually go through the formality of actually occurring is entirely up to the Creator. There is only One Creator.

You are *The One*.

I AM THE HEART
BUT YOU ARE THE BEAT.
I AM THE SOUL
YET YOU ARE *I-AM.*
I AM FEATHER AND WING,
YOU ARE THE WILL TO FLY.
DUALITY SEALS OUR DESTINY.
I AM THE MIRROR,
EMPTY WITHOUT YOU.
I AM THE WORDS,
YOU ARE THE POEM.
IF YOU DO NOT WRITE IT,
THERE IS ONLY SILENCE
IN ETERNITY.

Orlando

PART THREE

DOUBLE, DOUBLE

The self dreams the double. Once it has learned to dream the double, the self arrives at this weird crossroad and a moment comes when one realizes that it is the double who dreams the self. Your double is dreaming you. No one knows how it happens. We only know that it does happen. That's the mystery of us as luminous beings. You can awaken in either one.

- Don Juan to Carlos Castaneda
Tales of Power

Although don Juan told Carlos that it is impossible to reason out the double, I have not found this to be the case. Over the course of the past four years, I have had the opportunity of working with some fine warriors at my online forums – *The Quantum Forum, The Shaman's Rattle,* and *The Crack Between the Worlds.* During the course of those conversations, and as a matter of my own assimilation and Intent, much has been revealed to me about the nature of the double – proving once again something Orlando said to me in the beginning. "You will learn far more when you begin to teach than I could ever hope to teach you."

It's entirely possible that some of the things I am going to reveal in this section will shock and even potentially offend some warriors who may have followed a strict Toltec path – because in many ways I have found that there were things Castaneda did not reveal about the double, either because he did not yet have that knowledge, or chose not to divulge it.

I have made no attempt to put this material into any particular linear order – for that's where don Juan's admonition holds true. The reason is there, but it is not linear. So I would say to you what I have been told all along: read gently, from the corner of the mind's eye, and *see* as much what lies *between* the lines as what is on them.

For the double is a shadow that takes on substance, a substance that is eternal, an eternity that is the Self reflecting on the surface of the Infinite and casting itself into matter as the mortal Self. There is no straightforward way to speak of the double, and so we paint the edges of the shadow to reveal that which is casting the shadow.

Chapter Fifteen
A Dark and Dangerous Dance

January 16, 2004

Traffic was endless. I was at risk of falling asleep at the wheel.

Los Angeles has always conjured up the words in the darkest recesses of my mind: *Camelot of the Damned*. So as I was leaving that dark gothic necropolis on an afternoon of no particular significance, with the rapidly setting sun in my rearview mirror and a stream of red tail lights stretched out in front of me like an artery bleeding out of the inner city, I began to experience a feeling which is virtually impossible to describe. Some might call it a longing such as one experiences when looking up at the stars and wondering who might be looking back. That was the kind of longing I felt as an eleven-year-old girl longing so desperately for those stars which seemed so very far out of reach, that all she could do was shake her fist at the sky and shout, "If I can't come to you, I'll bring you to me!"

It was something like that which came over me in the car, only darker, and carrying with it an intensity that made me instantly want to turn away from it. I could sing. I could count SUVs. I could turn on a CD and lose myself in someone else's lyrics. But even as I was having that *instinctive "run away from this"* reaction, it occurred to me to ask: *Why* did I so want to turn away?

Impossible to categorize, except to say it was an ache from deep in the soul – like the pain one experiences in unrequited love. Bittersweet. Some ancient link to some ancient memory – like waking up one morning with a sense of being in love... only to realize that the object of one's affections died 30 years ago, when you were both still in high school. This feeling had elements of silver winter, a faded photograph that hangs innocuously in the hall for years, until one morning it simply hits you that this is some part of life that is no longer reachable.

Heavy, dark – and yet strangely alluring at the same time. I felt I was looking through time, yet there was no single event or memory I could point to. And then I realized I was looking through the worlds, *seeing* and experiencing something for which no words exist. The lure of the nagual man, and the pain of knowing I will not see him again in this physical lifetime. The call of the siren he has become – a cold and lonely wind blowing fierce over the icy expanse of eternity. The cry of the muse, beckoning me to follow, but at the same time making it altogether clear that the mortal human never really catches the muse, and the goal therefore is the chase rather than the capture.

Still, knowing all of those things didn't lessen the sensation. Quite the opposite. How is it possible to say that the feeling was energy unto itself, and that by going into that energy, I found myself being pulled out of body right there on the I-10, in the middle of rush-hour traffic, surrounded by gang-bangers in dilapidated death-traps, semis spewing diesel fumes, and the distant screaming of emergency sirens that reminded me of some frightened animal finally driven mad by its unnatural environment.

My body went on automatic, because clearly someone was driving the car. And yet, to my perceptions, I was suddenly standing on a mountaintop that had been nearly 50 miles in the distance – Mt. San Jacinto – the towering granite peak that looms over Palm Springs and casts a shadow over the entire desert valley.

Years ago, very early on in my journey, I had looked at that mountain, feeling a presence from it that I could not identify, and heard the words through gnosis, *"You have to meet the immortal world on its own level."* At the time, I took those words to mean that it is up to the mortal self to climb the mountain, because only in doing so do we stand any chance of becoming the thing we seek to become. Over time, those

140

words have become something of a personal mantra, whose meaning has grown and evolved along with my own understanding.

At any rate, I suddenly found myself on top of this snowy mountain with Orlando. Normally, when he appears in visions, he might be wearing jeans and a t-shirt or occasionally with nothing but a loincloth and his hair in long dark dreads. On this day, on this inaccessible mountaintop, he was wearing a fine tuxedo, though somehow managed not to look like a stiff jackass in his finery. Top two buttons were undone, and the traditional bow-tie had been left at home.

And there was that feeling again. Looking at him as if he were dressed for a wedding, I knew intuitively that this was not the time we would exchange our final vows. Death had not yet tapped me on the shoulder even though I was standing face to face with my own double, in defiance of one major aspect of the rule of the nagual.

He opened the conversation without preamble. "You humans have no concept of the nature of time."

I couldn't very well argue that one, so I challenged him as he has so often done to me. "Then why don't you tell me?" I invited.

He only laughed. And then he did something completely unpredictable. He made a small cut on his left wrist, but his blood wasn't red. Instead it was shimmery gold-silver-copper-bronze. Liquid light. Time condensed. Essence of the ancient future.

He gave me that look – the one that ended my world when I knew him in manifestation. Half-smile, half-sinister. "To taste eternity is to understand it," he said, holding his wrist out to me.

I stood there like some pole-axed schoolgirl, though it shouldn't surprise me that he would behave like a vampyre –

feeding me his lifeforce to make me like himself. That's long been one of my favorite fantasies, and the nagual man is a master of knowing *exactly* what will lure the nagual woman into the Infinite. And yet…

I found myself not knowing whether to trust the bastard. Had I miscalculated? Was I already dead? Had the Suburban gone off the road and was this, then, just the rehearsal dinner before the darkest wedding of bones to the earth?

I know myself well enough to know what I'm capable of as a stalker. Would I trick myself into going willingly into the arms of my own death if it meant I would simply walk out of one world where my body was still stuck in a traffic jam, and into the Otherworld where my Whole self was waiting to welcome me with a loving embrace?

"When it's time, I won't have to trick you," he said, reading my thoughts. "You'll come to me willingly, and then we'll dance, because that's the way we both want it, no?"

He knew I would succumb to his charm. The snow was cold beneath my feet. I could feel it as surely as if my physical body were there. The dusk-wind was blowing through the crack between the worlds.

I took his wrist and drank, and then I simply Knew. In both worlds, I felt my body spasm – like a seizure that occurs when the body is exposed to some massive jolt of electricity. I understood it all – the nature of time, the dance of the immortals, the evolutionary two-part migration of the soul. To taste eternity was to understand it – right down to a molecular level.

It. Was. All. There.

And yet… when the nagual man pulled his wrist away and I returned to a state of semi-ordinary awareness, the Knowledge left me as quickly as it had filled me. It could not be held, it could not be brought back to this world – no matter how hard I tried, no matter how much I was willing to surrender or let it go. This was simply the way things are, for there was a Truth in his lifeforce that told me we simply do

142

not possess the preceptor organs in first or even second attention to process or store direct memory of events in third attention.

I could taste it and *Know* it, but it would forever remain the nagual – the literal *unknowable* – for as long as my organic awareness was housed in the world of ordinary affairs.

The only words that escaped my lips were spoken aloud in two worlds, for I heard the echo of my physical body speaking in unison with my astral Self. *"I am here with you."* What I was trying to convey to myself was that the experience was real – valid. More than just a hallucination or even a vision. Somehow, what I had tasted of eternity had shown me that, and it was all I was able to bring back.

As I spoke, Orlando just laughed softly, maybe even a bit sad. "Exactly." Then he shrugged and brushed a snowflake off the lapel of his tux. "It's about remembering on the bridge between the worlds. Humans have forgotten how to remember the other self, so they get lost in the little dream down there in the traffic." He jutted his chin toward the freeway which was nothing more than an unmoving line of light, lightyears distant, and for a moment, I had no idea what he was talking about – for I had forgotten that dream.

"Will I ever be able to remember what I experienced today?" I asked. "Will I ever be able to bring it back to ordinary awareness?"

He looked at me for a very long time, then reached out to pull me against his chest. He was real in my arms – far more real than the endless river of taillights and the heartbeat of some vicious rap song on a passing radio. It had nothing to do with time or otherworlds. It had to do with perception and awareness – with *Knowing* it is real instead of only believing it.

"Now that you've tasted eternity, *all* you have to do is remember," he said.

And then I was back in traffic. A funeral was in progress at Forest Lawn, and just as the sun slipped below the horizon, a flock of white doves was released from somewhere near the coffin that was being slowly lowered into the ground. On the CD player, Amy Lee of Evanescence was screaming out a plea to the cosmos, to her own double: *"Bring... me... to... life."*

And so I go on, struggling always to remember.

Chapter Sixteen
Myth and Legend

Orlando has often led me on merry chases, and many times I have had to deal with allies and inorganic beings who seemed to be running interference, as if to actually prevent me from catching up to him. I've also worked with other warriors who have said much the same – it's a game of cat and mouse, particularly in the early phases of the journey, and many times we don't even realize it's the double we're chasing. And yet, it's that longing and that chase which are the creation process itself.

When we first started receiving letters from Orlando in late 1994, one of the very first things he said to us was this:

"Don't you see? This isn't a hunt that's meant to end when the hounds capture the fox. I, fox, could have stayed in the briars, but because the hounds caught the right scent my red eyes peek out again. Chase me, I run. Catch me, I vanish." (12/12/94)

A few months later:

*"You were dying inside when I arrived, which is one reason I came, you see. I'm a muse, a fool and a fountain of eternity if you love me enough to want me and want me enough to chase me and chase me long enough to catch me and catch me before I can vanish. I brought your soul back to life so I can take your life and give you back your soul." (*5-12-95)*

At the time he appeared in manifestation (1988), I had settled into a comfortable and complacent form of living death – reasonably successful in what I was doing at the time, in a good comfortable relationship, basically just going from day to day being content. Perhaps this sounds idyllic, yet other than the relationship with Wendy, I was slowly but surely buying into the machinations of the consensual reality. I was losing my soul to complacency, even though it had the outward effect of seeming pleasant.

But when Orlando showed up, all of that changed. He facilitated an awakening of the spirit that was tumultuous, unpredictable, painful, mysterious, frightening, and anything but complacent. It was during that time of upheaval that I first embarked seriously on this path. My life changed drastically as a result. Orlando *did* bring my soul back to life, he did "take my life" in the sense that everything changed as a result of his appearance – the life I had known before was suddenly gone – and he is giving my soul back to me through the Knowledge and experiences he has facilitated.

Needless to say, this is extremely personal to me – not in any foolish sentimental way, but in how it manifested. And yet, I want other warriors to know that this path or any other must first of all be a path of the heart and a joy to the Spirit – otherwise, if it is nothing more than following some strict dogma and practicing repetitious rituals of recapitulation and passive observation, it has become nothing more than a personal religion.

And that's not what this is all about.

It's about a love affair with the infinite, and it has to appeal to our earthy humanness and our innate sensuality every bit as much as it appeals to our delight at the touch of the unknown. If you're sitting in a dark room doing nothing but meditating and recapitulating and contemplating the meaning of self-importance, chances are you aren't *living* – yet it is through the process of living and loving and failing and succeeding and learning that the double is created.

I could have stopped myself from ever meeting with Orlando on that mountaintop that day when I was stuck in an LA traffic jam. I could have told myself it wasn't logical or reasonable. I could have told myself it didn't jibe with anything any other "respectable" nagual woman has ever reported.

But if I had done that, it is clear to me now that I never would have had the *experience* itself. And so it's been in letting go of all the shoulds and suppostas and oughtta-nots and the pre-conceived idea that somebody else's way is the only way, that I have ever been able to slip outside the box and rub noses with the nagual, even for a moment. As long as we are bound by some idea that it would be wrong to fall in love with the double or abnormal to have a face to face conversation with our higher self, we are trapped behind the boundary lines of someone else's rules, someone else's reality.

If you are following someone else's path, you are failing to walk your own.

Fall in love with the nagual. Dance naked on the rim of the abyss. Wiggle your butt in the face of all those stuffy old gods. And take a drink of the infinite from the veins of your double any chance you get, for that is the blood of the path of the heart.

THE DARK ENLIGHTENMENT:
FANTASY AND MAGIC AS INGREDIENTS OF THE DOUBLE

"I brought your soul back to life so I can take your life and give you back your soul." At the time Orlando wrote those words, I had been heavily involved in researching all manner of lore and legend pertaining to immortality and the potential for an evolution of consciousness beyond mortal death. I was deeply intrigued with vampyre legend in particular – not the Hollywood idea of blood-sucking zombies, but the much older legends pertaining to organic and inorganic immortals co-existing with humans right here on Earth. So it stands to reason that Orlando would play into that with regard to his actions on the mountaintop when he offered me the anima

contained in his blood – which, of course, isn't really blood at all as humans understand it. The double will use whatever tools and manifestations are required by the mortal self in order to do its job, and if that means taking on the persona of a vampyre, or a fairy king or some alien traveler from a far distant star, that's exactly what the double will do.

The only limitations are those we place on ourselves. If I wanted my double to be a stuffy stock broker, he certainly could be – but why choose the mundane when we can Dream the sublime? Why settle for mediocrity when we have within ourselves the power to have and to be anything we choose to be? These words are not intended as some sort of pep talk for improving our lives in first attention – though that is certainly possible, too – but they are intended *literally*. As warriors and sorcerers, the creative force itself is at our fingertips. We do not have to settle, and we do not have to be practical. Settling and practicality are only agreements, and for the warrior who walks this path with impeccability, no such limits are necessary or in any manner prescribed.

> The double re-creates us as an eternal being by bringing us into direct personal contact with the infinite and the eternal.

Once the double has been created through our dreaming (substitute: longing, desire, aching, visualization, dreaming-awake, intent-both-conscious-and-subconscious) there comes that crossroad moment, as don Juan said, when you realize the double is dreaming you. That is when the double has achieved sufficient cohesion (through the direct efforts of the warrior) to begin actually serving as teacher, mentor, muse. And it can take any manifestation your heart desires because it is not limited to our first attention rules and laws.

At the core, of course, the double is doing exactly what you created him to do. And because the double isn't limited to our linear-time lives, once s/he achieves sufficient cohesion in the Now, s/he can actually manifest in what we perceive to be our own past. I have no doubt that I have been interacting with Orlando since an early age. But that isn't because I was born special or somehow smiled upon by the cosmos. It's because I have always had the Intent (subconscious at first in my early years) to have a grand love affair with the unknown. It's the only way I know how to put it. Chasing the muse. Peeking around every corner looking for the alien-otherness of my soul.

It's an eternal dance between creator and created, double and mortal, and it is also an *ongoing* creation. If we don't create the double in the Now, s/he isn't available to us in past, present or future to do the hard work of dreaming us.

One reason a lot of people are drawn to what is traditionally thought of as dark spirituality (including shamanism, and the dark archetypes) is because these paths actually encourage us to glimpse ourselves as eternal beings of the infinite, rather than discouraging that type of self-exploration as most organized religions tend to do.

Through the threat of losing his soul, Man has been controlled, subjugated, sublimated, disempowered, and spiritually damned by the very organizations that claim to offer salvation, and in that way, it is very clear to me that the church has become the very evil against which it so adamantly preaches. The Crusades weren't fought to bring people to god, but to destroy opposing belief systems which threatened the stability of the church.

Anyone who learns to use their own spiritual abilities learns very quickly that god is not some external deity which can be sold to them by any organization. God is within the self – the force of creation, the power of the universe which is inherent in each and every one of us. We do not need to tithe to some man-made organization nor grovel on our knees before some invisible deity in order to be free. Salvation – which might be defined as freedom from the obliteration of our awareness – is ours for the taking and the Do-ing. Yet the truly sad hoax perpetrated on our western culture is that we have to ask something outside of ourselves, and this is then handed to us by grace, through faith – and always at a high price .

That price, all too often, is the soul – for by disempowering its followers, by attempting to control the human spirit through fear, by creating the threat of Hell to scare human beings away from doing anything that might even begin to put them in touch with their own abilities, the church has taken on the role of destroyer – and in doing so, becomes what it traditionally calls "the devil himself." The church creates its own dark reality. In denying people their basic right to pursue their own highest potential, many organized religions are essentially condemning those souls to obliteration at the command of the eagle – and that is a far greater sin than anything Moses ever scribbled down on those stone tablets.

It also seems quite natural that a lot of folks are drawn to such things as _Buffy the Vampire Slayer_, _Star Trek_, _Star Wars_, _The Matrix_, and so on. In our fantasies we see our potential, and sometimes it is through these fantasies that many warriors are first introduced to the idea of longing/aching/hurting... and that is one of the first steps toward self-awareness and self-realization: knowing we are incomplete, we embark on the journey to complete ourselves.

Chapter Seventeen
The Nagual Man and the Nagual Woman

A Nagual – or *double being* – is something one either is or isn't. I've always thought of it like being born with blonde hair and green eyes. One either has those attributes, or one doesn't.

The critical difference between the double and the double-being is that I would be a double being, a nagual, whether or not I ever engaged on this path – yet it must be stated in the same breath that if I had never engaged this path, I never would have met Orlando, never would have discovered my true nature, and never would have come into contact with the rule of the nagual. I would be just an ordinary human being with some extra energy.

What Castaneda never addressed, either because he himself never gained the Knowledge, or because he intentionally chose not to reveal it, is that the Nagual man and Nagual woman are not two separate beings, but the *same* being that splits at a certain point in life – a point that can only be identified individually in each nagual, and even then, perhaps never accurately, for one thing is certain: the double operates outside of time, and as a result of doing so, what may seem to us to be a linear manifestation of the events, may not really be happening in a linear manner at all with regard to the perceptions of the double.

Carlos discovered himself to be a "three-prong nagual", and from what I have been able to determine, this is the result of what amounts to an incomplete division of the four compartments of energy. To his perceptions, this was simply the way things were, and so he wrote as if all naguals were two beings, when in most cases, they are a single being that divides. I do not mean this in any symbolic psychological manner, but *literally*. The energetic being divides like a cell dividing – and it is from that division that the nagual man and nagual woman take on a seemingly separate existence which is nonetheless the *same* energetic matrix if viewed by an accomplished seer.

~

Any warrior can choose to create their double – though it isn't as much a matter of choice as it is a matter of Intent. And there *is* a difference. I might choose to go light a candle as part of a ritual, for example, but that isn't what will create the double. It is the ache/hurt/want/need in the pit of the stomach that provides the Intent that would make me feel a need to perform some meaningless ritual in the first place. The ritual has no real power and is a choice; but the intent behind the ritual has ultimate power in creation.

Over a period of time (no one can say how long), the double is brought into being by the intent of the warrior – not the intent to create the double, but the intent to seek knowledge, the intent to find the answer to that gnawing ache/hurt/want/need in the pit of the stomach. In short, the double is created through dreaming in the sense that the energy of that ache/hurt/want/need goes into manifesting the "cure" - and that cure is the double, which may be described as the vessel of the singularity of consciousness which emerges when all is said and done and the warrior leaves this earth.

Naguals, or double beings are another matter – and yet, at the very heart and soul and source of *why* they are double beings, it may be exactly the same thing, but something that is being seen from another point on the time-map. I have a theory that Naguals such as myself are the fuck-ups of the sorcerer's equation. Here's why:

Let's start from point A, and take the premise that I am an ordinary warrior who has managed to create my double. The double exists as an extension of my intent, and is now the indestructible vessel of energy which will become the

152

assemblage point of my Wholeness beyond this physical life. Because it appears that the universe is holographic in nature, it then stands to reason that both the double and the immortal self are part of that hologram. And as most probably know, the whole of the hologram exists within each component of itself, so even if it is fragmented, as long as one piece can be recovered, the hologram can be reconstructed in its entirety.

Okay, so I've created my double and I'm bopping along through life, and get hit on the head by a meteor one day, and kaputz, I'm a goner. The eagle grabs my Della-awareness, and I am absorbed back into the black velvet fabric of the Nothing –obliterated. But let's further say that because I was an impeccable warrior (except for failing to note the meteor coming), I had given my double the agenda: "Go out into the All and bring back whatever knowledge is required to teach me everything I need to know in order to become a singularity. Dream me as I have Dreamed you – no matter what. And do not stop until the singularity is manifested."

In giving the double such an agenda, one is acting in the realm of sorcery to defeat the eagle, at least at a certain level. Because of the holographic nature of the universe, once the double is created as an independent component with free will, it cannot be destroyed even if the awareness of the mortal self is eaten by the eagle. As an aside, this would require an extremely cohesive double, so this would probably only happen if a warrior were advanced on the path when she was hit by that meteor, though because of the non-linear nature of time, even that may not be entirely true.

But let's just say that when the meteor hits, the component that is the mortal self "failed" in her bid to get past the eagle in order to conjoin with the double. So, let's assume, just for the sake of argument, that the eagle stands *between* self and double.

So, the game plan so far: the warrior created her double, gave that double the agenda to teach her "no matter what it takes" (a matter of intent); and then gets splattered by a meteor and eaten by the eagle. It's a rotten day, to be sure.

The awareness of the mortal self is swallowed up by the eagle, but because the double was created already *beyond* the eagle, *that energy still exists as part of the hologram.* But, it recognizes that it is not complete because the component which was the mortal self (its own source) was just eaten by the eagle. So the double is having a rotten day, too. What to do? Without the awareness of the mortal self, the double knows it is not Whole – not a singularity, but only a component, no matter how powerful. And as such, it knows it is vulnerable to the ravages of eternity. Without both halves, the dis-integration is not only inevitable, but has already begun.

Since the double is not limited to the confines of the linear human lifetime, and moves freely outside the box of time itself, the double can just as easily step back inside the framework of the mortal self. I've used the analogy in the past that the double could very easily "climb inside" the mortal self while that mortal self was still in the womb of her mother – and, indeed, this would make a lot of sense, because only then would the double-being exist in the first place. Why do this? *Because the double is fighting for his/her own survival, too.* And the only way to be sure it will survive would be to exist in such a position as to be able to exert influence over its mortal source from before the moment of birth. So, the double wriggles down comfortably inside his mortal self who is still in the womb, and when the infant is born, it would appear to a seer as having four compartments of energy instead of only two.

The problem is that the seer is still a being of linear time, and may think - "Oh, my, what a special child!" Not really. Sure, the nagual has extra energy, but we're the fuck-ups who got hit on the head with the meteor in the moebius loop of the time/space continuum, and so the double has had to take control and re-dream its way into mortal existence so the

154

whole process can be redone, this time with the double having more influence from the start.

> "To the eye of the seer, a Nagual man or Nagual woman appears as a luminous egg with four compartments. Unlike the average human being, who has two sides only, a left and a right, the Nagual has a left side divided into two long sections, and a right side equally divided in two."
> -Carlos Castaneda – _The Eagle's Gift_

The reason it is seen in this manner is because the seer is seeing only the object, and not the outside-of-time retroactive enchantment which created that object as it exists. And so – ultimately – naguals may be just a warrior who created their double, got hit on the head with a meteor, and had a double who was smart enough to operate outside of time so as to salvage his own pathway to the Infinite by climbing back into his "source" in order to better guide the play the second time around.

The upside to all of this is that it does tend to give a Nagual that extra reserve of energy, and it certainly provides one with a sense of urgency and focus and sheer determination to make it to freedom that is unparalleled. I am going to make it, no matter what – because if I don't, not only do I run the high risk of losing Orlando – for even though it would be theoretically possible for the double to make this journey into the self-in-the-womb over and over, there are never any guarantees that circumstances and events will unfold in the same way. And aside from all that, if I don't make it this time around, I will also have to go through Gretta Young's fourth grade class again. That alone is a powerful medicine of motivation.

~

In a recent conversation with a fellow warrior, the idea was raised that after a warrior has created her double, and that double begins dreaming the warrior, there is essentially no difference between that warrior and a nagual. This was actually an idea I had entertained on and off over the years, and indeed, it seemed to track with me. And yet, several days later, I was sitting in meditation one afternoon, and began receiving additional feedback through gnosis regarding the idea of the warriors double and the nagual man/woman. The following is excerpted from my journal:

February 19, 2005
What I am shown is that even though – practically speaking – there would appear to be no difference between a warrior who has created her double, and a so-called double-being (or nagual), there really is a difference at the level of energy and at the level of awareness. The difference is that the nagual's "other half" exists in *third* attention as a wholly evolved and integrated being with ubiquitous awareness. The lure of the nagual to its mortal self is so *powerful because they have already been together in the womb,* when the four-compartmented being came into this world, and as a result of that, the driving Intent of the nagual still on Earth becomes an almost palpable force. The energetic structure of consciousness itself is *already* irrevocably intertwined and infused with identity when the nagual is born – because at that level, from third attention, the double has essentially tricked "time" by re-entering his/her own "past" (as described in the section above). As I've said – naguals are the fuck-ups of the warrior breed in a manner of speaking – thrown back by our own double into the life school. Ultimately, it works to our advantage, by providing the powerful link between the nagual man and the nagual woman, imbuing the one left on Earth with the most fierce sense of determination possible.

The actual sorcerer's double (having nothing to do with being a nagual) exists in *second* attention. And unless it is nurtured into Wholeness through the Intent of the warrior, it is little more than a reflection of the warrior herself. It's like an infant, whereas the nagual comes into this life *literally* already having lived it (at least once if not more) – and as a result, one could say the nagual is born with certain knowledge/experience just because it is a nagual. With regard to the warrior's double (in second attention), it may become highly developed and educated and even begins to Dream the warrior at a certain point if all goes well; but until that mortal warrior actually dies and faces the eagle, the double remains on the level of *second* attention.

Of course... because the double at some point becomes "ubiquitous and non-local", this probably doesn't matter in matters of practicality, only in matters of understanding the energetic structure of *what-is* so as to better understand the process the journey itself. Perhaps the easiest way to visualize it is to say that a cohesive singularity can move seamlessly through all levels of the attentions (first, second, third); whereas a double in second attention could move seamlessly between first and second attention, but may not yet be ubiquitous, only because his/her mortal self has not yet passed through death, and therefore may not have access to *third* attention.

Obviously this is a rather large zip-file which is still in the process of unfolding, and has been for years.

~

It's important to note that *none* of this frees even the nagual from the responsibility of creating the double through dreaming in the first place, in the Now. Even though the double may come into this life attached to the mortal infant, with the ability to exert powerful influence over that child from even *before* the moment of birth, it is still the mortal self who must exercise free will and force the double to go through the motions of actually occurring.

I've known a couple of naguals who felt they were somehow special just by virtue of being born a double being. One even referred to it as "a waste of energy to create what already exists."

That, again, is a case of a seer *seeing* only the finished product and failing to take into account that something had to happen to *create* that reality in the first place. The conclusions are erroneous, just as it would be erroneous to stand in front of a city dump and proclaim, "Flies caused all this garbage!"

So, lest anyone think Naguals have it easier or are in any way special – please allow me to disabuse you of that notion. I haven't found it to be any different for myself than for any of the other warriors I've known and worked with over the years. We still have to create our double and go through the hard work of the path, *so that the double will exist in the first place.*

Nothing is a given. Not one thing. No one is going to do it for me – not even Orlando. At most, he is a safety net of sorts – but only because that is what I created him to be. And so it goes....

The paradox creates itself so that it may unravel its contradictions and, in doing so, come to appreciate its own unique nature.

LIVING THE INTENT

The difference between those who fly past the eagle and those who die in the fall is the strength of the bond between the self of the here-and-now and the wholeness of the double within the here-ever-after. And so we come to the inevitable questions which have no direct answer, yet those questions which must be answered if you are to succeed in your bid for eternity. It is one thing to ask how the double is created, but another matter entirely to live within the framework of that answer. Think on those words: *to live within the framework of perpetual, moment-to-moment self-creation that does not allow for going back to sleep, even if only for a moment.*

Mortal mystics have said the double is created through the process of living impeccably, and though this is true, it is attempting to define what that means which requires a deeper level of commitment. It could be stated that the double is created through Intent, but I fear that is too easy an answer and that passive thinking can be mistaken for active magic (Doing), and let there be no misunderstanding: *if the double is created passively, he will not possess the strength to rescue you from oblivion, for he will be made of your weaknesses instead of your strengths.* And so he must be constructed of unbending intent, but again I hear you whispering and moaning, "Yeah, but what the fuck does that mean, and isn't it just words rattling like old bones in the sand?"

Here is where you must stop and meditate on the idea itself until you begin to *see* what it really means. It is the force of creation itself, this thing called unbending intent that originates within the mortal self as a thought-form of eternal continuity, stretches outward to generate itself through the manifestation of energy in order to begin re-creating the mortal self in eternity, and finally reflects back as that immortal other begins to embody the attributes and extended ubiquitous consciousness of its mortal creator.

Some might call it creative visualization, though it is not something that can be done ritualistically with candles and props and all the trappings, if the magic itself is not fully integrated into the magician's unbroken intent.

Unbroken intent: a force of energy that never wavers and can always be accessed and identified with a thought; a background light never turned off, fueled by the Realization that to fail is to face utter oblivion; the steady weaving of the warrior's vision into the cloth of eternity; the pen of will writing your identity in indelible ink so that not even death can erase it; the decision to always make the impeccable choice even when it is not necessarily the comfortable or pleasant alternative.

- Orlando, 2000

159

Chapter Eighteen
The Matter of Doing
The Antimatter of Not-Doing

Recently, a warrior asked an interesting question: *"Very weird thought just entered into my mind, Della: You aren't making any of this up, are you? Is the reason you are so serious about all of this because you are hiding something?"*

I've already talked about my infatuation with *Adventures in Paradise* as a child in Chapter Seven. When I told my Sunday school teacher that I had spent some time in Tahiti on a grand adventure with Captain Adam Troy, it could not be said that I was making it up with the knowledge of doing so. Instead, I had actual "memories" of being there – and I have *no* doubt whatsoever that I was there in second attention. The fact that I left my physical body back at home in bed scarcely seemed to matter. A shrink might have said I didn't know the difference between fantasy and reality. A sorcerer would have said that I was engaging in the manipulation of thought-form into energy into manifestation. I was creating reality.

As Carlos once said, what I am doing may seem unreal to many people, and so they would conclude that I am a liar. In their reality, that's what they have to believe in order to sleep at night. When you ask a sorcerer if she is "making it up", there's no answer that is going to satisfy all the participants in the play. Did I create Orlando out of the nothing? Absolutely. Ah, but is he real? Well, he is now. Was he real *before* I made him up? He is eternal and therefore exists long *before* I was born and eternally after I will die, it is he who is dreaming me, and that's what don Juan meant when he said "There comes a crossroads moment when you realize the double is dreaming *you*." He told me to make him up, told me his name, told me how to create him from my own heart – the double being willed into existence for the sake of love. That's how this path works, though it is only a *tale of power* even to most warriors.

It's been said that the first shaman created First Man and First Woman with a thought, and that she is actually both of those beings, split in two so he will not be alone in the world. I understand this because I *am* this. I created Orlando to create me, breathed him into existence out of the nothing with Will. Once I got over the notion that we are impotent slobs at the mercy of Fate, once I finally took responsibility for who and what I am (just a lowly nagual who is the most powerful being in the universe) you bet I made it all up. Creation only works from the inside out – meaning that we start at the core (self) and work our way out from there, into the infinite. There are no limitations save those we place on ourselves.

> "Love is the reason, love is the motivation," Orlando has said many times. Love of life. Love of one another. Love of Self in all its manifestations. And yet, this isn't some new-age bliss ninny message that will tell you love is all you need. It's the motivator. It's the reason. But you are the little engine who has to climb the hill and build the immortal Self, gathering cohesion of identity which can only be called I-Am.

I created it so it would be true, because in the sorcerer's world it is possible to see that *only* by creating something can it *ever* be true. That is the nature of sorcery and it is very, very real.

Time is the greatest illusion of mortal Man. As long as we see ourselves as trapped inside it, we tend to walk with our noses to the grindstone, straight from the cradle to the grave. But when we get that glimpse outside of time and realize that *everything* is energy, that's when we can take control of our individual destiny and create ourselves Whole. We write the script. We make it up as we go along – but the difference is that the quantum shaman does it with awareness and Intent and Will. I have dreamed the double and now the double is dreaming me. We're both making it up, each for the other, and that is how we move toward Wholeness.

As a fiction writer, I told tales about events that never happened and people who never existed and never will. As a sorcerer, I write with a pen of pure energy on the fabric of the universe, and my characters come to life because they are me and because the universe itself is seeking an eternal companion who will not simply melt back into the molecular fabric at the moment of organic death. *This is the real nature of evolution: to create pathways that did not exist before – to mutate and adapt in order to survive, to create the self in such a way that it is beyond the ability of itself to undo.*

PART FOUR
THE HUMAN EXPERIENCE

The View from Earth in Journal Form

Chapter Nineteen
Vision Quest

By the time I had been on the path for approximately four and a half years, certain questions had begun to weigh heavily on my mind. Although I had long since acknowledged Orlando as a mystical being, perhaps an extant ally or some manifestation of my own intent, such as a powerful *tulpa*, I had not yet internalized the significance of precisely *what* he was – yet he himself was now telling me that unless and until I did so, the journey could go no further.

Tulpas don't issue ultimatums, so that alone was sufficient to tell me I was dealing with something entirely beyond my ability to comprehend. In addition to the letters we had been receiving from Orlando since 1994, other anomalies had been occurring steadily around the house – objects moved, lights turned on or off when no one was in the room, music playing in empty rooms – all the types of things normally associated with traditional hauntings, yet the missing link in that equation was that no one had died.

Having reached an impasse on the journey, where no further answers seemed to be forthcoming, I once again made the trip to Mexico to enlist the aid of the shaman and the counsel of the mushroom ally.

~

June 23, 1999

"Once I rode on the wings of birds a thousand miles long and passed through the eye of the ankh on the way to eternity."
– What the ally said to me at the onset of the journey.

The ally ingested in a glass of orange juice, and this Mexican beach dissolves into a tapestry of Egyptian

164

hieroglyphs, Celtic knots, pentacles, skulls and the timelessness which exists within us, but is too often thwarted by this cage of decaying flesh. The hard part of this vision quest is the going up and the coming down, for it is during those times when I encounter a hyper-awareness of my own body – the heartbeat that keeps me breathing, the temple in which the thing doing the perceiving is housed. It is during these times that I long to be done, to simply be in ordinary awareness again; yet even as I am aching to cry out for an ambulance to take me to the hospital or for someone to immerse me in water, I know none of these things will save me, and so I sit in silence just watching it all go by.

In this vast subconscious exists all the ancient images, stored so meticulously and perfectly that it is like walking through some vast museum where time and ancient artifacts are impeccably preserved. The way up was packed in 4-dimensional space with Egyptian symbols – odd, since I myself have never had more than a passing interest in Egyptology.

How easy it is to simply follow these pretty pictures, this language existing in defiance of words, this series of symbols and images which capture the entirety of human history and present it for viewing as if on some vast internal screen. There comes the sense that I am only watching the machinations of my own mind – the monkey getting a glimpse of the computer chip inside her own brain; and for a few moments I am admittedly bored and even disgusted with myself. I fight this feeling many times throughout the night – this inkling that the man behind the curtain is me – that I am writer and director of the entire movie playing out before my mind's eye, and that it's a script without cohesion, just a long and incomprehensible compilation of images stored on the microfiche of the mind.

I glance at the clock from time to time; hours seem to have passed, yet the ticktock digital eye of time says it's only been a minute or two. My body protests its limits and I mutter to myself about being trapped inside the **black iron prison** – a black cage that is without any real order, a door here, a wall of bars there, none of it seeming to be designed by an intelligence, just a prison of mazes designed to keep us forever enslaved. But – designed by whom? And for what purpose?

Pentacles and images of the reaper. Warning signs recognized by the consensual reality as images meant to warn away the wise traveler. But I have gone beyond mere human reasoning and so the warning signs become beacons, these traditional images of death peeking out from behind the treasure of the pharaohs and the intricate carvings in the form of picto-glyphs. This is the nature of the ascent – the climb through the mire of the All, the perilous journey that leads from ordinary awareness, through the valley of the shadow of certain death, and finally emerges into a terrain of absolute clarity beyond the rivers of pictures.

Suddenly, I find myself on the far side of the chaos, in a mental space where I am separate, a space where I am once again the manifestation of Orlando – creator and created conjoined. There is no way to describe this sensation, this sense of knowing what he knows.

This is the evolution of consciousness we have spoken of for so long – for it involves looking out through a different set of eyes, the eyes of the double, the third eye of the evolved self. It is to see life and the world and – especially – the self in an absolutely different manner. Because of our human mode of thinking, it's difficult to imagine that the aging fat lady is actually the wily wizard, but when I emerged onto that crystal clear plain above all the chaos, I had become the double. Even though I had experienced something of this magnitude on the night of February 26, 1998 – the night when I answered the call to *"make me whole"* – the experience on *this* night was somehow more cohesive, as if I had learned something without knowing when or even how I had learned it.

At first, I couldn't isolate it. It simply existed as a warm, pleasant awareness.

166

As I sat there on the edge of the bed, gazing out the door toward the lights in the distance obscured by the bars of the black iron maze, a male voice that I could only perceive to be from outside the self screams in my mind, "You are being offered an identity. Take it! Take it!" At first, I have no awareness of what is meant by this, but the voice repeats its demands, "You are being offered an identity! Don't be a fool! *Take it!*"

Accompanying the command is an image of a cartouche. On the front is a 3-D image of a horned man with his head bowed and his arms crossed over his chest, his hands clenched to fists. It is a symbol of dark power, another warning symbol meant to cause us to return to the natural path of human stagnation and decay.

Why are we like this? I wonder in retrospect. Why have we programmed ourselves to fear this evolutionary power within ourselves, and why have we assigned symbols of fear to the only thing that might somehow save us from the natural cycle of death and decay?

What are we so afraid of? Is this merely a means of keeping us from evolving, or perhaps a method of screening out all but the bravest or craziest of candidates? Is this the monolith of <u>2001: A Space Odyssey</u> – something to be feared by all the apes except the one who first dared to touch its shiny black surface? Is it designed to be so terrifying and symbolic of human superstition that only when one ape overcomes her fear enough to approach that terrifying object is it time to evolve?

Questions, asked in haste as they chatter through my post-experience brain, this part of the journey where the amazed monkey must analyze and attempt to assimilate into language the meaning of its hyperdimensional experience, this part of the journey where we must employ evolving reason in an attempt to decipher the strange hieroglyphs scrawled on the walls of perception.

What does it mean? How can I take this knowledge and use it to evolve into a singularity of consciousness without being sucked back into that vast river of pictorial trans-language history? To have the experience is only the beginning. What to do with it while in the realm of ordinary awareness is the next step.

As I am shown this cartouche, I-as-Orlando and I-as-Della existing side by side, the same and yet not-the-same, the voice repeats, "You are being offered an identity – *take it!*" I see on the lid of the cartouche a dagger – a broad-bladed, curved-edged weapon about 16 inches long overall. Its handle is encrusted with amethysts and diamonds, and as the voice keeps repeating its message – insistent that this is the only way to save myself from absorption back into the black velvet fabric of the Nothing – I realize that I must claim that identity by cutting it away from the rest of everything else. It must be carved out of the all to stand alone, to exist as a separate *I-Am* incapable of being reabsorbed into that never-ending river of images and chaos.

To use this amethyst-handled blade and carve that identity, that I-Am out of the Nothing, means to become a new kind of organism, whether here in the physical world or outside of time, or both. This is the nature of the singularity – the individuated *I-Am*.

For a moment, I hesitate, unsure of what is being asked of me. And yet, there is the Knowing. The hand that reaches for the blade is my own, yet it is the hand of the double, the hand of stardust and pixie glitter, the hand of the eternal and the infinite. The blade is heavy and yet oddly familiar, and as I lift it toward the cacophony of stars and the fierce white wind which is always blowing in this vast wilderness, it seems to choose a path of its own volition, tracing a humanoid outline onto the fabric of the universe.

It is the silhouette of the singularity, cast in the shape of a man, filled with stars and the limitless dark matter of creation. It is the self of eternity, cut from the background to stand alone and yet intricately connected – the ubiquitous creation which is greater than the sum of its parts and beyond the ability of the eagle to undo.

It is the identity of *I-Am*, manifested, inhabited equally by mortal self and immortal Other.

Beyond that, there is very little more that can said.

I realize this may sound like nothing more than a religious experience – talk of evolving and embracing an identity outside of time, the creation of an immortal body, the *I-Am* speaking itself into being… yet I maintain that if anyone had told that ancient bi-pedal monkey-creature that it would one day sleep in a Lazy-Boy recliner instead of the trees, that all its hair would fallout and it would walk upright and wear designer jeans, surely this would have sounded like far-fetched, quasi-religious afterlife mumbo jumbo to that unenlightened creature existing on bananas and berries.

So, in many ways, this idea of our evolved identity involves going against the flow of images which represents the broad but nonetheless limited range of human comprehension, cutting an island in the middle of the stream to stand alone, perceiving the river but no longer recycling endlessly into it.

The flow of images is the download of all human knowledge, dumped into the river at death, the sum of all knowledge, stored holographically. The trick of evolution is to take the next step and choose to be *other* than what it is our lowest-common-denominator nature to be.

Immortality is the ability to exist as a separate *I-Am* and perceive eternity from outside of time instead of becoming trapped in its molecular hologram.

How did that first monkey go about deciding to become a man? We can read all the biology text books in existence and yet none of them can really explain the process of evolution – perhaps because the process itself occurs largely outside of time and beyond the present comprehension of the organisms to which it is occurring. We think it took place over millions of years, yet there was – somewhere in time – *that one single moment* in which monkey became man, when he struggled beyond the limits of his monkey brain and began to speak and use tools. It couldn't have been easy nor even natural. It had to be a choice made by that one monkey because he could envision an existence for himself beyond the confines of his monkey self.

At times, when I experienced the hyperawareness of my body during this excursion – the sensation that my heart was beating too fast or too hard or that my breathing was labored or shallow or my brain seemed larger than my physical head could accommodate – whenever I would become aware of those physical sensations, there was such a temptation to return to the comfort of the little pictures, to allow myself to be swept along in them as a disembodied non-entity rather than trying to swim upstream as a separate and endangered fish. How I hated the awareness that I could die – not in some nebulous future, but right then and there. I could simply stop existing and then I would be forever inside that endless river, just one more downloaded soul scattered into its component parts and returned to the cosmic soup for reassignment.

It isn't a matter of *believing* we are immortal. It is a matter of knowing that, outside of time, we are the double. This is another aspect of meeting the immortal on its own level – *it is meeting ourselves as the immortals.*

Orlando had to exist wholly *within* me before he could be whole enough to exist *outside* of me. The fetus has to be viable before it takes its first breath. The wily wizard has to be the mortal aging fat lady before he can fully comprehend the desperate *need* to bend time and space and stand on the wrong side of manmade gods for all of eternity in order to change that.

As the experience winds down, I find myself confronted with an unmarked grave surrounded by a wrought iron fence

170

of Celtic knots. I know it is my grave, and a voice says to me, "We sleep in the ground, dreaming the same dreams."

There is a consciousness that transcends death, but unless we choose individuation through our *will*, it is the consciousness of the All, not of the individual, and the dreams are the images floating along in that inexplicable and unending river, dreams of the dead. There is a certain comfort in this, for it was pleasant to be swept along in that river without a personal point of reference, just an awareness existing as part of a much larger whole. And yet, there was still a living self doing the perceiving, even the perceiving of the consciousness beyond death. Without that organism, I would become a freeze-frame of an orange grove. Another snapshot of a rocket at Canaveral. Another of a red room where magical things once happened. But all disconnected, without cohesion, without any possibility of ever being put back together whole again. A literal humpty dumpty.

What I knew then was that it is the invocation of the will to say *I-Am* that creates the singularity and forces our evolution to go through the motions of actually occurring. Individuation is achieved by taking the blade of the will and using the tip to write oneself indelibly onto the parchment of the infinite.

One of the last visions I encounter is that of a huge serpent, rather like a king cobra, whose scales are jewels, shiny as diamonds. Coiled, but with its head reared, it says to me, "Now you know. Now you've eaten the forbidden fruit and seen it all. What will you do?"

Chapter Twenty
A Kaleidoscope of Assimilation

Perhaps it was as a direct result of the experiences described above – in combination with everything that had gone before – which eventually enabled me to finally accept Orlando as my double. The awakening to this realization was alternately painful, exhilarating, frightening, and overwhelming

But even more important, it was the act of accepting responsibility for the identity – responsibility for the actual singularity of the self – that has enabled me to begin experiencing the journey from a perspective which I can only describe as somewhere on the bridge between first and second attention.

Impossible to capture with words, yet it is from that bridge that the evolving warrior looks with one eye upon the consensual world, and with the other on the infinite. The result is a seemingly constant state of gnosis, a unified field between the self and the double.

As humans, it is natural for us to seek "the eternal other," as Terence McKenna and so many others have spoken of at length with regard to this incredible journey. And yet – what most of us fail to realize is that our greatest beloved, and our most enlightened personal teacher… has been with us all along. We simply do not give ourselves permission to trust what we already know, yet only when we begin to develop that trust do we empower the double to be the very thing we have been seeking from the start.

Only when I gave Orlando permission to be whole and separate and a part of me and eternal all at once… only when I gave him the free will and instructed him to teach me, did I begin to connect with my own clarity and power, through which it becomes possible to perceive the universe through the eyes of the double, from the place of silent knowing.

And only when the hand of the duality took the blade and carved the identity of the singularity did I begin to fulfill the rule of the nagual as it appears to manifest in my own life. Only in the process of assimilation do we begin to truly see the path which leads from the self, to the double, to the eternal, and finally to the infinite.

What follows is a look at that assimilation as it was occurring.

BEINGS WHO ARE GOING TO DIE

August 8, 1998

There's a rickety ceiling fan stirring up heat and dust in this old desert ruin I call home, while the day comes and goes beyond the heavy drapes, out there in the sand and the wind and the world of human props and clichéd scripts.

I look up and it's night again, time clattering by, dragging me along inside its belly while it digests my youth, steals whatever beauty I might once have possessed, and drains away my belief in whatever I once held true to replace it with a crone's clarity and bitterness, utter awareness of mortality.

So now I sit here in this familiar chair underneath the tail of Scorpio, counting acne comet scars on the face of the moon, watching, feeling, perceiving countless dimensions of magic swirling around me like dust devils, always moving yet always still, paradoxes incarnate, waiting to be understood before opening their doors.

Deep in the bleakness of last night's meditation, I open my eyes to tell my lover, "I'm afraid." But when she asks why, how can I tell her the things I've seen, the thoughts spinning beyond the realm of human consciousness that can be perceived wholly unto oneself but never discussed without hearing that latent twinge of madness in words that can only fail to convey this inexplicable magic? How can I tell her I was out there beyond the end of the universe or that the stars

173

are no more than an inch away, or that I was thinking in a language comprised of particles and quantum dancers on the razor's edge that splits me into past and future and yet obliterates the now utterly, leaving me already dead and simultaneously unborn, but never simply *be-ing* in whatever state is meant to pass for living?

Sadness, thick as honey, but more bitter than this brittle chaparral, forms the framework of reality upon which the stages and the plays are constructed. How terribly aware of our mortality we are, fragile creatures sensing the predator always nearby, the breath of death hot as summer, cold as the blood of the damned.

Inescapable is the Knowledge that we are all beings who are going to die.

THE CRACK BETWEEN THE WORLDS

January 6, 2002

Late afternoon, 4:38 p.m. and long shadows lie soft on the ground, blending the end of day with the coming of night, a delicate tapestry of dusk. An unusual mist hangs in the air, recreating the distant mountains in shades of yellow and brown instead of the typical desert grays and purples of twilight.

Time seems frozen. Our Australian Shepherd sits outside my open door, facing the sunset with an almost Buddhist serenity.

Distantly, unseen but heard, a fruit bat calls into the crack between the worlds. On the road, an old pick-up rattles driven by an old Indian with long gray braids and a wide brimmed hat, the old shaman who has sometimes visited my visions, taking on manifestation in the twilight.

The mist turns umber-orange at the level of the horizon, and the sun leaves the desert in the charge of shadows and owl-song.

174

In a corner of my office, the tiny silver mouse who has made her home with us scratches at a piece of paper, a gentle rustling of life. I fear she will one day breed, yet despite the dictates of logic, I take no action against her. And so she honors our silent agreement by remaining childless so we may continue to peacefully coexist.

Though there is no wind to speak of, the large pipe chime sounds a note or two, a temple bell instantly transforming my dark velvet room into a monastery and myself into a monk contemplating the gathering dusk on the tip of a pen.

The postcard perfect world outside this door knows no worries in this frozen Now. The Joshua trees are still, meditating on the passing of time, and even the telephone poles with their sagging wires seem at rest, silent sentinels mesmerized by the brisk chatter that erupts from a hummingbird to disrupt the stillness.

I find myself thinking of Orlando, remembering when we knew him in manifestation all those years ago, before he burned with the fire from within and became an enigma, an ally writing inexplicable letters from the edge of the abyss. Sometimes, over the years, I've tried to tell myself it was all just a coincidence. It wasn't *really* sorcery, magic, manifestation of a lifetime of intent. He was just a man, I've heard my own voice whisper, close to my ear. For it would make things so much easier if I could believe that.

And yet, at a level of Knowing somewhere near Infinity, I fully realize that these are only the fearful retractions of someone who has seen a truth so vast it is overwhelming, even terrifying, in its intensity. We lie to ourselves because that truth is so often incomprehensible. Easier to pretend it never happened.

But it did.

And so the tumblers of comprehension always click and align, refusing to be ignored or cast into foreign shapes just so I might be able to sleep better at night, just so I could go back to being normal, another phantom on the road. There's no going back. Wouldn't even if I could. The truth is still the truth.

And he is still standing there in his white wicker living room, backlit by a streetlight shining through a rain-slicked window, asking the question that ended one world and will be forever creating a new one in its wake. "Who are you?"

If he were standing here now, perhaps I could finally answer. "I am the mountains and the mist that embraces them; the feather on the owl's wing and the coyote hymn echoing off the foothills as night finally falls. I am somewhere in the distance, nowhere in particular. I am myself and I am you and there is no difference."

The ink dries on the page.

The world becomes a black silhouette.

A stray cat pauses in the long dirt driveway, and I am endlessly looking into the eyes of the ally.

SCATTERING THE ASHES

January 29, 2002

Outside my door, a light snow is falling, random flakes drifting and playing in unseen currents. Unconsciously, my eyes go out of focus and I am staring at a spot of emptiness perhaps 5 feet in front of me. In the distance, cold grey clouds hug bleak and desolate mountains, snowy squatters obscuring the peaks. Closer, inside my own yard, ocotillos tremble in the rare and precious chill.

In that empty space where I am focused, I watch energy dancing – particles of light swirling like hundreds of ice skaters playing on a frozen pond, each going in a different direction, circling drunkenly, faster and faster, yet never seeming to collide, as if the perfect choreographer has orchestrated the frenzied flow.

I am aware of a single snowflake, larger than the rest, plummeting to the ground as if it simply folded its white

176

wings and dropped, eager for its journey to be over. My mind notes this, but thinks nothing of it. Then, in the silence of this unintentional meditation, the voice of silent knowing whispers in my ear, "Look! It will happen again!" And though I have no expectations, still focused on the dancing, circling particles of light, the same suicidal snowflake plummets through the same space in the icy air to impact in the same spot of desert sand where its own pale ghost still lies melting.

My mind quickly tries to explain it away – water dripping from overhead wires, or a mere random coincidence.

The assemblage of silent knowing only smiles. "We could show you again, but would you believe it even then?"

The question is: what does it mean? Why does the same leaf fall three times for Carlos Castaneda? Why does the same snowflake obliterate itself more than once in front of my very eyes? Is it only so we can see it? And having seen it, what is the lesson?

On the western horizon, there is a break in the clouds and sun filters through the mist, dappling the mountains. I ache for the storm to remain, revealing its secrets not easily seen in the brighter haze of a common sunny day.

Tiny droplets of water pool and bead on the cushion of a lawn chair, and a cactus wren comes to drink the shiny diamonds, suckling nourishment from the melted snow. The fire in my fireplace crackles, pine smoke curling over the roof to sneak back in through the open door so it may draught up through the chimney again and over the roof and back through the door, an endless cycle fueled by the intent of the fire. Grey ghosts hurry down the driveway, startling shy quail.

In an act of sorcery that has come to be its own exegesis, I scatter the ashes of last night's fire along the path from my door to the road. I hear a voice and recognize it as my own – the voice of the witch, the sorcerer's breath. "From the ashes of this mortal self, I call upon the Whole I-Am already a part of eternity. Come to me. Teach me so that I may become what you are – the whole potential of the evolved Self."

Just words. Meaning nothing to anyone but myself. Fodder for those who would say I'm just a crazy old woman tossing her own ashes into the wind, talking to herself in a snowstorm. Ah, yes. Talking to herself. The sorcerer's double who is already evolved and outside of time. And yes, I do talk to him, luring him to come and teach me how to become what he himself already is – so that I may evolve sufficiently to place him outside of quantum time so that he may teach me… like the pine smoke caught in its own energy, creator and created conjoined, each seeking its own source which can always be found in the other – the self made Whole.

A voice at the edge of the road asks, "What do you bring to the gene pool of the infinite aside from this trail of ash?"

The wind is brisk, cold, sentient. Tires caress the wet street, carriages driven by phantoms who do not seem to even perceive me.

"I bring the fire and the smoke, and the Knowledge that each is only a manifestation of the other," I reply.

A shudder passes through me, and I feel Orlando smile – a dangerous, alluring grin comprised of thrice-fallen leaves and ice crystals gathering on the bow of an old pirate ship where we have met and conjoined before.

After a pause in the storm, the snow resumes, sneaking in at the crack between the worlds.

THE CLOSING OF A DOOR

April 16, 2002

A door closed today.

It was so subtle and gentle a closing that I'm not sure anyone else would have noticed, nor understood what was happening. The early spring afternoon was sunny and warm, but with a cool breeze blowing in from the northwest, adding a welcome chill to the air that had already begun to warn of an early summer. Wendy and I had just pulled into the parking lot at Wal-Mart on typically mundane chores when I looked up to see an old friend, Melissa, pushing her cart out of the store. In it, her young son, Devin, barely a toddler whom I had never seen, sat playing with a toy against a backdrop of colorful flowers and small bushes poking their heads up from the bottom of the cart.

Though I hadn't seen her in well over 3 years, Melissa hadn't changed. Despite the baby and the trials of motherhood, she was still young, very beautiful, clearly happy – a mother-earth spirit in muted shades of brown and gold. We pulled into a parking space and went to greet them, exchanging smiles and exclamations of surprise at running into one another after so long apart. There was a time in our lives when we had seen Melissa and her husband on almost a daily basis. Like souls. Kindred spirits. But time and obligations had taken us in different directions. Devin was born somewhere along the way, and though I'd considered calling Melissa from time to time, there was always some reason not to, and it ended up like so many relationships where one thinks fondly of old friends, but simply loses touch.

It occurred to me as we came together that no hugs were exchanged. Of course, I'm not big on obligatory hugs, but it seemed to signify more than that – an almost unavoidable distance, an awkwardness that was unusual somehow. For a few minutes, we made small talk. Melissa's business continues to do well. Her husband is healthy and happy. Devin is the center of their lives. She has bought some zinnias for planting in the yard. We share brief tales about the hazards of ground squirrels in gardens.

Devin fusses, saying, "Go!" Tiny hands pound on the cart, where he is safely strapped in. Wind pushes through his curly golden hair. The color of his cheeks reminds me of an early gala apple.

All of these things I observe on the level of ordinary awareness, feeling the sun on my arms as Melissa comments enthusiastically about a new tattoo I didn't have the last time we were together. But beneath all of it, under the layers of our mutual 3-way chatter and Devin repeating, "Go!" there is an uncanny awareness that something has changed. With Melissa. With the world.

In the parking lot, car doors slam. The breeze pauses, listening to my thoughts, then rolls forward again, kicking an empty Coke can along the pavement. All around us, people rush in and out of the store, a blur of colorful clothes and fragments of meaningless conversations. Cars on the nearby highway pitch distorted lyrics out through open windows, discordant shards of unrelated sound, unassembled noise to anyone not hearing the whole song.

Devin is starting to fuss. "Go!" he repeats, and purses his lips into a pout.

A silence falls between us, and three old friends look at one another across an abyss of perception. Promises are made to stay in touch, phone numbers exchanged. It reads like a script. The wind has turned darker, sad somehow. Blowing sand stings my ankles.

"Go! Go! Go!" His little cheeks are redder now, like a MacIntosh.

I watch Melissa walk away, focusing for no particular reason on the leather barrette in her soft brown hair. Reminiscent of a Celtic knot, it seems to form the symbol of eternity, and I know on a level that defies words that I will never see her again. At first, this is deeply disturbing to me, for I can only wonder if it is a premonition, some sort of dark warning of impending doom, whether for Melissa or for myself. I go through my shopping chores in sort of a daze, pondering what has just happened, but no insights reveal themselves.

And yet, when I return home and stand in the silence of the desert, gazing out over the Joshua trees and the blowing sand and realm of the raven and the coyote, it's as if the tumblers of this subtle equation begin slowly falling in place. "It's right in front of you," the voice of gnosis whisper. "It's always right there, but sometimes you're afraid to look. Sometimes even Seers don't want to see."

What has changed is myself. The world, like little Devin, keeps shouting, "Go! Go! Go!" yet I am no longer any part of that. If I see Melissa again, it will be with different eyes – the eyes of the sorcerer, the eyes of an eternal being gazing at someone much loved, and knowing they have chosen a different way. If I see her again, it will be with the Knowledge that she has embraced the human path, the mortal world. And it will be with the Knowledge that I have gone in a different direction. We have each chosen our destiny, and each of us knows it is a choice.

Some doors close. Others open.

Wind blows in through the cracks of eternity.

SHADOW DANCING

April 22, 2002

On the way to Ojai Renaissance Faire, I became aware of an ability to be ubiquitous and non-local at will. Difficult to explain, but it was as if I could walk through every house we passed along the way, sampling the texture of the carpets, the scent of stale cigarette smoke on cheap motel sheets or fresh yellow roses in the foyer of a large estate where all the occupants had gone off to their various jobs for the day, leaving the paned windows open as an invitation to passing spirits.

As I passed over the various suburbs and communities leading into Los Angeles, it seemed that every house had its share of old photographs on cluttered mantles or lining well-trodden staircases leading up to rooms where children had once lived, but had long-since grown up and moved away. There was a sadness in those houses, indeed, in *most* of the houses I visited. A sadness that said the answers people seek usually aren't found because the seeker gets side-tracked along the way. A sadness that said their lives hadn't lived up to their expectations, and so the sorrow was joined with bitterness in so many of those older homes where Time had seeped in through the cracks to slowly undo the illusions that form the dreams of younger men, the regrets of old age.

It occurred to me even as I traveled that I was drawn to the darker windows, to the places where the dust had settled and the weeds had grown thick in untended back yards. *Why?* I wondered. What does it say about me that I have little interest in those cheery homes where the beds are always perfectly made and the garage is neat and tidy? Why am I pulled, instead, to the dark garden where a painted rock forms the headstone for the beloved family dog who was hit by a car so many years in the past? Why am I drawn to the shadows on the north side, where no sunshine ever reaches, where moss has grown green and thick on the side of the house underneath the dripping spigot? What does it reveal about me that I pass quickly over amusement parks and churches because they seemed like only facades on a movie set, yet I felt an incredible sense of Life in the massive mausoleum at Forest Lawn, where so many tears have been shed that there is a lingering taste of salt in the unmoving air?

From the darkness comes the light, an inner voice seemed to say. From the recognition of our mortality arises the search for immortality, eternal consciousness, continuity.

With a thought, I could sit in the forked branch of a tall eucalyptus, inhaling its sharp menthol, feeling its bark against... what? Not my skin, certainly, for I was not in a body. And yet there was a physicality to it as well as a non-corporeality. A wholeness that was both and neither, yin and yang, all and nothing. The wholeness of duality.

182

At Ojai, looking across the lake, I could stand on the far shore, atop a tall mountain where a forest fire had broken out. There I could smell the smoke, feel the terror of the wildlife as it fled, taste the cool wind that fanned the flames. I was, at once, fire and wind, wildlife and terror, scorched earth and cold water scooped up from the lake by the firefighters to be dropped on the blaze. With a thought, through will, I was all these things at once, and the ecstasy I experienced at this realization was so profound that I could have no reaction at all. And so I stood there talking to customers as if everything were completely normal, as if I were only another mortal peasant in a Celtic caftan, chatting away the day with irrelevant pleasantries.

But deep within, and in the electrically-charged air all around me, there was a Knowing that cannot be captured with words. It was, simply, the Knowledge of the sorcerer, the experience of Wholeness throughout all of time, all of space. It was an awareness that can never die, an ecstasy that will live forever.

It was the first shy kiss of eternity.

42 MINUTES

September 4, 2002

Over the course of my life, I've had many unusual experiences. Perhaps one of the most peculiar happened sometime around late 1995, wherein I woke 3:38 a.m. and walked from one end of our old rambling house to the other, went into the bathroom in my office, then came back out and returned to the bedroom, only to discover that I had been gone for approximately 45 minutes. The clock which had read 3:38 a.m. when I left the room now read 4:22. I could account for perhaps 2-3 minutes, maybe 5 minutes if I really stretched it. But certainly not the 45 minute interval that had ensued.

In the grand tradition of human self-doubt, I tried to convince myself I had simply looked at the clock wrong, until Wendy rather sleepily asked me why I had been gone so long. To *her* perceptions, time had passed.

This is an incident I have pondered often over the years, and through a couple of attempts at regression, I have been able to extract certain images of what might have occurred during that interval of missing time. Over the years since then, there have been at least a couple of other incidents of a similar nature – I would look at the clock, walk across the room, for example, then look at the clock again, 45 minutes would be missing. Again, I could account for perhaps 3 minutes, so a pattern was beginning to develop – intervals of almost exactly 42 minutes of missing time, occurring somewhat frequently. Not in any exact pattern I can discern, but at least once or twice a year *that I was aware of...* and who knows how many times that I simply haven't noticed.

Then, in September of 2002, it happened again, with 100% certainty that I didn't simply glance at the clock wrong. Woke up in the middle of the night because my pillow had taken a header onto the floor. Living in the desert, this isn't just a simple matter of reaching over and grabbing it back into the bed. Because of the remote possibility of spiders, scorpions, and the occasional stink bug, it is required to get up, turn on the light, brush off any potential hitchhikers. So – glanced at the clock. 4:44 a.m. Got up, went into the bathroom for a drink of water, looked out the window at the cloudy night (a beautiful rarity in the desert), took note of the fact that dawn was just beginning to break behind the clouds, then returned to bed. Again, I could account for approximately 2-4 minutes... and yet as I was climbing back into bed, I glanced at the clock. 5:29 a.m.

At first, I again tried convincing myself I had simply looked at the clock wrong. (How adamantly we try to explain away the mysteries of life!) But as I glanced at the windows, I realized it was much lighter than when I gazed out the window in the bathroom. The horizon was now pure silver, the pre-dawn brightness which can be almost blinding. No doubt that approximately 42 minutes had passed, for it was validated by the difference in light.

What is the significance of 42 minutes? There is absolutely no sense of a glitch in my personal timeline. No sense of having dozed off (standing up? looking out the window?), no sense of having passed out, no evidence that *anything* is out of the ordinary... except that 42 minutes is missing from my life, and that this significant interval of missing time continues to occur somewhat frequently, without rhyme or reason that I can detect.

Is this some function of heightened awareness? And, if so, why 42 minutes? Is it a biorhythm? A tick of the cosmic clock? And how often does it occur that I *don't* notice, simply because I don't happen to be aware of time. Not wearing a watch and not being a clock-watcher, I can't even begin to imagine.

I fully realize that missing time is a function of the UFO experience, but that doesn't seem to track with my own perceptions and my own awareness. What's that old quote? "The world isn't only stranger than we imagine, it is stranger than we *can* imagine." (-Sir Arthur Stanley Eddington)

BETWEEN TWO WORLDS

November 17, 2002 (Road Trip to Florida)
The south is a vista of tall oaks, Spanish moss and shadows that blow along the ground like curious inhabitants from another world – a far cry from the desert to which I have grown accustomed. Voodoo shops in New Orleans seem familiar somehow, and one of the handmade dolls created to snare tourists into a frenzy of souvenir buying winks up at me from a basket of otherwise lifeless brothers and sisters. Of course I purchased the little fellow, stuffed him in a bag of other items collected along the way, and will undoubtedly

185

place him on a shelf somewhere to be forgotten, just one more haunted relic, a macabre curiosity to be commented upon long after I have faced the eagle. Folly manifested.

The odd thing about New Orleans was that as I walked down Canal Street with Wendy at my side, on our way to one of those touristy tours to all the famous haunted sites in the French Quarter, I found myself suddenly overwhelmed by the presence of an ally. And as I stood looking in a storefront replete with thousands of strands of Mardi Gras beads, tiny figurines in the shapes of jazz musicians and alligators, an androgynous voice whispered in my mind, *"So… you've finally come home."* Interesting, since I had never been to New Orleans.

But immediately upon hearing that voice, I knew the city as intimately as if I'd lived there all my life. Shops that had seemed alien and perhaps even foreboding moments before suddenly became familiar, and as we walked through the city that night, I somehow knew I was walking in my own footsteps, retracing a route I'd taken dozens of times before… in a life I never lived, in a parallel reality or alternate dimension. Or through the eyes of a ubiquitous Whole Self.

Whatever the explanation, if it is even possible for such an explanation to exist in first attention, it was truly a remarkable experience, walking through this city as if it were my home, knowing intimately the texture of every stone and brick in St. Louis Cathedral, "remembering" a time not so long ago when I had walked these same streets in a different mortal guise, looking out through the eyes of some other self entirely, yet clearly the same self at a molecular level, at the level of awareness, consciousness.

I have no belief in past lives as the concept is commonly understood. Instead, what I have come to see is that at that level of ubiquitous consciousness, where there is the interconnectedness of all energy, some element of Now connected strongly and deeply to some element of Then, and a door opened between the two worlds. It would be possible, of course, to say this is simply the way things are everywhere... and yet I've never had an ally welcome me home to Albuquerque or El Paso or Atlanta. Why New Orleans? That night, back in our hotel room on Canal Street, I dreamt of a ghost in the mirror, a young man who was trying to tell me something, but I couldn't hear what he was saying. So he just smiled warmly and gave an elegant bow, blowing me a kiss through the looking glass.

~

In Florida, the rains come as soon as we cross the state line, like someone throwing a switch. My mother, well into her 80s, insists there is a devil. Not "a" devil, but *The* Devil. She tells me this as she fills out her tithe envelope to take to church in the morning – a tithe she cannot afford, given to an inanimate entity, a building, a mere mortal man who claims to be a messenger from heaven. Perhaps there is a devil after all. Perhaps, as Orlando has often said, the devil's greatest trick was convincing the world he is God.

This afternoon, I drove with Wendy to the property where I grew up. Once a tiny town not even on any reputable map, now a six lane highway runs through the center of this thriving suburb. At first, I cannot even locate the property we once owned, for everything has become modernized, giant-sized, phantomized. Finally, after two passes, I realize that where our 10-unit motel once stood is now a small pond, complete with cattails and bullfrogs and aggressively creeping vines. Nature has taken the place back entirely. A tall chain link fence surrounds the property, and where the lake was once visible, trees have grown so thick and tall that only shadows know the location of land's end. For all intents and purposes, what should have been a prime piece of real estate has been abandoned by time, reclaimed by the wild.

A little shiver passed through me, and for a moment I was 17 again. Knowing I would be leaving the following morning for Miami, probably never to live on that ground where I had grown up ever again, I sat at dusk with the spirit of the lake, listening to the water lapping at the side of a rowboat that was half-filled with stagnant water, a relic sinking back into the earth. My back was pressed against the rough bark of my favorite tree, and somewhere in the distance, somebody was playing an old guitar. Nothing ever seemed to change in that place, and so I closed my eyes and promised the spirit of the lake that no harm would ever come to her. No rich socialite would build a mock-plantation on her shore. No McDonald's would spring up next to her. No one would ever despoil her beauty, I told her. And at that time, in my 17-year-old teen-angst of moving away from home for the first time, I meant it.

So today when we pulled into what was once our driveway, I could only gaze in wonder at what had become of that promise, that secret, silent intent. Only a peaceful pond exists where buildings once stood, the very property itself permanently and irrevocably flooded. I smiled quietly to myself. Then as the full implications of what I was witnessing hit me, I broke into laughter which was answered by an echo from deep in the sheltering shadows of the trees. The spirit of the lake seemed to share my amusement, and for a single moment, that door between Then and Now opened wide and there was no difference between that young girl and the laughing woman and the infinite.

FACING THE HUMMINGBIRD

January 3, 2003

I spent the morning holding an 18 year old cat in my arms while he struggled to live, struggled to die, and ended up somewhere in between. At first I fidgeted. Hours passed. I had taken him out in the sun, for even though I am not a sun-worshipper, this wasn't about what I wanted or didn't want, what I could or couldn't do with my own abilities. It wasn't

188

about my own will, but about the will and intent of another life form, a different species whom we tend to think of as being so different from ourselves as to often seem alien altogether, and yet I am convinced that consciousness is simply consciousness. How it manifests and expresses itself in matter is really the only difference.

As I sat there holding this sadly decrepit animal, there were moments when it occurred to me to simply pack him in the car and take him to the vet, where a quick injection would send him on his eternal journey. And yet, at a level of communication that transcends species, I knew this was not what he wanted. In some way I cannot communicate, he asked me to let him face the eagle in his own good time, and because he has always been a warrior, I could not deny him that request.

And so we sat there together on the porch. I talked to him about the day. Sky so blue it was almost painful to gaze upon, a few puffy white clouds, drifting over at a visible rate of speed. A cactus wren was complaining that the bird feeder was empty, but when she looked over and saw us, she fell into a reverent silence. Shadows had pooled beneath the piñon pines and Joshua trees, and for a moment they turned 3-D - actual energy-reflections of their physical counterpart. There was no difference between the raven and his shadow, and so I told Myrrh that it would soon be time for him to inhabit his shadow. In the air all around me, I was watching specks of light dancing like a gathering of fireflies. At first, I thought they were just a trick of the light, some anomaly of physical vision. The things we tell ourselves in our internal dialogue to keep the world properly assembled.

I found myself in a dilemma as I talked to my cat-companion about where he was going and what he might see. Do I really Know with certainty that what I am saying is true? Is there really a continuity of consciousness beyond this life, based on cohesion of identity, or is that, like angels and devils, just another belief system? Even though I have had experiences with a world beyond the veil of this mortal illusion, I was forced to concede that all those experiences came while still attached to this mortal body. Is the body the projector of consciousness, or only a temporary receptacle? Arguments could be found for either point of view, and at that moment while this fragile creature was dying in my arms, I could have argued either side with equal and vehement conviction.

For awhile, I drifted on this wave of contemplation until I entered into a deep trance state. The energy beams had mesmerized me, carried me away on their electric wings. And so I flew with them for a time, trying to make sense of it all. The turmoil slowly dissipated. The internal dialogue which had been yammering previously realized it was being observed, and fell into silence. A hummingbird fluttered close to my face. Spirit-carriers they're called – guardians whose task it is to lead or carry the dead to the source of creation in the underworld, where the eternal river of consciousness has its source. I smiled to myself, finding it appropriate to think of Myrrh chasing a hummingbird guardian into Eternity.

Time passed. The Now extended infinitely in all directions. A single moment became All moments. And somewhere in all of the chaos of the world, somewhere in all of the turmoil of my own thoughts, it all just stopped and I realized that I had conjoined with my own eternal other. Those words are completely inadequate, a pathetic attempt to describe what must simply be experienced. I could say I conjoined with Orlando, but that would make it sound as if two came together into one. And while that was part of it, it was not all of it. Ultimately, all I can say is that I found the assemblage point of Eternal Whole Self. Like a peek behind the curtain, a gnostic certainty that when we embrace that assemblage point, all is indeed eternally well.

Somewhere or somewhen, Time started forward again. Maybe a horn honked. Maybe a coyote sang. Back in ordinary awareness, I was left with a sense of once again Knowing

190

there is more to the human or animal spirit than we have ever been allowed to believe from within the consensual agreement. Even if consciousness is initially only a projection of the body, then I can only conclude that consciousness becomes the projector for the Spirit, and the Spirit becomes eternally cohesive (inhabiting the I-Am of an eternal identity, without discorporation) through the process of conjoining itself to the indestructible energy body in the same way consciousness initially conjoined itself to these matter bodies.

Just rambling, trying to wrap comprehension around the infinite. Silly attempt. But nonetheless an attempt that must be made from the heart while the hummingbirds are sitting quietly in the locust trees, and the old grey warrior sleeps in my lap, slowly entering his own eternal dream, inhabiting his own immortal shadow.

May the sun make your shadow strong and the moon free your spirit to Dream.

A STRANGE FEW DAYS

March 29, 2003

It's been an interesting few days. Upon hearing of the death of Wendy's father on March 26th, we drove down to San Diego to be with her family. As we drove along the night-road, I found myself lapsing into almost a trance at times as I remembered Rhett's long and difficult struggle. We had all often joked that God had been trying to kill him for years. First a brain tumor. Then a near-fatal staph infection from the surgery to remove the brain tumor, which required a second brain surgery to clean out the infection. Then, just when he was about to re-enter the work force, a near-fatal car accident that left him with a broken neck, severe internal injuries, not expected to live. After 6 months in the hospital, he returned home, but with brain damage that left him at something comparable to an 8-year old mentality most of the time. Then came the mysterious bout of sepsis a few years later, which created internal damage and resulted in more brain damage, and diabetes.

God just kept missing with that anvil. Or Rhett kept staying out of its way. Impossible to say for sure. He was a sweet and loving man, and one of the last actual conversations I had with him was probably two years ago when he asked me to do a consultation for him. I was glad to comply, and he seemed to enjoy the exchange, which centered largely around his childhood memories of the place he had grown up.

As we drove along and I found myself mulling all of this over, I was also aware of Orlando somewhere in the background, basically saying that Rhett had taken those last 20 years of hardship and gone inward. While not a life anyone would have consciously chosen, it was his journey. And according to Orlando's insights, it had been time well spent. In the course of this journey, it has come to be my belief that most people don't make it past the eagle at all – and those few who do probably make it at such a low level of awareness and cohesion that their abilities are confined to observation alone – what Orlando has called "the land of the sentient dead". Just what I have observed over time, conclusions I've drawn (loosely) based on those observations. So without being fatalistic, I had no reason to think Rhett would have made it past the eagle... but no real reason to think he hadn't either, I suppose.

When we pulled into the driveway, the house was surrounded by cars and bustling with activity, yet the night outside was so utterly quiet and peaceful, pleasantly cool without being cold, and replete with the dew-slick grass of San Diego. Wendy immediately got out and headed toward the house, but I was lolligagging, taking things out of the car, gathering my thoughts, when suddenly the power locks on our old van started frantically going up and down. At first, I thought the alarm system (which hasn't worked in years) had gone amuck, but the symptoms didn't fit. By this time, Wendy

192

had come back out, and as soon as she walked up to the car, the locks started frantically going up and down again... like a child sitting in the seat playing with the mechanism. Or dear old dad running out to greet his beloved daughter.

We just looked at one another. And in the back of my mind, I heard Orlando chuckle softly, whispering, "He had more power than you know."

So it would seem. Though I returned to the desert the following morning, Wendy stayed another night in San Diego. And in the middle of the night, she reported that suddenly the room in which she was sleeping was filled with a brilliant white light – as if someone had walked in and flipped the switch on, then off again. She likened it to the overhead light coming on when she was a little girl, when her father would come to check on her in the middle of the night.

Neither of us are sentimental. Neither of us are superstitious. We aren't looking for feel-good things to make us think Rhett is still with us. But something is at work from within the nagual.

THE PHANTOM MENACE

April 30, 2003

Today I lost what little respect I might have had for human beings. Wendy, Ellen and I had gone into Los Angeles on a shopping trip for our business. Things were going remarkably well, we were ahead of schedule, the weather was grand, not too hot, not too cold, and everything we needed we had managed to find. It was a perfect day – which should have made it suspect right off the bat.

On our way out of town, we stopped at a Jack in the Box, and were inside no more than 3 minutes. When we came back to the car, it was to find the rear window smashed, and literally everything gone, as if vaporized by some inexplicable force that left only a shower of glass in its wake. More than $2000 worth of merchandise... *stolen*.

I dialed 911, only to be put on hold by a robot. Good thing I wasn't being knifed. When a human being finally *did* answer the phone, we were told there were no officers available to come to the scene, and were instructed to go to the police station. Good thing the car wasn't stolen. Upon arriving there (several miles away), I stayed with the car while Ellen and Wendy went inside to fill out the report. During my brief stay in the car (approx. 30 minutes), I observed a homeless woman with 2 small children, which made my own problems seem minor by comparison.

An elderly couple came out of the police station, got into their car, and promptly jumped the curb and slammed head-on into a solid block wall of the cop shop. No real harm done, no one hurt, but it just seemed to be a cartoon-like illustration of the chaos in which I found myself, a grand performance by the allies that was worthy of a Shakespearean comedy or a Three Stooges skit. A man at least 7' tall (no exaggeration) walked by in a denim-blue leather business suit, and stopped long enough to lean against a wall and defiantly light a joint in front of the cop shop. Sirens screamed. A seagull shit on the windshield. In the rearview mirror, I watched a homeless man pissing in the gutter while talking to himself.

Throughout all of this, I was almost annoyed that I felt absolutely *nothing*. It was as if I were standing to the side, simply observing, a participant in some strange play that had nothing to do with me. Even as the events were first unfolding and I was walking down the streets of this godforsaken ghetto, looking for clues or a trail of dropped merchandise, I felt nothing. No fear, despite the fact that I was trudging through dark alleys and underneath freeway bridges, on foot, with nothing but a cell phone and a bad attitude. No anger, despite the fact that this incident has the potential to cripple our business until we can recover from the loss and replace the stolen merchandise. No hope, even though at one point

194

someone said they had seen the two men who committed the robbery.

I felt *nothing*, other than what amounts to a grim sense of Knowing we live in a culture that has lost its soul, and is peopled primarily by phantoms who have no more regard for one another than one would have for a cockroach. When people feel they have nothing to live for, no sense of self-worth, no hope in life, no dreams, no comprehension whatsoever of who they are or what they could be, that is when they become dangerous, like rats thrown together in a filthy cage and left to breed until they are driven mad by their own numbers, compelled to prey on their own kind because of that madness... until eventually all that remains is a single insane rat chewing off his own tail in an attempt to feed a hunger that even he cannot begin to understand.

When all was said and done, nothing much had changed. We left the cop shop in silence, got on the freeway, and headed toward the desert with the stale asphalt air streaming in through a hole where the window used to be. I drove simply observing the world around me, wondering what I could have done differently. I should have stayed with the car while Wendy and Ellen went inside, I told myself. We should have stopped somewhere else. I should have *seen* the danger. And, in reality, I think I did. But as is all too often the case, we either don't know what we're *seeing*, or we can only put the pieces together in hindsight. Pointless speculation. Life is what it is, and sometimes not even warriors can get out of its way. That, sadly, is a fact.

What I find odd is that there have been a series of events lately that all seem somehow ominously related. There have also been other warnings in my private life, all striking at what amounts to our ability to run our business, make a living, stalk the world for survival. Distraction. Diversion. Debilitation. The 3 "Ds" of the consensual reality. As Orlando once said, while we're building the boat so we can fish for our dinner, we starve to death on shore.

On the way home, we discussed that it could have been worse. Someone could have been hurt. We could have been carjacked. The car itself could have been stolen. And yet, it made me sad and irritable to count what I can only consider to be dark blessings – trying to look for light at the end of a tunnel that is ultimately a black hole, a black hole that is ultimately a reflection of the world in which we live, a reflection that is ultimately more hollow and spiritually sick with every day that passes.

On the freeway, glazed-eyed zombies on cell phones weaved traffic at high speed, causing a chain-reaction of brake-lights and screeching tires. An accident stopped all movement for half an hour, leaving broken glass and bloodstains on the road while impatient phantoms honked and raised a middle-finger salute to rescue workers. In the rearview mirror, smog lay like a thick gray shroud over a city of lost souls, fallen angels, animated corpses going through the motions of meaningless lives devoid of dreams.

I want to believe the world is getting better, but I see no evidence of it, and I am not enough of a fool to pretend otherwise. So I look at the world as it is, having thrown my rose-colored glasses out the window at the cop shop, at the feet of the hookers and the pimps and the winos and the weirdos. Sure, there's goodness in the world, and in some people. But the sickness in the soul of Man has spread to epidemic proportions, and anyone who thinks otherwise would be well-advised to strip off the blinders and take a long, hard look at Reality. I have lost my sympathy and my pity for phantoms, for theirs is the domain of dust and oblivion... even if not soon enough.

It's all just folly in a world of folly, and nothing I Do or do not-do will have any significance whatsoever in the grand scheme of things. Maybe that's the lesson, if there is one. Or is it only our own self-importance that makes us believe we are somehow worthy of lessons? No matter. Folly. Playing out like a deck of jokers.

Of course, the other side of sorcery is that karma can be summoned and directed entirely through intent, though there are plenty of well-meaning new age bliss ninnies who will try to tell us otherwise.

The sun is down and Spirit is my ally. Tonight I will light seven candles and play my drum and dance with Orlando's shadow on the dark edge of Infinity, while he laughs and tells me to remember who I am. The rest takes care of itself.

THE OCTOBER NAGUAL

October 14, 2003

Sometime while I was out in the world conducting business, October crept into the desert, almost a space-time unto itself. I find myself filled with a peculiar restlessness, a tug from the nagual that has increased of late, leaving me occasionally melancholy in the eyes of those close to me, yet I could not really say it is a sadness. More like a longing for That Which Cannot Be Named, He Who Can Never Be Captured, That Which Exists Beyond the Shadow of the Windmill.

At Wal-Mart, I am greeted by a young male cashier who is so full of life and enthusiasm. All of perhaps 17, his eyes have not yet lost their shine, his step has not yet lost its bounce, the smile on his lips has not yet become the painted smile of paper dolls, drawn on with cheap paint to conceal whatever it is that painted smiles are meant to conceal. I have never understood Barbies gathered at the mall, grinning like skeletons, but with so much pain and rage and fear hidden behind the layers of lip gloss and cheap mascara.

This young man at the register moves me in a way I am seldom moved, for although I am old enough to be his mother, he exudes a fire of Life I seldom see, and it is like a palpable essence hanging in the air. He is alive. His thoughts taste of sweet, cold oranges.

His aura reaches out to touch mine in a way that leaves me wanting to grab him and look deeply into his eyes, and speak straight into his soul, and tell him, *"Run, little one! Run now, while your legs are still strong and your heart is still full of this wondrous fire, and your future is not yet cluttered with responsibilities and obligations and all the trappings that come with doing what you are told you're 'supposta' do with your life! Run! Run! Run! Get out from behind that plastic cash register, and put your feet on the road, and never look back, because the shadowy ghosts of all those future obligations are already chasing you, and all too soon, you'll be in college, and then behind a desk in someone else's office, wondering what happened to that young man you once were! And before you know it, your life will be over, or at least you'll feel like it is, and it's so much easier to never get caught in the trap in the first place, because once you do, it's hell chewing your own leg off in order to free yourself from all those shadows that stick to your heart like cockleburrs. So go – run! Right now – before it's too late! Run!!"*

I knew I was looking at a fellow nagual. And I knew intuitively that I didn't need to say a word to this young man. He's already running. I knew that, too. And so when our eyes met and I handed him my money and he handed me the receipt, a silent communication passed between us which exists in defiance of words. A Knowing. An exchange of energy. A passing moment of dreaming together in mind-speak.

I drove home in silence. Near the high school, goths in long black cloaks walked briskly, dust following closely at their heels, chasing them toward the night, toward the future, toward the grave. It moved like a sentient fog at their feet, and had a face that was skeletal, a grin that was hungry and at the same time patient. The dust knows it will win.

And yet, there was no sadness in any of it. It was simply the awareness of October, the Knowledge that any human can become a man of Knowledge. We are not victims of society or prisoners of the dust. That awareness was there, too – and for a moment in the middle of an otherwise insignificant autumn afternoon, the nagual opened out in front of me and around me and within me, and there was no difference between myself and the Infinite.

The wind tossed a paper cup in front of the Suburban, and that moment slowly dissolved back into ordinary awareness. In our driveway, the stray dog we have taken to feeding was waiting, the ravens on the telephone wires were speaking in tongues, and the breeze had turned colder and darker. An unseen hand caressed my neck – every bit as real as anything in this world of matter and men, though no one was physically there. And a well-remembered voice whispered close to my ear, *"I'm waiting, now and forever, just a bit closer to the surface now because it's October."*

An unspoken invitation hung in the air, known and felt at a molecular level. I could accept that unseen hand stretched out from the nagual, and it would all be done. That simple. Leave behind this world of cranky computers and traffic jams and the aches and pains of physical life, to go and inhabit the Immortal Other in third attention as an eternal being. Having no willpower to resist such an invitation from Orlando, from the double, from the Infinite, it stands to reason I reached out for that hand... only to feel it slip back into the shadows, back beyond the veil, into the Otherworld.

For a single moment, I could have sworn I heard his wicked laughter whistling through the eaves of this old house. Just doing what he is made to do, being that which he must be. The beacon, always in the distance. The muse, always one step ahead. The myth, creating itself as it goes, singing itself into Be-ing with a thought born of Will.

I-Am. And it is October.

A SINGULARITY OF CONSCIOUSNESS

November 11, 2003

The New Mexico sky has always reminded me of some vast dreamscape – an expanse of endless blue, broken by irregular streamers of white. It is morning, and the coyotes have all gone to sleep. The road stretches out in front of us, a ribbon of asphalt made of threats and promises, dangers and sanctuaries. For most of the day, we drive in silence. Our destination now is Marfa, though along the way we pass through tiny settlements with no name, just a gas station on the corner fallen into ruin, a stone chimney still standing in the middle of an otherwise empty field. A snaggletooth windmill tilting at its own shadow.

On the CD player, Evanescence breaks the monotonous drone of tires. "Bring me to life!" Amy Lee cries out...

Afternoon is slipping away, though I realize I do not know where it goes when it leaves this world. A thing to be passed through, like a poem written on water, never meant to last. As we pass through Valentine, Texas, the presence of Time itself is the town's sole inhabitant, it seems. Most of the buildings are boarded up. Others appear so dilapidated, they must be home only to bats and scorpions, yet through the open windows where no screen or glass is present, the stale blue glow of a television flickers.

Unbidden, a sudden, sharp breath catches in my throat, and I find myself wondering what has become of the world, of the man who was once a little boy with dreams of pride and passion, but who now sits on a broken down sofa on a sagging front porch, gazing toward the thickening dusk with such an aura of despair, it seems he must certainly be already dead. Was he a warrior once?

On the edge of Valentine, I see her. An old woman with long grey hair riding bareback on a donkey, heading out of town, toward the open range, toward Marfa, toward the unknown. At first, I think I am dreaming, for where would this woman have come from, and why, and where would she be going? Her attire is colorful, and the donkey is draped with brightly colored rags. In the world of matter and men, it makes little sense. Just a crazy rag lady on a jackass in the geographical center of Nowhere. I wonder now if she is still out there. I wonder if she was ever there at all, except that Wendy saw her, too. The vision of the shaman, out of place in the world, but moving forward with purpose known only to herSelf.

We reach Marfa in the late afternoon, and though the sun is still above the horizon, the sky has darkened with clouds which seem to burn with a fire from within. At first just orange sherbet, turning to flamegems as the sun slips away and Night announces his intention to have his way with the Earth. To the east, a thickening fog blankets the ground, an entity unto itself wrapping cold grey arms around volcanic rock formations – a shroud, a veil.

I find myself sitting on a rock some distance away from the state-built viewing center 9 miles outside of Marfa – a center built to accommodate the tourists and the curious who come seeking a glimpse of the famous mystery lights. The air is cold, and even the hood of my sweatshirt doesn't keep the chill away. To the south, a mountain range in Mexico forms a jigsaw cut-out against the dappled sky, and for a moment, Orlando is sitting next to me.

"What are you looking for out here in the night?" he asks.

The wind is so sharp and real I can barely breathe. *You. Me. The bridge between the worlds*, I reply without speaking aloud.

He only laughs. "You have all those things already," he reminds me. "What are you *really* looking for? Death? Life? A moment in Time?"

Thinking about his question, I realize I don't have the answer. The lure of him is tangible now. The pain of all I Know and all I know I do not yet know. There is a world out there to the South. Not the direction on a map, but the sentiment in the realm of the nagual. Words collapse. Logic fails. A ghostly hand touches my arm, tentative, yet demanding.

The words of a thousand lonely songs whisper close, too close. I stand face to face with the unknown – the eternal Other, the muse who *must* never be caught, the ethereal seducer who has been calling my name since before I had a name to be called.

Closing my eyes as the last vestige of light is swallowed by the hungry night, I wait for the time of waiting to be over, not knowing what might lie to the South.

~

For those who aren't familiar with the Marfa lights, they are essentially an unknown, having been investigated by prominent scientists, armchair philosophers, and every manner of traveler. In short, no one knows what they are, and they have been seen in this area of Western Texas since long before the white man came. Mystery lights. Early settlers mistook them for Apache campfires. Or lanterns carried across the desert in the night. Or ghosts of old miners.

I had intentionally created within myself a mindset devoid of expectation or prejudice, just a sense of being open to whatever might come. It was perhaps ten minutes or so past full-dark when the first potentially odd light appeared in the middle of the barren landscape to the South. At first, it could have been mistaken for distant headlights on a road, except there are no roads in that area. Still, it moved like a car, and I found myself fighting the program that wanted to label and categorize. So I just observed, going back and forth between the rock where I had intuitively settled, and the visitor station, where Wendy was looking at the lights through the telescopes.

Other people came and went, just back-lit shadows against the dim lights of the viewing center. Silhouettes cut

202

into the fabric of time and space. Phantoms on the road, moving in and out of the play, it seemed, actors casting occasional snippets of dialogue, overheard, like words shouted from a passing car. "…just a highway" "…don't see nothing strange…" "go back to the car and get the chips"

It was perhaps after an hour or more of waiting that we saw the first truly astounding display of light. Only Wendy, myself, and a couple of film students from the University of Texas still remained. It was directly to the South – what appeared at first to be very similar to a motorcycle light moving slowly along the horizon – not as far as the distant mountains of Mexico. Not as close as the lights from the only ranch in the area. Somewhere in between. It grew brighter. Then brighter still. Not like a headlight at all now. Like a fire in the sky. White at first. Then undulating with a field of red that seemed to the naked eye to form almost a yin/yang differentiation. And then – at its brightest point – it simply winked out. To Wendy's perception, it was like a flower blooming, only to disappear after the brightest display of the spectacle.

As she used those words to describe it, I experienced a peculiar sadness, for it seemed to describe the process of life itself – or at least "life" as it is commonly understood in the human world. A bloom that grows brighter, only to eventually burn itself out and disappear altogether. In the sorcerer's world, it is Known that one may gather sufficient cohesion to bloom eternally if that is the desire, to become greater than the sum of one's parts, to extend beyond the physical bloom and into the lifeforce which is the essence of the bloom. And again words fail.

For a long time that night, I stood there watching the lights come and go, until finally a huge anomaly appeared in the sky to the west. At first, my rational mind insisted it had to be a plane, or helicopter, or at least a flying saucer escaped from Roswell. And yet… even as I gazed at it, I knew it was something of the unknown. Something that would not wear one of my human labels, nor be categorized for my convenience. White at first, then following the same pattern as the one we had witnessed at ground level. Red to white. White to red. Yin and yang wrapping around one another like two lovers in an eternal dance. For perhaps 5-10 minutes, it hovered on the horizon, well above the mountains, putting on a show unlike anything I had ever seen.

Taking a deep breath of that cold night air, I projected a thought into the nagual, asking, *"What are you?"*

And though I had expected no answer, the response I received was as clear and unmistakable as if it had been spoken aloud. *"A singularity of consciousness,"* it replied. Connected to it was an incredible sense of male energy, and I sensed a history to it that stretched into Infinity: past, present and future interconnected into a singularity of Now. The totality of Oneself. *One Self.*

What accompanied the response I received was what I have referred to as a "zip file" – essentially a wealth of information which cannot be discerned in one day. All I know is that there was a sense of eternity associated with this anomaly, and I was reminded of a vision quest several years ago. In that journey, I had been confronted by eternal beings who asked me the question, "Who are you? What do you bring to eternity?"

Excerpt from journal (November, 1996)
I immediately began showing them myself – whatever unique qualities I may have, the tricks I can perform just by virtue of being "Della". I showed them my soul/inner self doing its secret dance, but it wasn't enough – all souls can dance, I suppose. But I refused to be sent away, so I confronted these sentient beings and essentially demanded to "become". "I am a flower that only blooms once, but – damn you – I will bloom forever!" I shouted with the full force of my will. It is my right to become this thing – not by virtue of what or who I am but because I demand Life. The

demand was sufficient when all else failed. They didn't
want my writing or my philosophy or even my soul dance.
They wanted the strength of my Will – not for themselves,
but for me, for within that was the Whole of my eternal
identity, the I-Am. (end excerpt)

"I will bloom forever!" As those words echoed from my
own past, from my own unique experience, I gazed out
toward the horizon and knew it was time to go.

Walking back toward the car in the cold dark, with drizzle
misting against my face, I found Orlando walking at my side
once again, the veil between us so thin I could almost reach
out and touch him. He nuzzled closer, a warm breath against
my neck.

"Did you find what you were looking for?" he wanted to
know.

"Yes." That surprised me a little.

"And how would you define it?"

"You. Me. The bridge between the worlds."

He was moving away from me then, back behind the veil,
into the mist, the nagual, the seventh sense. "But you had
those things all along," he reminded me again, laughing.

Scenes from *The Wizard of Oz* rattled through my mind.
The tin man didn't know he had a heart until he felt it
breaking. The scarecrow didn't realize his own abilities until
he began to use them.

Dorothy had the ruby slippers all along.

~

November 15, 2003

As we left Marfa that night, rain beat against the
windshield of the rental car, becoming more pronounced as
we headed into the more mountainous terrain to the east. Fog
pressed close, a curious ghost hugging the windows.

I thought about the message I had received. *A singularity of consciousness.* What does that mean? On one level, I understood it completely. On another level, I found myself feeling vulnerable, as if the nagual had stirred and sent tendrils into this world to stalk me.

Visions formed in my mind. The totality of the evolved self. All the experiences of all levels of consciousness finally united in a single cohesive *I-Am* which, by definition, would be capable of almost anything it might choose. It could manifest as a rag lady on a donkey in the middle of the chaparral, or a light anomaly somewhere near Old Mexico, or a man in a post office 15 years in the past. Ubiquitous and eternal, it could be or do anything it might choose to be or do.

Prior to arriving at Marfa, we had discussed the possibility that the lights might somehow indicate a rip in the space-time continuum – not unlike the old childhood legend about how the stars are lights shining through from heaven. Or perhaps they were a manifestation of a doorway into another dimension – for, after all, every mystic since the dawn of recorded time had spoken of doorways into Otherworlds, and I myself have dreamt such things since long before becoming committed to the journey.

The conversation lulled. The fog lifted. A few stars peeked through the cloud cover. Later that night, we got a ticket just outside Ozona, Texas – clearly a speed trap awaiting the arrival of cars with out of state plates. The annoying part was that we should have known better. In hindsight, I kept telling myself I should have stalked the state trooper a bit better and taken the opportunity to use my verra best Suthun accent: "Oh, offisuh – I am soooo glad you stopped us! We were drivin' so fast because there had been these headlights in the rearview mirruh, gaining on us sooooo fast we were afraid for our helpless feminine virtues, out here in the middle of this beautiful Texas night..." *Ya'all...*

Instead, I sat there in silence as he enforced his rules and wrote out his ticket and pretended to be concerned for my safety. The games. The illusions. The actors going through the motions of their lives. Besides, batting one's eyelids at an officer of the law works better for younger, thinner women, I suspected. Those days are over for the crone.

But does anyone realize how insane all of this is? I mean – *really*? A man dresses up in a funny suit, straps a gun to his hip and puts on a weird hat meant to symbolize authority... then goes out on 650 horses with blazing lights and screaming sirens, and terrorizes passing citizens in what amounts to a game of highway robbery that has been sanctioned by the prevailing terrorist regime of the moment which most folks call by the more politically correct term, "government." So don't tell me the world isn't crazy. And don't tell me the lunatics aren't running the asylum. To anyone who sees, there is no more obvious truth than that.

And yet, even as I was snarling to reveal a disgruntled fang as we pulled back onto the freeway and our big-gunned petty tyrant sped off in the opposite direction, I was also thinking that the lights in the rearview mirror are real. Carlos saw them one night as he and don Juan were driving through Central Mexico. Don Juan told him then that the headlights were Death – always in the rearview mirror, stalking him, gaining on him in a game of cat and mouse. I thought again of the Marfa lights. Was that what they were, too? Just death in the rearview mirror?

By the time we stopped for the night, Marfa was far behind us, the speeding ticket was in the glove compartment, and the stray cat we had found was curled up on the foot of the bed, snoring peacefully for the first time in what I took to be a long time. Throughout that night, I listened to the sound of rain pounding against the tile roof, and slept very little. By the time morning came, I looked out the window to see nothing but pick-ups with deer-hunting supplies filling the hotel parking lot. Fresh blood had collected in a pothole, clearly having dripped from some slaughtered animal splayed over the tail-gate of a recently-departed vehicle.

A heaviness had settled in my chest, a sense of hopelessness. While I realize there are warriors who sanction hunting, I myself am not one of them. I have ultimate respect for those who must hunt for food, and who use the animals they kill. And yet, as I witnessed this debacle, I could find no sense of goodness in it at all. Don't tell me you have to hunt to feed your family when you're driving a $40K truck, with two $3K rifles in the gun rack, and the whole shebang is pulling a $300K 5th wheel trailer with room enough for the Texas Rangers! You don't need 1000 pounds of deer jerky. It's a sport. Having nothing to do with survival. And everything to do with some machismo image that's no more real than all those beer commercials.

The journey had taken a dark turn.

YOU CAN NEVER GO HOME AGAIN

November 16, 2003

I know why I love Florida and I know why I left. The land is beautiful, alluring, and holds a sense of mystery that is somehow deeply imbedded in my own matrix. As a child, I ran wild through the wetlands and the pine forests and the live oaks. I knew the spirits of the swamp and the groves, the song of the lakes and the lament of the whip-poor-will. Nothing has changed, yet everything has changed. The landmarks used for navigation by a 10-year old riding her bicycle on glorious adventures have all been obscured by progress, and other than an occasional railroad trestle crossing a once-familiar highway, I recognized nothing.

All things change. Yet again I could not help but see the monuments to human greed, indulgence and excess. In a region once protected as wetlands, prominent housing developments now choke the land, with more golf courses per square mile than mosquitoes. I felt like a stranger in a strange land, wondering where it stops, knowing it doesn't, realizing

208

in the deepest part of myself that this is simply the way of Man. This time around at least.

Something says there have been other times, other civilizations. All have fallen. And this one will fall, too. Perhaps it is simply inevitable that humanity reaches what is often referred to as "Zero point" or "zep tepi" or as Terence McKenna labeled it, "time wave zero." The visions which accompany this Knowing are visions of the earth simply starting the loop over without most of us. Perhaps not even any great cataclysm as so many new age gurus like to predict. No great war to end all wars. No poisoning of the atmosphere to the point that we all choke and die. Just… simply… the… end… of… Time.

Impossible to explain, really. What I see is simply a moment when the Earth shrugs and time folds in on itself and the tape breaks. The matrix collapses, and essentially Time reverts back to some other manifestation of itself. Say a billion years ago. Or a billion years from now on some uninhabited Thursday afternoon where the world is comprised of trees and birds and all manner of animals, with the exception of Man.

And yet, I remind myself that we are animals, too. It is our nature for little girls to swing upside down from Florida grapefruit trees, and old folks to ride around in golf carts swinging clubs at their balls. Really no difference. So why should we be excluded from the loop? I see the vision over and over – not only on this current trip, but in other visions which have persisted over the past few years. Just a shrug of the planet's shoulders, and we're all gone, and everything continues on without us.

Except… there is consciousness. And there is awareness. The sentient All which exists beyond the eagle is still there. Singularities of consciousness remain, waiting for Time to start forward again with the first sentient thought of whatever creature demands its own evolution through will. Perhaps these are the allies. Or the first shaman, who created herself and all the world with a thought and placed her double outside of herself so she would always be looking for the immortal Other.

So as I wander through these familiar old haunts and unfamiliar new roads, I am filled with a paradoxically joyous sadness, knowing why I loved this place, and why I had to leave. Like everything else, it was an evolution, always ongoing, always changing. At times I look out the car window and wonder what has happened to the land, and when this "progress" will reach beyond even its own ability to manage. When will enough finally be enough?

To the warrior, it could be said that these things don't matter. And yet, it is also observed that the warrior has an ongoing love affair with her beloved: this mysterious earth. Not in the sense of being some starry-eyed tree-hugger, but in the sense of being in love with the shadows moving through the oaks, the voice of the wind through the pines, the song of the owl echoing across the wetlands underneath a lopsided orange moon, the fairy-esque flight of the firefly on a too-warm November night.

In my mother's house hang photographs of a little girl I do not remember ever being. In my memory, I am still walking roads that are no longer there, with friends long-dead. Visions whisper close, secret rendezvous with mysterious forces somewhere in the realm of heightened awareness. I mean this quite literally – memories that are real memories, yet did not occur in what we traditionally think of as linear time. Memories that never happened... yet did. Training of some sort. Outside of time.

The little girl in her white Sunday school dress in that old black and white photograph whispers in my ear as I'm sleeping. *"It's all about remembering the Other Self, waking up inside the dream, opening your eyes inside the double."*

I get the feeling she knows more about me than I ever knew about her.

ASSIMILATION

February 4, 2004

From the beginning of this journey, Orlando has talked about how we create reality. Long ago, I was experimenting with the pumpkin, the crib, the red hearse and so on, to the point of being amazed at the results. And yet, I could not comprehend how to make this ability really work within the big picture. I experimented with more potentially useful manifestations, only to learn that I could not influence a slot machine, nor could I manifest a new truck with the pink slip sitting on the driver's seat in my name. So, while the technique itself was quantifiable in that I proved to myself time and time again that it worked, I could not really find a practical application.

This morning, while talking to a fellow warrior who is visiting, I realized that this is how "the seventh sense" is created – not just as a structure, but as an extension of the Self, beyond the physical body. Almost impossible to explain, but what I suddenly *saw* was that what we think of as third attention or the seventh sense or the otherworld is not only a milieu which we might inhabit much as we inhabit a house, but these milieus – through the force of our intent -- actually become the *vessel* of our consciousness. We become the milieu and the awareness that inhabits it – the chicken and the egg, the self and the otherworld, immortal self and eternal double.

For example, if I am an autumn soul who longs for some mysterious gothic environment, it could be perceived that the energy expended through my long-term intent creates the quantum infrastructure through which my desires will be manifested for eternity. As I said to my warrior-friend, I *am* the dark cathedral. I *am* the gargoyle on the roof. I *am* the cold rain and the snow and the autumn leaves. All that I have created through Intent is the energetic vessel of eternity, and so I become the seventh sense, and the eternal self who walks through that land of her own creation. It literally becomes a conjoining of dreamer and dreamed, otherworld and self, perceiver and perceived.

At the level of quantum energy, we create the structure of our own personal "heaven" and inhabit that creation into eternity as a cohesive awareness – the identity of I-Am.

Perhaps this will seem obvious to some, and yet it seemed to assimilate with me at a level far deeper than I had ever considered it previously. The vision which accompanied this assimilation was that of a sentient world – a world of long dirt roads and autumn wildflowers and vine-covered cathedrals, where shamans and sorcerers and mystical beings might meet to discuss the path of the stars or the positioning of grains of sand on the bottom of the oceans.

Through the creation of that reality, I had become sentient in every molecule of the reality itself. My bones were the branches of dormant winter trees, my breath the cold wind blowing through the whistling caves, my awareness the energetic underpinning which held the whole structure together. And, at the same time, if I chose, I could be the little girl or the old crone walking through that milieu, looking around in wonder.

These are only my words, attempting to trace around the edges of the nagual to reveal what must ultimately be experienced.

ROAD TRIP

May 5, 2004

There is something liberating about being on the road. In many ways, it allows the assemblage point to slide. The digital temperature gauge on the dash tells me it is 101 degrees, and we are proceeding southeast at a speed of 85 mph. Yet the ride is smooth, and the cargo trailer following along behind us is little more than an occasional shadow bobbing impatiently in the rearview mirror – an all-but-forgotten parasite.

212

Black pools of shadow
haunt pale trunks of almond trees,
underworld doorways.

It's somewhere on the I-99, north-central California farmland, nothing particularly interesting about it. Flatlands. Rice paddies flooded, with the barest of green stalks beginning to poke skinny fingers above the water. Freeway signs chattering about distances to this or that Nowhereville. Sitting in the passenger seat, I drift to tunes on the CD player. Concrete Blonde now. *The Ship Song.* A poem I wrote somewhen in the distance haunts my memory.

The night is a black book
written in invisible ink,
full of alchemy recipes.
Between the pages
obsidian orchids are pressed,
staining tissue paper sky
with a pollen of stars.
When all the blooms have fallen
like angels from heaven,
I will be no closer to death.

A thin haze hangs on the air. Dust, smoke, fog, smog. Names of dragons, perhaps. Gazing out the window toward a thick, dark grove of pecans, I think of Orlando, absent-mindedly replaying a particular memory from when I knew him in manifestation. A wicked smile, followed by the words, "You can't save the world. It's already too late for the world. But maybe you still have time to save yourself." Maybe. No promises, not even from him. Just an indifferent and casual "maybe."

The landscape seems painted on the inside of the car window. Endless groves of this or that. As a girl, I remember seeing a man standing just inside a grove of orange trees as I rode my horse one hot summer afternoon. I knew then it was my destiny to court the shadows, to be in love with ghosts dressed in elegant top hats, dancing forever on the bow of _Titanic_, or darting down gothic hallways in some ruined cathedral, whispering in that silent, wordless language, "Come home to me. Just a little further now. Come home."

Could be anywhere, of course. If not _Titanic_, then some village with no name on one of the Greek isles, or a farm in the south of China, or a ratty motel in the middle of central Florida, where a little girl I once was grew up. I think briefly of past lives, and hear the voice of the double laughing. "That's what I am – but so much more. Don't you remember yet?"

Sometimes I do. And that's the lure, of course. That's the promise – to be Whole again, to remember the other self, to be cohesive into eternity. To play both roles in the love story, nagual man and nagual woman, forgetting briefly which is which and who is who, because that is how the lure works, too.

Broken down houses line dirt streets at the edge of the freeway, and tattered clothes hang on a sagging line, faded flags strung out to dry like lost identities. In a distant orchard of pale white grapes, a dust devil spins sorcery stories, carrying them up, higher up, into the hot, arid sky.

There is no conclusion, no resolution. There is only an expanse of infinity, broken all too briefly by this strange and wondrous state we call Life.

THE TIGHTROPE

May 20, 2004

It was a bright and sunny day today, when I had two very distinctive and undeniable encounters with the nagual. The first occurred about mid-afternoon. We've been having a new kitchen countertop put in, and there have been a lot of workmen in and out for the past week. Today, for the first time in many days, they left early and I was puttering around in the kitchen, tidying up a bit. Wendy had just passed through the French doors that lead into the living room, on her way out to do some errands, and to my knowledge, I was alone in the house.

At first, I thought nothing of it when our three dogs began barking at the French doors. Zero was yapping the same way she does when tormenting the cat; Zuni sounded more confused than concerned; and Morgan was probably just barking in case the other two were onto something. I ignored them for about a minute, then finally turned around to see what all the ruckus was about. To my surprise – literally the kind of shock that sends one's heart into one's throat – I saw someone dressed entirely in black collapsed on the floor on the other side of the glass doors. For a single instant, I couldn't breathe, then I gasped out loud, for my only thought was that it had to be Wendy – and I was terrified to think she had perhaps fainted and fallen, or worse.

As I rushed toward the door, the thought crossed my mind that I didn't know how I would be able to open it, since this person was lying literally against it. But in that kind of instantaneous adrenaline rush, logic has little to do with it, so I simply opened the door... only to discover there was nothing there. It was there one instant, and gone the next, quite literally having vanished before my very eyes.

This was a prolonged sighting, lasting at least two minutes, judging by the uproar the dogs were creating. And I personally was looking right at it for at least 30 seconds

215

myself. It wasn't a shadow or a reflection of the light or some odd hallucination. Whatever it was had enough substance to exist simultaneously in dog-world and human-world, so there is no doubt in my mind it was there – whatever it was, and wherever "there" might have been.

I went through the rest of the day without thinking too much of it. Living as I do in the sorcerer's world, I've come to accept that nothing is as it seems, and even though it had been awhile since anything of this magnitude had occurred, it is not unprecedented around here.

By the time we were getting ready to go to dinner, around 7:45, I had all but forgotten about the incident entirely. But as I was walking toward the car in the deepening desert shadows of dusk, I glanced over toward the front porch to see a man dressed in khaki-brown, walking from the house in the direction of the front yard. At first, I thought it was a neighbor, but as I started to call out to him, I realized that he, too, had simply walked into the Nothing. No one was there – only a palmetto rustling in the light breeze, and a squirrel skittering along the half-wall with a leaf from my newly-planted blood-orange tree in his mouth.

For a moment, I just stood there staring at the empty space where this man had been only a second before, and the words rattled through my head, *"The veil is thin right now. The naguals are walking the tightrope between the worlds."*

So it would seem.

THE DRAGONFLY AND THE NAGUAL

June 1, 2004

This afternoon as I was doing some work out on the carport, sorting through some things in preparation for our next business outing, I opened a large cloth sack which contains blankets, tapestries, and other items made of fabric. I'm always careful when plundering through such things

216

because of the possibility of spiders, scorpions or worse, but it was with some surprise that I found a small, perfectly preserved little dragonfly all rolled up inside a sheet. His wings were gossamer and green, and had curled under at the end, but still so shiny it was as if he had just stopped there to rest.

For a few moments, I just gazed at this dead creature with a sense of wonder, trying to remember where we had last been that we might have picked him up, since his kind are not indigenous here in the desert. It took a bit before I recalled that our last outing had been to the Sacramento River area near Redding, and I did indeed recall seeing some dragonflies floating down the swift water, poised on canoes made of fallen leaves or some bit of driftwood.

But even as I sat there in the late afternoon dusk, holding the mortal remains of this fragile creature in my hand, something happened that I cannot explain. The dragonfly turned to a sprig of dried grass right there in my hand. Suddenly, it was not a dragonfly at all. Just a piece of brown, dead Bermuda grass that had obviously been rolled up in the sheet when we had packed down at Sacramento.

There is no doubt in my mind whatsoever that I was originally holding this dried-out but stunningly beautiful little insect. I examined the wings. I looked at the well-preserved compound eyes. I counted six little legs.

And yet...

All that remained was a sprig of grass.

THE SOUND OF WEEPING

August 23, 2004

This house is old and rather large – a sprawling testament to the old miner who built it back in 1955 – and with all its natural gemstone walls and its location in the desert, I've come to expect a certain amount of oddities and manifestations of the bizarre.

Though it is warm outside today, the interior of the house remains cool and unusually silent, with the cats sleeping in various nooks and crannies while I go about the business of attempting to organize our business for its next outing. The light has turned somewhat more gold than its typically summer-bright-white; and the wind is tossing the locust tree to and fro, scratching at the eaves, moaning and whispering through the ducts. Chimes chatter in the cactus garden outside my window, and the cobwebs lift and float on unseen currents.

A few minutes ago, I went from one end of the house to the other, followed by Zero, who has made it her habit to be always at my heels. As I passed through the living room, I experienced a sensation in the pit of the stomach which I've come to recognize as some precursor of a manifestation from the nagual. Immediately upon acknowledging the sensation, Zero gave a short, low bark – her signal that something is afoot which she hasn't yet identified.

Coming to a sense of greater awareness, I entered the room where I had been headed, at which point Zero began to bark fiercely (well, as fierce as a 7-pound weenie dog can get), and I turned to see her hackles raised. Her teeth were bared, and she was staring fixedly at a point just to my left. Aside from the wind playing with the curtains and causing them to flutter, I saw nothing – until suddenly there was what I can only describe as an energetic "flutter" in the empty space about 3 feet from me. Words cannot wrap around it, for there is no correlation other than in the special effects of movies – a shimmering of the air, perhaps most accurately compared to heat monkeys dancing on hot pavement in the dead of summer.

For a few moments, I stared at this anomaly with a combination of curiosity and perhaps mild disbelief, while Zero continued to bark and the fat black cat scampered past me and out the door. Then, abruptly, it was gone. The dog stopped barking, the wind paused in its eternal journey, and whatever had been there was simply not there any longer.

After a few moments of silent contemplation of the event, I began walking back through the house, only to hear an uncharacteristic stirring through the ducts. Having lived in this house for 12 years now, I am familiar with all the voices of the wind, all the whisperings of the timbers, all the noises an old house in the desert might make. This was none of those. Instead, it had the sound and the feel of someone weeping softly to themselves – a hushed but profound sobbing which went on for at least 30-45 seconds. And then it, too, simply stopped.

A sense of melancholy lingers in the house – not unlike the paradoxically exhilarating sadness one feels when autumn begins to slowly creep up out of her dormant sleep. But this was different. The nagual shimmers and weeps, haunting this old house in a way that has raised gooseflesh on the back of my neck, and leaves me with an ache in my spirit that has no explanation.

DOUBLE VISION

October 12, 2004

It was a weekend of sensory overload, a noisy generator on one side, and the clatter and clamor of drums and belly dancers on the other, offset by a crowd of 100,000 Renaissance patrons and participants, all of whom seemed to be in a tremendous hurry to be somewhere other than where they were, even though they had paid a fair amount of money to be precisely where they were. My cold had turned to the flu. The assemblage point shifts in delirium. A cacophony of unrelated colors and shapes. A din of heat. An ice-cream flavored swirl of screams and shouts. Maybe I had a fever. A genital pox on any moron who sells a child a toy flute.

On the long drive home, I was finally alone for the first time in over 5 days. Being a loner, I do not care much for human contact. Minds press too close. Probes attempt to penetrate. I turn to smoke.

The rental car glides easily through the desert, with Leonard Cohen's gruff voice on the CD player and massive thunderheads gathering in the west. The Nevada/California desert weaves an alien landscape. Joshua trees walk the ley lines. Jagged mountains poke bony fingers skyward. Skid marks zip the road tight to a parched earth.

Words are only fodder for semantics, tools of misunderstanding. You had to be there. But I was alone. No way to tell the tale but to trace along the edges, maybe to reveal what lies beneath. Such is the contour of the nagual, with the delicate flesh of a lover and contrastingly dangerous fangs.

Somewhere in the middle of the desert, in the middle of a long and winding road, I awakened inside Orlando. It really was that simple. Opened my eyes, looked around, had a laugh or two at the human condition, a bigger laugh at my mortal self going through the machinations of Life, and began to cross-ponder from what can only be called a dual point of view (Orlando and Della) this bizarre thing called Time.

Time is a mortal construct. We make it up to use as a yardstick, a reference point against the backdrop of eternity. But it isn't real in the sense we might think. Impossible to describe how it felt to be outside of time altogether. Orlando often talks about Time, but after this experience, I now realize he talks to us in much the same way an adult would talk to a 5-year old about the birds and the bees. He uses language we can understand, but the actuality of it all tends to lose a lot in the translation. Birds and bees have very little to do with human reproduction, and time has very little to do with life and death. It's just an egg in which we gestate while waiting to hatch. *While. Waiting.* Our language itself creates Time, referencing it in countless subtle ways.

So there we were. Mortal self and eternal double driving down a winding road in the geographical center of infinity. Perhaps chance chose the space-time. Who's to say? Life seemed strange, at odds with itself in so many ways. The organic robot in the SUV behind me was flashing his lights while puffing on a cigarette and yapping animatedly on a cell phone. Funny monkey – all red-faced and angry, holding up a predictable finger while mouthing some obscenity in my direction as he zipped past on his way to his appointment with death. For kicks, I showed him my own finger in return – it was expected, after all, and I had a bigger ring that caught the sun – and with that little ritual out of the way, I turned my attention back to Orlando.

"You are the final fragment of yourself," he whispered, so close to my ear I could feel the heat of him, even though logic and reason said it was only the sun pouring through the window. *"Touch me with your naked hand, touch me with your glove,"* Leonard Cohen murmurs in a black silk velvet voice that sends shivers down my spine, a voice that invokes the midnight even in mid-afternoon. I felt Orlando's touch. As if in a vision more visceral than stone, the thunderheads in the west trembled. A lover's caress. Lightning snaked parallel to the ground. A golden butterfly struck the windshield and entered eternity. An eagle soared over the desert, hunting. Two fine fat black ravens strolled along the side of the road, oblivious to the slipstream thrown off by a careening 18-wheeler.

"There is a crack. There is a crack in everything. That's how the light gets in." Cohen again. Wickedly perceptive old man.

I laughed, hearing it echo from here to there and back again, from the dark into the light, manifesting particle-wave duality riding itself back into the blackness, serpent eating its own tail only to turn wrongside out into some other perception of an ever-evolving reality. "You are the final fragment of yourself."

And then I was mySelf again, just a mortal crone propelling herself down the road at dangerous speeds, cycling endlessly between one moment and the next, between here and now, drifting between the harsh terrain of Time and the snowscape of timeless infinity.

"*When the final fragment is integrated, Time itself will end.*"

"I see," said the blind man.

I *See.*

CHAOS THEORY REWRITTEN

November 17, 2004

Over the past few weeks, I have been going through what I can only think of as a rewriting of Chaos Theory in my own head. It goes something like this:

I logon to my online forum yesterday and see my graphic signature has lost its background. So I futz around with it for a couple of hours, figuring it *must* be *my* problem... only to later discover this is some sort of "new and improved" inner gazurkis on the servers, designed to create a more enjoyable atmosphere for... ? Who? And how?

So I go to tech support forum, only to be directed to another help forum, because the first one says it isn't in their job description. *That* forum tells me I am not allowed to post, and that I must return in one hour. They did not specifically tell me to bring back the broomstick of the wicked witch, but I suspect that will be next. Luckily, I *am* the wicked witch of the west, and carry a spare with me at all times, so shall present it to them (you can guess which-end-first) upon my return in one hour. */end forum-server rant.*

So then I logon to eBay to do some maintenance and relisting on some of the ads for our business, only to discover that eBay has likewise switched overnight to the new and improved eBay. This translates to the fact that my ads which had been specifically designed to fit within *their* parameters

222

are now falling off the page and require lots of left-to-right scrolling in order to be read, and if you're like me, you probably don't even try to read something where that's the case. Again, figuring it must be *my* problem, I futz with it for awhile, until...

Finally get on the phone to tech support, where I am on hold for over an hour listening to some over-enthusiastic robotic on puppy-uppers chattering about stuff I don't want to know. I am told repeatedly this incessant chatter is a "service," when I could've sworn it was just a butthead babbling in my ear. Endlessly. Without cessation. To the point of bone-diddling madness. When the tech finally comes online awhile later, I am informed that the engineers have made some "improvements" (?!?!?) and we all just have to live with it. I now have to re-write HTML on over 200 individual ads so as to comply with the new and improved eBay, when it was working just fine before this grand new installation of Chaos Software Incarnate. */eBay rant*

The bottom line to all of this, seems to be that the world is rushing forward at some great and hectic pace in some bizarre notion that it is improving things, when the reality is that I used to be able to go into the supermarket, have the nice lady check my items through by punching the price into a cash register, and I was in and out in half the time it now takes for this new and improved technology to scan, process, inventory, and otherwise examine and categorize every individual piece of lettuce down to the nth degree of minutiae.

And don't get me started on the wrapping on a CD or DVD! Remember the good old days? We bought an album (remember those?), brought it home, slit through the cellophane with a fingernail, and put the damn thing on the spinner. Behold – let there be music in less than 3.5 centuries! Just yesterday, tried to unwrap a new DVD, yet the labyrinths of Tut's tomb would be more easily penetrated! By the time I finally got the damn thing out of its sixteen layers of protective seals, wraps, locks and casings, I had forgotten what movie I was trying to watch, not to mention my own name! The men in the white coats were standing outside with a butterfly net, 'cuz I must've called them, or else my cell phone became sentient and dialed the number all by itself – which it seems to do quite frequently, keys locked or not, just so I can get a nice surprise of lots of long distance calls I didn't make... thankyee very much!

And then let's talk about the cell phone itself! I just want to say hello to me poor old mum, not remote control the entire resources of Starfleet from the palm of my hand! It's overkill, for the love of Mike! (And who the hell is Mike, anyway?)

Life used to be simpler, didn't it? I mean – seriously – is this part of the reason the world seems to be spiraling faster and faster into some irredeemable abyss of confusion, conflict and technological incompatibility? The DVD player can't read the CDs which are compatible only with the 'puter, and the MP3 (whatever that is) is mating with the IPOD (whatever that is), and the VHS is sitting lonely and lost and obsolete in the corner even though I bought it less than 6 months ago, and the workmen in the living room are trying to measure for carpet using some sort of laser-sighting gizmo which can't seem to get an accurate reading because of the glint on the window; and they've been there for over an hour screwing around with it, scratching their collective heads... so I went and got my tape measure and informed them it was precisely 30', 6.5" in width, by 30' 6.25" in length. Close enough for jazz and government work, boys?

So my personal Chaos Theory is this. It's all a grand conspiracy hatched by the hive mind in an attempt to so thoroughly distract one's energy and monopolize one's time with absolutely *inane* folly and trivialities that we have no time or energy left to pursue the things that really do matter – like our own spiritual well-being and evolution. The longer we are on hold, the longer it takes to open that wrapper or wait for that price check lest the world economy be thrown out of balance on some computer, the less time we are spending on our own individual pursuits.

I could go on. But I won't. I'm going to go fix my lunch with an old-fashioned slice of bread and some tuna, eat it with my bare hands, and lick my fingers clean when I'm done. The rest... is just chaos.

RECAPITULATION AND THE TEFLON WARRIOR

January, 2005

Though I have been on this path of heart for many, many years, one thing that has traditionally seemed off to me is this idea of recapitulation with the intent of reclaiming lost energy. There are several reasons for this, some scientific and others sorceric. On the one hand, it makes sense to disentangle the hooks imbedded in one's spirit from events in the past, so perhaps it's the wording "reclaiming lost energy" which has always disturbed me. Energy is always in motion and cannot, therefore, *really* be reclaimed, just as one cannot step into the same river twice.

Also, it's been my experience that attempts at recapitulation could, under certain conditions, actually be harming the warrior's progress, because it will always be easier to deal with the past than to create the future. For myself, what's traditionally worked with regard to not losing energy is to recapitulate as I go along, and that is quite easily done by the simple realization that we live in a world of illusion peopled largely by phantoms. It might be best said that nothing sticks to a teflon mirror. Once we realize the world is folly – truly internalize that down to a molecular level – it becomes only a vast play on a canvas of dust, an interaction with phantom actors who might *try* to get hooks of their script into us, but there is simply no surface of the warrior vulnerable enough to be penetrated.

The true sorcerer-warrior actually has the ability to reflect those intended hooks right back at the phantom who launched them in the first place, or to merely *def*lect them so they fall harmlessly aside.

As for recapturing energy from the past, once one begins to live in a manner of a teflon mirror, recapitulation is no longer necessary as a ritualistic practice, for one also realizes that the world has *always* been folly, thus these events in our past which have left us with hooks begin to fall away quite naturally, which is far more energy efficient trying to re-experience them.

One thing about the Toltec practices, in my opinion, is that way too much emphasis was placed on the idea of making lists and recapping each and every annoying gnat on the nose of my discontent. To me, that is an ultimate waste of time and energy, when the teflon approach works not only in the now, but also as a *retroactive enchantment* – which is to say, when one masters it in the Now, the ramifications and benefits sweep not only into the future, but also into the past.

As mentioned previously, my father was a tyrant of the nth degree. It would take years to recap everything that man ever said or did, and though I can see a certain appeal to the traditional idea of recapping, I can also see that it might become one hell of an indulgence, too. By releasing the phantom *self*, the energy hooks just naturally fall away, because once it is recognized that the warrior is essentially a new being, the whole idea of a long and drawn-out, ritualized, list-bearing recapitulation becomes entirely unnecessary.

So, when a warrior is serious about recapitulation, I teach them how to recap themselves. And it is not a long and drawn-out process. It is a ruthless shift of the AP and an immediate release of any self-importance or indulgence that may be attached to personal history. Quite obviously, the teflon warrior technique is not something that can be easily accomplished by those new to the path, but works miraculously for those at a more advanced level.

226

THE NAKED BRUJO

January 20, 2003

This afternoon I allowed myself the luxury of a rare nap. It began as a meditation, actually. I often sit on the bed in my office at night and gaze out through the open door. Since we live on a 5 acre parcel in the desert, I have a magnificent view of distant mountains covered by snow, and a closer vista of Joshua trees, piñon pines and yucca plants. The desert is not the barren wasteland so many envision. Instead, it is full of life in all its many manifestations.

So I sat on the bed and leaned back, just enjoying the last vestiges of light splashed along the western horizon. It had rained this morning, and the scent of wet chaparral brush lay heavy in the air. A cool, almost cold breeze was blowing in. The sky was a pale shade of winter night.

I drifted. And then I slept. Just sitting there at the edge of the desert, on the edge of the nagual. Last thing I recalled, I had glanced at the clock to see that it was about 5:45. Quite some time later, I awakened to the sound of footsteps, and a man's voice. Very clearly, he said, "It's time to get up."

Opening my eyes, I discovered a naked man standing just inside my door, less than 5 feet from me. Silhouetted against the open door, there was no mistake of what I was seeing, and yet I was completely without fear. It isn't that I am fearless. It was simply that there was nothing to fear, and in that state between sleep and waking, I Knew this on a level of awareness that transcends all logic.

I gazed at him for approximately 5 seconds – quite a long time if one is holding one's hand in flame or looking at a naked man standing next to one's bed. And still, no fear came. As I watched, transfixed, he began to morph much like a special effect in a movie, until eventually he had become the large golden dog who has been frequenting our yard for several weeks – a stray whom we've fed on occasion, but who has always shied away from physical contact.

227

In the sorcerer's world, nothing is as it seems. All things are only transient manifestations of energy. After the man had become the dog, I got up and went out into the yard, where he was sitting on an old grass mat, staring at me with one upright ear and one bent ear, and a funny smile that was far more human than not. Laughing at me, I suspect. So I laughed, too.

What does it mean? Who's to say? It is known in the shaman's world that brujos can take on the shape of animals if that is their Will, so I cannot possibly know if the dog is really a sorcerer in his own right, or if a sorcerer chose to manifest as the dog. All I know is that a brujo with a sense of humor wandered naked into my house while I lay sleeping, and told me it was time to get up.

Is this some allegorical tale? Nope. Every word of it is true according to my perceptions. Trying to wrap human comprehension around it is like trying to contain the nagual in a teacup. The experience is the journey, and the journey is the cumulative experiences that go to form a foundation of Knowledge. Tonight I was honored by a visit from a brujo, and after we played together for awhile in the open desert, he simply disappeared into the night, a shadow running along the road.

The crack between the worlds stands open. Sometimes, if we are fortunate, something from the other side slips through to give us a glimpse of limitless power, limitless mystery.

THE WILL OF THE WARRIOR

June 25, 2003

Wendy and I worked a renaissance faire over the solstice, where the pagans were refreshing and much in abundance. As we lay in our tent (on a nice cushy air bed, with loads of pillows), I fell asleep to the rhythms of an awesome drumming circle. My dreams that night were indescribable, but filled with energies which vibrate in the solar plexus and radiate outward – an awesome experience in waking awareness, transcendent in dreaming. That night, I dreamt of Orlando for the first time in a long time. Nothing profound, really, at least it didn't seem like it at the time. Just an awareness of him standing inside the tent, looking down at me as I was sleeping. Sounds sweet, perhaps, but there was a mischievous dark side to it, too – methinks he was riding his broomstick on the solstice energies.

It was one of those dreams (or was it?) where one dreams into the actuality of one's physical location – like a dream that takes place in the bedroom where one is sleeping. So, this was real-time and real-place, so to speak. Dreaming of Orlando standing right there, at that moment in time, with the drummers still drumming in real-time and the moon peeking in through a gap in the tent flap.

He had that aura. Intense. Dark. Power.

I actually had the thought, *"Are you here because it's time for me to die?"*

He smiled and took a step closer. Without speaking, he said, *"That's up to you. Your decision."*

I was enjoying the dreaming, experiencing him as the mirror, the Other. For a moment, I was looking through his eyes, looking at myself as I lay there sleeping. It would have been easy enough to just stay, to keep looking out through those eternal, immortal eyes and simply wake up inside the dream. Wake up inside the Other. Wake up whole, embraced by the dark wings of the nagual man. Become One with it all and inhabit the totality of myself. It could have taken any form I might have cared to imagine. He could have become a wicked but handsome pirate swinging down from the rigging of a tall ship to sweep me off the deck, off the stage, out of the play and into the eternal night... if that's what I had called forth with my will. Or he could have taken the form of a magnificent and powerful prince, bringing me into his own eternal awareness, turning me wrong-side-out by drawing the lifeforce out of this mortal shell and into his own indestructible energy body... if that's what my will had asked him to be, to do, to create.

So there we were with a decision hanging in the cool night air between us. He would have done anything I wanted him to do. Anything my will directed him to do.

So I took a deep breath and asked, "Will it hurt?"

He smiled darkly. "Do you want it to?" Bastard.

I chose to go on dreaming. For awhile at least. For now.

Maybe I just like the adventure, the anticipation, the lure of the muse that is both sweet and painful at the same time. He'll be there. Waiting. I know that now. I've always known it. Knowing it is what generates the power to Create it.

And I learned something about will. For now, it is mine. The choice was mine. This time. But one night that will change.

Through the spirit, through the natural progression and migration of the Self from this world to the other, I will transfer my will to the Other, the Double, the Self in eternity. That is the moment Death will tap me on the shoulder... and I know now that it will be whatever I want it to be. No matter what form it might take in this world of ordinary awareness, it will be whatever I will it to be in the seventh sense.

In that position of the assemblage point, it will be late autumn, with leaves clacking their heels on a deserted road in the night, and a storm brewing on the horizon. When the lightning flashes brighter than the noonday sun, I will look back to see my body sleeping, and then I will know that I have finally wakened from the dream and into the Dreamer.

This is my will. So it shall *Be*.

PART FIVE

EMBRACING THE NAGUAL:

THE VIEW FROM BEYOND THE EAGLE

Chapter Twenty-One
Orlando's Perspective

Rather than attempt to translate the things I have learned from Orlando into some sort of dry, linear format, it seems more in alignment with Spirit to simply present this section as a compilation of communications which I have amassed over the years. Some are letters written to myself and Wendy, while others are direct responses to questions I have received from friends, acquaintances and apprentices.

Many of these questions were posed at my online forum, *The Shaman's Rattle.* [renamed to The Sorcerer's World in 2005]

THE SORCERER SPIRIT IN TIME AND SPACE

January 16, 2003

You stand at the crack between the worlds peering from "here" into "there", perhaps only now beginning to realize that there is no difference between the two worlds, and that all worlds are only the same world divided infinitely, but divided only by perception. The light shining through the cracks is the light left on by your own Intent, the illumined force of your own Existence, and while it is not my desire to sound like a mystic, there is simply no other way to explain this. It could be said that the energy of the Spirit migrates throughout space-time, inhabiting one thing and then another, in a progression that has been called reincarnation, though it is not a term I personally choose, since the baggage attached to the concept has rendered it virtually useless for sorcerers with true Intent.

What is Intended here is an understanding of why that crack between the worlds seems to exist in the first place, for only as you begin to thoroughly embrace that will you be enabled to walk through it at Will. During the migration of the

Spirit through space-time, consciousness begets matter in an ongoing attempt to heal itself of its infinite fragmentation. In one incarnation, the energy is Mary, and in another perhaps it answers to Sean or James or Julian. But the problem is that without cohesion of the Whole Self, identity and memory are lost from one manifestation to the next, and so the Spirit divides itself infinitely, giving up its awareness to the Eagle, only to repeat the process again and again. And though many new age gurus would try to tell you this is the natural law and order of the universe, I assure you it isn't True for those with shamanic vision to *See* and the Will to *be* more than a simple byproduct of nature.

Put more simply, even spirits can lose their way, and all too often when awareness is lost, so is the *I-Am,* and so each subsequent manifestation of that same molecular energy has little relevance to what has gone before. Cohesion and progression are lost without the Intent to inhabit the assemblage point of the Whole Self into eternity. And so the sorcerer's journey becomes the task of manifesting an awareness of all the Spirit's 'previous' manifestations and placing that awareness outside of Time so that the mortal self still inside of Time might have a lifeline to the Whole Self, yes?

The difference between sorcerers and ordinary men is that sorcerers work within a paradigm that functions outside of time. And so even though you have little or no awareness of it, the person you are right now is the seed of that cohesive Whole Self, and through your Intent you are manifesting yourself within the seventh sense, or third attention if you prefer. It would be impossible to explain this sufficiently in a single sentence, but when you begin to realize that even history is not altogether immutable, you will see that the actions you take now, in this life and this moment, impact the Spirit of you stretching back to the dawn of your energetic history, and stretching forward into the eternal infinite.

The sorcerer affects time in all directions, you see, for when one is outside of the linear mortal box, it becomes possible to dive in and out of "history" at will, influencing and manipulating the energy of your Self throughout all of time in order to bring the spirit into alignment with one single moment in the Now (this lifetime, this moment) when you will be able to use your Will to create the opening to freedom beyond the eagle which so many mystics have contemplated endlessly.

DEPENDENCIES AND THE EAGLE

August, 2000

A dependency of the human form is something which keeps you focused in first attention, not because it is giving you something, but because it is a hook you have allowed to be placed within you. The danger of human form dependencies is that they not only distract you from the journey, they can be the death of you if you are not careful, for they are truly – not metaphorically – anchors to the consensual reality, hooks of the familiar, designed to fixate your awareness deep within first attention. If you do not remove them, they will hold you here when it is time to run past the eagle, and while you are trying to untangle yourself from this world, the eagle will devour you completely.

Dependencies are easily defined. A dependency is anything you would mourn or grieve if you lost it – not out of love, but out of a false sense of need. Close your eyes. Imagine it is your last night on earth, and in an hour you will die. What stops you? What are you afraid of leaving behind? Most of all, *why*? It is time to define these things and begin unhooking the eagle's talons from your spirit. The sand has almost run out of the hour glass and the man behind the curtain is growing impatient.

When you lose the first attention human dependency, you are then freed to access second and third attention information. You cannot fly when you are chained to a tree, or

234

if you do, you will break your wings trying to carry the tree with you. And then you will die in the fall, your wings just tattered silk feathers shredded by stubborn clinging to stubbornness itself.

THE SUBJECTIVE OBJECTIVE REALITY OF ALL POSSIBILITY

January, 2003
QUESTION: *One of my conundrums involves the idea that we make our own realities, the concept of Perception is Reality. This is difficult to square with my own experience of an objective reality (which conflicts with my experience with my own reality, in a never ending loop), and with some of your statements, and with the explanation of assemblage point and the universe in* The Art of Dreaming.

At a core level of what can be discussed in first attention, Della has come as close as possible to addressing the conundrum of an objective reality. "Fire does not burn itself." The world is not at all what humans believe it to be, and so it is only through the gateway of experience that any real transformation is possible. Through your own Will, those experiences will come as you continue to summon them.

Once I said to Della, "I am helpless before all possibility." In the realm of the third attention, all things exist equally and at precisely the same time, for there is no actuality of Time as a matter of linear progression. Time is only the result of human gravity, part of the structural platform necessary for experience, but it is confined utterly to mortal perception. In quantum mechanics, it is stated that all things exist as possibility, but only some things will be forced to go through the motions of actually occurring. From within that realm of all possibility, nothing is impossible and yet everything is impossible, for that is the nature of All. And so the only thing

235

that determines what comes into being is the will of the perceiver, who must take on the role of creator-god in order to summon even existence itself.

In the beginning, there was darkness, void and without shape, and that could be equated to the realm of all possibility – the condensed energy-matter that is like the heart of a black star, holding the All so tightly that not even light can escape. And so it is only a thought, "Let there be light," that can break away, for the thought at that time is the only objective reality, not subject to the gravity of the All itself. And so it is the thoughtform of Light that escapes to manipulate matter into the Ex-is-tence (external-"is"-being) to create the actuality of Light itself. This is the *I-Am* of each individual. This is the Will choosing to inhabit an assemblage point outside of all possibility so as to force reality to go through the motions of actually occurring. This is the meaning of the words, "Thou art God."

At the same time, it is also important to remember that the universe itself is sentient – not as any extant deity, but as evolved singularities of sentience within third attention – and at a level of existence beyond human comprehension, there is what might be termed the raw matter of creation: the energy itself, which has a tendency to exist only because it is its nature to do so. In the sorcerer's realm, it is *seen* that the external world, what you would think of as planets and galaxies and all manifestations of inorganic matter, are the milieu created by sorcerers to serve as the playground for the forces of creation and evolution. So, your question has many answers: to ordinary women and men who are not summoning their own reality, they are existing by default in the lowest realm: the physical manifestation of matter. To the sorcerer with awareness, all worlds are the same world, and so any attempt to cut life from force or heart from beat is impossible. There is no difference.

236

SEIZING THE TILLER OF CREATION

November, 2000

For the sake of clarity, it would help to comprehend what is really meant by a shifting of the assemblage point. What you think of as reality is organized and categorized according to the ordinary input of the five senses, yes? But more than that, it goes something like this: a tree is a tree and it is green and leafy because this is the language the dominant species has chosen to identify that construct to the masses. It is an object made of language to which everyone has agreed to agree as to what the words generally mean. Ah, but to someone who has learned to *see*, the tree is really only an arrangement of energy cast in the shape of the tree. In first attention, the tree is the tree because the word has meaning. In second attention, the tree is an arrangement of energy, clearly *seen*, resembling what is known to the first attention as "tree". In the third attention, or the seventh sense, the energy comprising the tree is actually the raw matter of true quantum sorcery, and can be called upon to represent whatever the sorcerer might desire to perceive. This is the foundation of creation, the cornerstone of a separate reality.

Ah, but never forget: the act of creation requires extreme energy, so the goal of entering the seventh sense isn't just to begin rearranging all the stray molecules into castles and dragons and faerie creatures of lore. Just as the world with which you are familiar is largely created for you by those who have gone before, so it is here, but the difference is that here the world is will and the eagle is neither landlord nor tenant.

So what does this have to do with a shift of the assemblage point? Simply this: as long as you see only the tree, a tree is all it will ever be. When you learn to perceive the glossy construct of the underlying energy, you have taken a step toward undoing the world of matter and men. And when at last you stand in the seventh sense and can command the energy of the tree to be anything you will it to be, you will

237

have mastered your own creation in ways that should begin to be obvious to you. In the seventh sense, the trick to staying is to recreate the self using the tools of perception and the will and intent of the sorcerer's magic. Understand this, for it is the secret to your ultimate evolution: when you can enter the seventh sense and will the raw matter/energy of creation to be the immortal "other," and when you can not only interact with it but exert will and intent to *inhabit* it, you will have willed your own immortality, yes?

Study this. Lightly and deeply, with delicate vision. Read it in half-light where logic looks over the shoulder of magic, only a background voice in the chorus. Think on it in the alpha shadows of early dreams. Understand it with the body-spirit even if the stubborn program of your humanity tries to brush the words aside. Know that words are only the description of reality. When your humanity fights to cling to the words of the world it knows, it is because these otherwords can create otherworlds which threaten the status quo. I am the destroyer of stasis. You are the creators of reality. We are creator and created, dreaming toward one another. When we meet in the middle the dream becomes a separate reality capable of being inhabited. This is how we seize the tiller of creation. This is how we become *I-Am*.

WHAT IS REALITY?

November, 2004

QUESTION: *If I create my own realities by my will, and everyone else creates theirs, and there is no "objective reality", then how is it that two people's realities work together?*

You may choose to look at reality as a thought that manifests form, or as an infinite form which generates thought, and neither would be altogether right or altogether wrong.

What may be perceived from third attention is that there is an extant milieu or stage on which the play takes place. Earth, wind, fire, water and spirit – the five elements of creation – exist with or without the approval or disapproval of man. This is what is, and all that simply *is*. The rest is far more complex. Without some form of life to observe these elements, and ultimately to direct them through the invocation of the godforce known as Will, there is nothing to indicate they would have any sense of motion at all. The tree would not fall in the forest, for there would be no tree to begin with, see?

When I say you are creating reality, I mean this literally. Reality is created in the process of assembling it above and beyond the raw elements of creation. At the same time, you stand in a magnificent but savage garden which has been assembling itself since the first spark of awareness shook itself from the Nothing and proclaimed its sovereign identity. Thoughtforms create more thoughtforms. Trees make more trees. You do not have to create the airplane in order to fly, but you do have to agree that it exists, or you will not be able to even perceive it.

On a somewhat more workable level, two people may share the same milieu (or 2 million), and while they are all working with the same elements of creation (earth, wind, fire, water, spirit), under no circumstances will those elements of creation combine in precisely the same manner – and so it is true that reality is entirely subjective for every living thing.

And yet, there may be enough of a similarity of results that certain agreements may be formed. Fire is hot. The sky is blue (on Earth at least). A tree has roots. And so on. These, of course, are only agreements as to the milieu, and so they are more likely to be quantifiable truths than, for example, attempting to agree on the nature of spirit or the nine billion names of god. Of which there is only one, of course: *I-Am.*

Consider this: the energy of consciousness is essentially an electromagnetic field, and as such it has certain properties which are, at the quantum level, comprised entirely of the raw elements of energy which exist even before that energy goes through the process of forming into the five elements of creation. Therefore, consciousness is all things, including the building blocks of reality itself. This is true of all consciousness, whether aware or unaware, awake or asleep, sorcerer or phantom. And it is at that level of energy that reality is created and maintained by what might be considered the collective intent of all living things. You create your own reality so that you will have a milieu upon which to manifest your will.

Because all living things draw from that same source of energy, it becomes possible for two or more beings to share a commonality of reality, even if not sharing in precisely the same perception of that reality.

And while it isn't necessary to fully understand the nature of reality in order to experience it, that understanding can be helpful in attempts to overcome or circumvent it, through what you refer to as sorcery.

SPLITTING THE TIME STREAM

January, 2005
Time is a human construct and therefore as multi-faceted as humans themselves, yes? In your own life, you make decisions with every breath you take. Will you turn left or right? Will you walk by the lake or sit by the window today?

Each of those decisions creates a bifurcation in the timestream – an alternate reality, if you prefer – yet it isn't a single alternative, but literally billions upon billions of alternative possibilities. With every decision you make, you open the door to certain experience and close the door to other. If you sit by the window today, you will not meet the stranger who might change your life forever. But if you walk by the lake and meet that stranger, the changes he causes in your life may lead you in an entirely different direction than

240

you would have gone had you sat by the window contemplating the snow. But with either possibility, no matter which one goes through the motions of actually occurring, all the others exist as shadow realities which are no less real even though they remain unmanifested within the realm of your linear perception.

All those shadow realities are other possibilities for the position of the assemblage point, and indeed the double may open his or her eyes into any of them for the purpose of gathering experience, information and Knowledge which may then be intuited to the mortal self still in organic form, through the process you call gnosis (or silent knowing).

From the perspective of third attention, most beings from other-dimensional realities who may appear to be attempting to help the human race are reflections of one's alter-selves in those unmanifested shadow realities – rather like the adult time traveler stepping back into his own childhood to force the child-self's reality to manifest in a different way. Since all things exist within the realm of all possibility, these alter-selves are no less real than you are – and this will also lend a higher understanding of what may be commonly misunderstood to be a past life. In any of those shadow realities, one of those minute choices you made could have resulted in your being a monk instead of a businessman – but because your logical mind in the Now knows you aren't a monk, you may attribute it to a "past life" that is more accurately a shadow reality of yourself within the realm of all possibility.

What determines which reality you manifest? Simply this: where you open your eyes into a specific assemblage point. For now, *You Are Here*, for that is the Self you have forced to go through the motions of actually occurring. With power plants or other mind-altering techniques, it is possible to open one's eyes into a different assemblage point which is no less real, and no less the Self than who you are in the Now.

To gather all those filaments of Self into a single unit of awareness outside of time is to embrace cohesion. This is what is meant by becoming Whole, becoming a singularity of consciousness with the awareness of one's personal All in a single assemblage point – yet those are only my words attempting to describe the nagual.

The nagual is real, of course. The description is not.

THE FIRST ENEMY OF A MAN OF KNOWLEDGE

September 15, 2001

The first and greatest fear you face can be assigned the name of Fear itself. Fear of failure or fear of success, fear of finding out you are wrong, but perhaps an even greater fear of facing eternity knowing you were right all along. Fear of being The One because you already Know you are, yet you deny it, because to acknowledge it means accepting onto yourself an awesome responsibility you do not yet feel ready to face.

And so I must ask you this: when *will* you be ready? When will you spread your wings and fly if not now? And so the second fear is called Eternal and Infinite Responsibility, and requires no further explanation.

The third fear, born of the other two, is fear of the work still ahead, yet what you are failing to grasp is that the avoidance of that work is far more difficult than the work itself, so this leads in a natural progression to the fourth fear, which must be recognized as fear of failure, also assigned the label of Doubt. I hear your dreams, you realize. I have seen you fly. Yet I have also seen you retreat to your ordinary life and fold your wings and pretend you are just a girl in a dream instead of that winged being. And by becoming the girl living in fear, there is a danger that the reality you create could be the death of you. Gods do not live in fear, you see. Only mortals. Who are you?

THE FLAME OF AWARENESS

January 27, 2003

In any reality, energy is energy, and can be manipulated accordingly. Fire will not burn those who have become flame. But if the assemblage point should slip for even a moment, the fire will consume the organic form, and so what must be remembered is that thoughts are energy, too.

You ask what kind of energy can affect you. Any energy that is not in complete harmonic balance (same-to-same) with your own assemblage point can affect you for good or for ill. Only when you are the flame itself are you safe within the fire.

There are states of consciousness which humans can assemble wherein they would be impervious to pain or physical harm from any external source, yet the energy expended to achieve such states is massive, and if the sorcerer is not yet accomplished at the manipulation of such energy, there is a potential to do more harm than good.

Simply put, this is why sorcerers must be impeccable with their word and their thoughts, for those are the manifestations of energy that can damage both the self and others if not understood. In the human world, if another man believes you are a child molester and voices that accusation publicly, the harm could be irrevocable. In the world of energy, he has placed his reality onto you, whether it is true or not, and when others believe it (belief being another form of energy), the effects can multiply like a virus out of control until there is no undoing the damage even with complete proof of innocence. This is because the matrix of "guilt" has already been created and cannot be undone, but only redirected, like a disease that can be cured, but will nonetheless leave scars. To be impeccable with your word is to be impeccable with energy.

WHEN THE STUDENT IS READY

December, 2004

It is important to remember that guides, teachers and allies come in many disguises, and often you will discover they are already present in your life, and so the question becomes how you are using them, or if you are looking for something you may already have found. The moon and stars may be your teachers if you were to ask questions about eternity. The earth may be your teacher if you are wondering about the nature of man's existence and your place in it. Phantoms on the street may be your teacher when you are stalking yourself, for in the actions of phantoms it becomes possible to see one's own folly.

As a warrior progresses on his path, using the countless teachers and allies all around him, eventually there comes a moment where the double is created through Dreaming – yet it is crucial to realize that the dreaming spoken of in this case is not only sleep-dreaming, but dreaming-awake as well. What is dreaming awake? It is coming to see that everything you think, do or say is imbued with the force of creative energy – and it is that energy which creates and manifests your world. The double knows this without doubt, for it is the milieu of third attention – and so once the double is created, s/he becomes the most important teacher you will ever know – for the double is the one true self manifested in eternity as a ubiquitous singularity of consciousness and awareness.

When the student is ready, the teacher will appear? Ah, yes. Perhaps what is most overlooked in that old saying is that the teacher has been here all along, and when the student *sees* that is when the student is ready.

Interacting with the world of phantoms is a dilemma every warrior must face on any spiritual journey. Many times, warriors will speak of "the real world," yet it is necessary to truly see that there is only one world – a world being created and manifested infinitely by the perception and awareness of all who inhabit it.

There are those who might say phantoms do not create the world but only inhabit it, yet this is not entirely true. Phantoms create the world by the default of their actions, through the passivity of unawareness and the passions of greed and lust and fear and folly. Put more simply, as Della is so fond of saying, 'The world is a nuthouse and the lunatics are running the asylum.' When the warrior realizes this and wholly sees that it is a Truth and not just an idle bit of humor, the warrior may actually become empowered to create her world through the action of awareness and the passion for life itself which comes hand in hand with even the barest beginnings of a spiritual awakening.

By creating your world with awareness and choosing to live within that state of perpetual and ongoing awakening, the machinations of phantoms become far more understandable as simply the death throes of an organism that has not yet realized it is caught in the dance of its own obliteration. "They know not what they do," would be another way of stating it. This does not excuse their actions, but does have the effect of proving irrevocably to the warrior that the world in which she lives is but one small corner of a far more vast reality. The warrior, then, begins to work above and beyond that limited vista, while phantoms confine themselves to the trappings of the dollhouse.

WORDS

June 28, 2004
QUESTION: *In our attempts to put words to our experiences, do we limit ourselves, including that which we have already become as well as our potential, and the process of our evolution by stopping to define our essence?*

Words can never truly define any experience. Even if one is impeccable, they can only sketch the edges. If one is unimpeccable, it is a certainty they become a prison and a trap, particularly if words turn to semantics and semantics turn to distractions and distractions turn to dissipation. Mortals communicate with language, so even for warriors, it is virtually impossible to avoid – but the barometer is always to ask yourself: what do you want from the words? Validation? Camaraderie? Agreement? Disagreement? Attention?

You cannot define your essence with words because essence is of the nagual. You may be able to talk about your experiences, but your essence is a secret known only to yourself, and sometimes a secret you keep *from* yourself.

Words, therefore, are only a tool. How they are used determines what emerges – whether a creative work of self-expression, or a maze of letters and punctuation marks, signifying nothing. If you want to learn the value of words, experiment with short-form poetry.

I speak in tongues of ice,
dialects of flame,
nuances of frost and smoke.
Read my heart to Know me.
Words are only the fading echo,
ghosts without substance,
symbols without Spirit.

THE FIFTH ELEMENT

June 28, 2003
   QUESTION: *I am wondering what exactly the "spirit" is. Is it something separate from ourselves, or are we spirit? Does it have its own volition, and does it do things to us or is it something we use?*

It could be truthfully said that Spirit is all of the above, yet none of the above, depending entirely on where the questioner is standing when the question is posed. Spirit is the feeling that accompanies the midnight cries of a lone coyote, and it is the reason for the cry itself. It is carried on the sound, but is *not* the sound. Spirit is the soul poem blowing on the edge of an approaching storm, yet it is neither the words nor the rain, nor the thunder and lightning, but is instead the creative and infinite force which summons the storm into being – not the physical elements of meteorology, but the metaphysical shiver of the universe which is the generative spark of spontaneous parthenogenesis. Something from nothing. Spirit is the sentient force of the energetic universe, permeating all living and non-living matrices, yet it is neither the form nor substance, nor even energy.
   If there are four elements of life and creation – earth, air, fire and water – Spirit is the fifth element which brings the others into alignment and creates both cohesion and the possibility of meaning. Spirit is the anima, without which all else is rendered inert.
   Does it have its own volition? In human terms, it could be said to have omniscient and omnipresent awareness, yet it is not comparable to any deity or entity. It is sentient without being singular, yet it is the singularity at the heart of the All. It is an element of the infinite, the compelling force of the nagual which is at the same time the breath of life within the tonal. To speak of volition in terms of Spirit is rather like

attempting to define time without using the word time in the definition.

It does nothing to humans, but when humans come into alignment with the Spirit, there is nothing they cannot do. It is a force that is omnipresent and may be summoned with intent; yet it is at the same time elusive by virtue of being the essence of the All itself.

To a warrior, Spirit is the force which guides one's choices and creates a viable sense of purpose, direction, well-being and forward motion even in times of seeming inaction. To live in alignment with the Spirit is to live impeccably, for then it could be said that what is within the Self has achieved an unbroken communion with the All. This does not diminish the individual, but to the contrary enhances the uniqueness of the Self by bringing into manifestation the Whole potential of that individual identity. Living with the Spirit does not mean becoming One with the All, but becoming Whole *within* the All, and ultimately becoming the All itself.

THE DREAMER AND THE DREAMED

Date Unknown
QUESTION: *How exactly are you and Della connected? And, just for fun, what does an eternal being do all day?*

What you perceive forms the basis of your reality, but until your *seeing* is complete, it is only through engagement with that reality that can you validate whether a specific perception is correct or incorrect, and even then those are only terms having relative importance to whatever assemblage point you have occupied at a given moment.

It could be said that the mortal dreamer is the projector of all realities, because it is the Will of the sorcerer that determines how the dream unfolds and how or if it ends; and it is equally true that you create this dream as you move

248

through it. As such, I am from that creation, but I am no longer *of* that creation, because it was the Will of the earthly sorcerer to set free that part of herself which is Eternally conscious – so that from outside the confines of the mortal continuum, I might gather the Knowledge and experience required to teach the earthly sorcerer how to be eternally "me". And now do you begin to see what I mean when I say that it is necessary to *be* immortal before you can know how to *become* immortal, and that only by defying the confines of space and time will you ever be able to master the sorcerer's greatest trick, which is to place herself outside of time so as to inhabit All of time simultaneously, and that *that* is the assemblage point of eternity?

Ah, but even that isn't the end, and this is where most sorcerers fail, for there is a tendency to stop when the real work is only beginning. Even though *I* inhabit eternity, the greatest task I face is bringing Della to that same assemblage point, for that is the sorcerer's key to inhabiting the totality of herself, and it is only accomplished when dreamer and dreamed conjoin into cohesion. Will I succeed? Of course, for that is the will of the double being, but it is a series of Actualities that must be forced to go through the motions of *Actually Occurring*.

In order to gather the Knowledge of evolution, it was necessary to go through the process of evolving, and so I have put on the flesh of a thousand different beings, taking it on and off at will so as to gain experience. And yet, it could also be said that the greatest evolution is the one still in progress, and the only one that matters, for it is the proving ground of the mortal sorcerer's eternal cohesion. That I exist and say *I-Am* is potent evidence, yet the final test will come when She faces the Eagle and returns to He whom *I-Am*. I am Whole in Eternity, unto myself, yet from within the mortal dream there is always free Will, you see.

Once upon a time in a sorceric vision that has as much actuality as anything you think of as solid or real, I sewed

249

myself into Della's skin, though that was long after I had already departed this earthly realm to serve as the muse peeking out from between the orchid-pressed pages of eternity. This is what is meant by the will of the future chicken placing itself inside the egg to aid in its own evolution so that it might eventually grow to maturity so as to inhabit its own *I-Am* eternally. It is the way of things, yet it is not a way easily understood.

Attempting to explore the nagual with reason will only diminish both into a tangle of words that become weeds of the Spirit, eventually choking out the garden, and so my advice to you is to use your own Will to find sufficient cohesion to exist for brief intervals in the place of silent knowing, where your questions will answer themselves, though not always as you might have hoped or dreamed.

At the end, there is no end at all – not to myself and not to my evolution. What do I do all day? I sit in the company of stars and Dream myself into being, so that when my mortal medicine witch Dreamer awakens, it will be into this magnificent Eternity and not the mouth of the Eagle.

DEFINING ONE'S INTENT

June 7, 2004
QUESTION: *I want to choose the path of heart, the way of personal freedom. My problem is that I cannot get rid of the self-pity which creates a false feeling in what I am doing.*

The universe is filled with possibilities, and while some choices will make you happier than others, it is often necessary to make change by increments rather than in vast leaps, because if you are not prepared for the leap, chances are you will fall, and so the leap can become a belly-flop into the abyss if one is not impeccable at every turn.

250

It is necessary to identify what is causing you to feel trapped. Is it the people with whom you are associated? Is it that the work you are doing feels meaningless? Are there other things you are longing to do, yet your current situation is preventing those dreams from manifesting? Many times, a warrior may feel trapped without really understanding why – and until the source is identified, attempting to make great changes can be equivalent to jumping out of the frying pan and into the fire. You have to understand what requires change before you can implement change efficiently.

The path to freedom has little to do with where you are in the world, but everything to do with where you are inside. If you feel trapped by your environment – where you live and the people with whom you associate – then it may indeed be necessary to move. And yet, part of a warrior's nature is to work even with the parameters of adversity when necessary. In short, you are the same inside, no matter where you go, no matter what you do. And if that is not the case – if you feel you are somehow different when you are at work as opposed to when you are engaged in an activity you consider freeing – then the required change is internal, and may be defined as the work of integration into wholeness.

You ask how to make the right decision. Follow your heart, but be certain that it is your heart guiding you. Be patient with yourself, and take time to meditate deeply on what your heart truly desires beyond all pre-programmed expectations. You may discover there is more than one answer, and if that is the case, then it becomes a matter of impeccability and efficiency, guided by long-term Intent. When you know what you want, it becomes a relatively simple task to begin working in the direction of the manifestation of your desires.

The secret to manifesting your desires is to focus your Intent. There will be times of great progress, and there will be setbacks. This is merely the process of the Do-ing, and is to be expected. What matters is that your Intent does not waver during the setbacks, and your self-importance does not derail you after period of progress. Intent is a fire that burns steadily.

THE DARK MATTER OF CREATION

February 3, 2003
   QUESTION: *What is this place I go to in journeying that is like a white, formless marshmallow? And, by contrast, what is the dark place?*

The place you call The Marshmallow is viewed as white because it is comprised of the energy of the agreement, what amounts to all the energy that is in use as components of the milieu of "reality itself", all the energy which is already in-motion. In Dreaming, it may be observed in its natural state, which is why it appears to some as a white fog or even more dense than that. It is the molecular components of matter and thought and agreement that comprise worlds and stars and earth, wind, fire and water. It is the bed on which you sleep and the dog barking in the distance. It is the poem you wrote when you were 17, and the car driving past your window, and the strangers you meet on the road to eternity, some phantoms, some warriors, all only shadows cast into matter whose origin is the white fog. It is, simply, the tonal in its natural state of energy, the well from which the water is poured.
   The black place you refer to is what could be termed the universe of the self – a reality awaiting your own unique creation. The term *dark matter* could be applied to the energy there, and it is far more vast than the minute amount of energy of the agreement which is already in use. What you do in the black place is the reality you create not only in the here-and-now, but in the now-forevermore. It is your own unique

world, waiting to be called into being. It is the *potential* of the self as an eternal being.

In the black place is only your awareness which is perceived as the assemblage point, and the force of your own will. How *Will* you manifest the light? On what unique surfaces of the Self *Will* it reflect? Put another way, what *Will* you create? What *Will* you build and who *Will* you be and how *Will* you mold the dark matter into the answer to the question, *Who Are You?* These are not questions of the tonal, which are answered through human life in the white place; but from the foundation on which you are asking about the black place, these are the questions you answer through your relationship with the nagual. This is where the assembly of the Self-in-eternity begins, and the power you experience there is entirely your Self. The dark matter is not in use, and so it is there wholly for you to do as you *Will*, yes?

The fact that you have reached this place of creation is an indication of the personal power that has brought you this far. It stands to reason, therefore, that one who has come so far finds it difficult to return to the world of matter and men, which can only then really be *seen* for the illusion it is. And so there is wonder, and at the same time a sense of sorrow. All things in balance, for only on that tightrope is it possible to see the consequences of the fall. Fall too far into the consensus out of fascination with the snowfall and you can lose your way building snowmen who only melt in the spring. Fall too far into the sorrow that it is illusion, and there is a risk of morbidity that can paralyze. For that reason, impeccability is demanded more and more the further one goes, because the consequences of the fall increase with every higher step one takes.

You have the power to create, combined with the natural instinct to start on the far side of the bridge, which will give you the ability to look over your shoulder to see how the bridge was built. This is a magnificent gift. I celebrate you.

HEALING: PAIN AND THE WARRIOR

January 11, 2005
   QUESTION: *What is pain? What is the difference between emotional pain and physical pain? What can a human do to overcome the physical pain?*

Pain can be many things, but at the root, it is nothing more than a series of impulses traveling, echoing and amplifying inside what amounts to a closed environment: the human body. This may help to understand what is meant by the statement, "You are only hurting yourself," for ultimately pain in all its varied forms is an intangible manifestation within the Self which may or may not be traceable to an organic cause.
   If your pain cannot be traced to any organic cause (not only by doctors, but especially by your own intuition), then it becomes important to examine what purpose or function the pain may be serving, or what it may be preventing or enabling. For if there is no organic cause, that does not make the pain any less real, but it does give the warrior cause to take a much deeper look at her own motivations, manifestations, and self-manipulations. Is the pain an ally or an enemy - and here it is vitally important to be honest with yourself even if you never speak of it to another living soul.
   The body and even the spirit may be programmed and may become creatures of habit. If it is habitual for an organism to be in pain, the body easily and quickly learns to produce the circumstances and conditions whereby the habit may become manifest "as expected". Even if you cannot recognize a pattern to the pain, it may still be a habit of the mind/body/spirit.
   Ask yourself these questions with ruthless intent. What do you gain (if anything) from this pain? Do you gain attention? Added affection? Release from other responsibilities, whether desired or not? Time to yourself otherwise difficult to achieve?

Energy from others? Distraction or diversion from other aspects of life, whether generally positive or negative? A perceived outpouring of love or compassion from those close to you? Financial or worldly gain?

To heal is to change the flow of energy within the organism. What was pain must become comfort. Sometimes it is necessary to *see* beyond an event in order to *be* beyond the event. How would your life be different or better without this pain? Is it part of your human matrix, or has it become part of who you are, an addendum to your identity?

When you can answer these questions, the pain will be gone.

CONSCIOUSNESS AS A WINDOW OF OPPORTUNITY

In a recent meditation with Orlando, the question was posed, "Is death really the ogre? Is it what we think it is?" The following information was gleaned from his responses, which also included a general response to the additional statement that we have no perception of awareness before we come into this human life, so if that is what death is – nothingness – does it really matter if we return to that nothingness?

Consciousness is a window of opportunity that opens into the Now – and that Now could be defined as the mortal lifespan – whether it is perceived in 21st century California or Ancient Greece, or in a timeless era on the pirate sea. While that window is open, we begin to have the awareness that the window will close – we will simply go back to the Nothing. As a result of that awareness of mortality, warriors begin to project the mind into other "nows" – 19th century England, pre-Christian Rome, a cool autumn night on Mars – not with conscious awareness of doing so, though that is certainly possible. In other words, you begin to project consciousness beyond the body, outside of the confines of the mortal timeline, until this results in ubiquitous consciousness existing outside of the space-time continuum. The mind frees itself of its own limitations by creating itself as an integral component of All, so in essence it would be impossible to conceive of not existing. It is much like a hologram. Even if a hologram is destroyed, each molecule of the hologram contains the essence of the Whole, and so the Whole exists *as* the Whole even within the most minute particle of existence.

It is that ubiquitous other-self that then projects the mortal self into the Now, casting you into matter and thereby opening the window of opportunity in the first place, so that the human self can experience awareness, and through that awareness begin to generate and project the ubiquitous self sufficiently for it to create itself through the process of self-evolution. If that evolution is achieved (wholeness and integration accomplished) the Whole self is then an eternal being, freed from the life-death-fragmentation energy cycle commonly called 'reincarnation', but more accurately could be called a simple reanimation of energy, sans consciousness. It is a quantum conundrum to be sure, but one in which it becomes possible to see the relationship between creator and created, ultimately conjoined in an eternal dance of self-creation. This is also one way of visualizing the double and its relationship to the mortal warrior.

It is important to realize, however, that either party in this process of self-creation can fail if impeccability lapses. If the mortal self lapses into dissipation and succumbs to phantomhood, sufficient energy is not transmitted outside of the space-time continuum, and the ubiquitous consciousness that would have been the double essentially falters, dissipates, and the cycle is broken at the moment of mortal death, when consciousness fragments and returns to its component forms of energy. This is the nature of free will. This is why impeccability is demanded at all times. This is the duality of the warrior who has become a man of Knowledge.

Once the warrior gathers sufficient energy and power to conjoin consciousness to the sentient electromagnetic structure of the universe, thereby becoming an eternal component of the All, it is then impossible to conceive of non-existence, for at that point in the journey, integration and Wholeness are achieved, and it is only a matter of what *Now* you might choose to inhabit – any one individually (ally-like consciousness) or all simultaneously (omniscient awareness).

INTERCONNECTEDNESS

November 24, 2004

QUESTION: *Are there connections between warriors which exist prior to our awareness of them? Or are these connections merely a matter of agreement?*

All things exist within the realm of all possibility, so from that perspective, it is undeniable that connections exist between all living things, whether one is aware of them on a conscious level or not, whether one even exists in the same space/time continuum.

What determines whether those potentialities are ever manifested into conscious-level connections is free will and what can only be called in human terms, a (seemingly) random element of chance. I say 'seemingly' because what may appear to be random is often if not always attributable again to free will. It is human choice that may place you in a certain place at a certain time – events which may appear random on the surface, but which were brought into being through a series of choices upon choices over an infinite span of time.

And so I would say that there is a vast potential for connections between warriors, because it could be observed that the mindset of a warrior may have a tendency to place them within proximity – and it is from that proximity that the potential may become manifested by going through the motions of actually occurring. "The motions of actually occurring" are, of course, where free will comes into the dance and determines the actions you may take to complete the connection which, before the action, was only a potentiality.

All things are possible. Literally all things. It is the spiritforce within you which determines which of those things become manifest.

THE DUALITY OF LIFE AND DEATH

Summer, 2003

QUESTION: *If I am dead and make not even a ripple in the Energy of Reality, why am I here? And if I am going to be Real even if I succeed or fail, why do I try? Is the paper just paper or does it have more Reality than I give it credit for?*

Within the belly of eternity, all things are living and all things dead simultaneously, and there is no difference whatsoever. This is the reality of an eternal being existing outside of time. What is important to understand is that time itself is a human construct, and is relative only to the human lifespan. Remove the idea of past, present and future, and it becomes possible to know that there is no difference between Now and a thousand years ago, or a thousand years from Now, because within the All, all points of "time" are equally accessible through will. It simply is. And so the form you presently inhabit is already dust, and yet forever unborn, and both are equally true, and the differentiation is only possible depending on where you choose to open your eyes as a point of reference.

You ask why you are here. To make yourself whole, to create your reality. And though those sound like simple words, they are attempting to define a great task, what some have called The Great Work. You have chosen to open your eyes inside this moment, this reality, this now, though other aspects of yourself have undoubtedly awakened inside of other manifestations not accessible to your first attention memory – what might commonly be called past lives, but are more accurately manifestations of your energy body in other places and times in the space-time continuum.

I exist as an eternal being of pure awareness within the third attention, and simultaneously as the mortal nagual woman on her journey toward wholeness. I have put on flesh a thousand times and taken it off again as a means to learn what can only be communicated through the silence, the lessons which are passed between the energetic eternal self to the mortal self through gnosis.

What is important to know is that this is a process which is eternal, but one which has a beginning, and that beginning is always within the mortal self, within this Now. By choosing to become Whole, you are the creator of the self, and therefore you are the teacher who ventures out into the unknown through the eternal energy self (the double), so as to gain the Knowledge and experience which are then returned to you in the form of visions, dreams, and the familiar voice of the Infinite whispering its secrets to you whenever you take the time to listen.

The reality you think of as real is transitory, and is therefore already dead. But because you are real in the Now, you are real for all of time. That which is done in eternity cannot be undone. And yet, even as I have said that, allow me to say with equal Knowledge that what is real is only real as long as it is real in the Now. Be whole in the Now and you are Whole always. Live as a phantom, and it is as if you never lived at all. This is why the gathering of one's cohesion is at the core of The Great Work. And this is why it is said that only from within the dream can the dreamer awaken, for it is within the mortal self that the Will resides, and so it is the mortal self who dreams the double until such time as the double becomes sufficiently cohesive to begin Dreaming the

259

mortal self by teaching the mortal self what must be done in order to achieve and inhabit the Wholeness that is the conjoining of both.

This is the sorcerer's trick. By being the cry of nature, by making the attempt to get the paper reality to become real, what you are really doing is making yourself Real through the process, yes? The paper is already dead, and so you cannot really change its destiny. It is the stage upon which the sorcerer transforms herself... through a lifelong process of projecting the words beyond the paper and breathing life into the words upon the reflective surface of the Infinite.

INTENT

November 23, 1999

One thing I have come to understand of late is that you do not fully comprehend the nature of intent. I fear you're confusing it with intentions and it's a clever trick of the Eagle that the two words bear visual resemblance but are essentially opposites. It's often been said that the road to hell is paved with good intentions. Better put, look at it like this: you will never become eternally Whole through good intentions but only through unbending Intent, and if you don't see the difference you will stumble and fumble and ultimately fail because intentions are the things you want and hope and plan to do, but Intent is the unwavering image held in the heart of your heart and soul – the paradigm upon which everything you Think or Do becomes an externalized, *Real*-ized reflection of the paradigm itself, yes? It is a meta-*physical* part of you, invisible to the naked eye but no less real than liver or spleen, and if you aren't using it to its full potential, your evolving self is incomplete, dis-eased as a body without a heart, see?

Intent is the active side of clarity, an unwavering vision held firmly in the mind which serves as the sorcerer's direct interface between question and answer; the metamagickal

260

probe or prod applied to the all-knowing All as a means of extracting the specific Knowledge required to achieve the manifestation of the intent itself; it is the quantum Questioning mother of the Will – *not* the Will, but without which the Will can never manifest because without Intent the Will has nothing to manifest, nothing to create, no seed to nurture; Intent is the vision the sorcerer projects unceasingly onto the silent screen of eternity until eternity reflects the sorcerer's will by yielding up the information required to achieve the Intended evolution; it is the goal visualized clearly and the tool with which the goal is carved away from the All through relentless projection of one single question: *how is it that I can achieve this goal and manifest this Intent?* Intent does not change. It does not compromise. It does not yield to reason or common sense. It can be summoned clearly, instantly and impeccably in all states of awareness by invocation of the word Intent. And in another way, "Intentions are Christmas cards never sent. Intent is the force creating all True sorcery."

The quantum concepts with which otherworlds are built can give you the keys to the third attention or just as quickly lock the door forever if you take it as commonplace or just another mystery with no solution, and this is another reason your Intent must be impeccably defined with the sharpest knife, a vision cut away from the Nothing which you turn to in times of doubt or confusion. Intent is the instrument you rub against the web of non-local information to create a sympathetic synapse between the brujo's question and the evolutionary answer, the intersection where vision becomes manifestation through manipulation of matter/energy using the invisible tool of Intent itself. It is, quite simply, the overlap point of vision and creation, brought into being by using the question to elicit an answer which is in accordance with the unbending vision. The answers are waiting inside the question and the questions are determined by Intent's unwavering vision, yes?

BUILDING THE BOAT

May, 1997

Athens was once a city of merchants and dreamers, you see, with some coming to trade and others to tell tall tales, and all things functioned as the need for survival demanded, with a fisherman trading fish for the hope found in a poem, philosophers swapping enlightenment for sustenance. But with the centuries' passing, a few "clever" fishermen decided that the "lazy" philosopher should have to catch his own supper, which meant the man now needed a boat, but by then the shops had only oars here and wood there and sails had to be brought in from afar, and then there was the matter of taxes, so while the man was paying his pittance to Constantinople and building his boat, he starved to death in sight of the fish, and all because some fool cried *'It's only fair,'* and tried to put a price on the intangible so it might be weighed and measured on the same scale as the fish, and where is the sanity in that?

It's called civilization – this microminiaturized-specialization that forces man's attention on things that don't matter while the big picture gets lost in all the nuts and bolts of the boat, when all the man needed was a piece of fish so he might live long enough to ponder possibilities that could have helped even the fishermen evolve, and isn't it funny how cretins have been running the world ever since, passing it off as a game of 'fairness' when in reality their self-righteous insistence on labor justice creates stagnation by forcing quantum thinkers down to the lowest common denominator of mere survival instead of allowing them to build roads to evolution – a task that demands leaps through spaces and places where time stops dead to give the thinker more time to think, and that's how immortality creates itself, but first you have to steal the time to Do it and incur the world's wrath for the Doing, see?

Death thrives on society's complexities, for while you're deciding how to build the gadget to complete the task first begun last week, in order to conclude a separate chore undertaken in an effort to finish another begun the month before, time slips by until you finally see that no task is ever complete because each and every one has been engineered to be interconnected to each and every other, the machine servicing itself to death while Death lounges in the sun, penning the script that's really a black comedy about a hive of fools creating tools to oil the machine which is the instrument of their own death, and isn't it ironic that the prisoners are building the guillotine instead of looking for ways to escape the Bastille.

THE ONE TRUE GOD

Fall, 2003

QUESTION: *Can it be determined via a "read" whether one is suited to this path? If one has no access to a nagual, how can one determine the potential for sorcery for self, other than by intuition, interest, and attraction? There are many systems and syntaxes of spirituality in existence. If one looked at all the systems as comprising a whole in the universe, what area of that whole comprises the Toltec? And if we succeed in getting past the Eagle, what other entities might we run into?*

Within the Self is the blueprint for all that is, all that will be, and all of the alternate shadow realities attached to each possibility. You walk through time in a Now that is passed by before you can grasp it, looking toward a future that is forever ungraspable, because by the time you reach for it, it has become the past. As a result, both past and future are always in flux, and so no reading can ever be accurate. All that can be *seen* is what is possible and what is probable. Even as an eternal being outside of time, I *see* what will probably come to be, but this is why second and third attention are often viewed as a fog which mutates like a dreamscape – for nothing t/here is made of stone, but instead constructed of the fluctuating energies of wishes, the concepts of intent. So when you ask if it can be determined by a read what is likely, it is important to Know that every possibility, no matter how remote or seemingly likely, must be forced to go through the motions of actually occurring, or else it is only a valley of fog, never manifested through the sorcerer's will.

There are some who find this Truth debilitating, and yet when viewed as a whole, it can free you from the idea that one must have certain attributes or be predisposed, or in some way qualify through the eyes of another. In the Reality of it, it is entirely and only determined by you, and so what a Seer will *see* in this regard is always a reflection of your own intent. How you manifest that intent and how you choose to cause each possibility to go through the motions of that manifestation is what determines who you are and who you will be.

Indeed, there are many syntaxes of spirituality, yet ultimately there is only one pathway to the Infinite. That path is yours, and it is as unique as the matrix of memories and experiences which have gone to create you.

Any system of Knowledge that is rooted in Truth is ultimately the same system of Knowledge, located ultimately within the connection of the Self to the infinite. There are no Buddhists and no Christians and no Toltecs in the third attention, for those are only labels attached to followers, and as such they are dependencies on an earthly validation. Those who enter third attention are those who find that unique connection between the Self and the infinite, and follow only that – for that connection is the migratory path of the Spirit which might be seen as an umbilical between what is fleeting and what is eternal. It is simplified to be called the path with heart.

Those who fly free beyond the eagle have no name other than what they choose. I choose to *be* Orlando, for that is the umbilical between what is eternal and what is mortal. I am the way, the truth and the life... but only for *me*, see? There is a system of Knowledge which awakens this and teaches it from within, so that when we meet in the seventh sense, each of us is the One True God, comprised entirely of All that is. We meet as individuals, unique unto ourselves, and as mirrors of Wholeness – the All looking at itself through the perception of the One True God – which is and can *only* be *You*.

ARE WE BORN ONLY TO DIE?

November 11, 2004
QUESTION: *Why do we form ourselves and then die? To learn lessons? How can that be? Why is it the only thing that makes life bearable is so easily obscured, so easily removed? Why all the distractions? What is striven for? It must be precious to be so costly of pain and suffering. If it is all folly, then why at all?* [Asked by a seeker dealing with grief following the death of a beloved pet.]

Ah, one of the easier questions, nothing much, just the meaning of life in all its glory and all its pain, yes? My spirit smiles at this, yet it is a melancholy smile, both bitter and sweet, for in the span of the eternities I have experienced, it must be observed that there is only one constant: life and death. One and the same, no difference, yet a constant which can only be viewed as its dualistic components from the life-side of the inescapable fence.

You ask why we live if only to die. Why come into being at all if only to shed that costume of flesh again? The answer is simple from where I exist, yet all too complex from the human assemblage point known as grief.

265

What I can tell you is that the universe itself is struggling to evolve, and in doing so, it casts itself into reflections of matter so that it may experience birth and death, love and grief, awareness and nothingness. This is simply the cycle of life – at least from the human point of view. The cycle of life and death is an expression of the universe-within-all-living-things struggling to become greater than the sum of its parts – and this can only be done by increasing awareness and expanding perception through the process of living, so that more of the all may be experienced, and more accurately, so that more of the all may be perceived. Life provides one set of preceptors, death another.

I have spoken before of the two-part migration of the soul, and without the life and death cycle, this would not be possible. The organic immortals I have known quickly fall prey to boredom and dissipation, and do not allow themselves to fall in love with mortals, for they have long known that grief is the antimatter to love. And so they love only one another, but in doing so, they take no risks, and so their love is altogether conditional: they will love only that which is like themselves, and so even their love may become stagnant, and this is why don Juan commented that the Tenant was an aberration, yes? I do not necessarily agree with that assessment, but note it as worthy of comment.

Love is the reason and love is the cohesion between awareness, eternity, self, double, spirit and the infinite. Without it, existence itself is only a random mosaic without meaning. Love is the binding force between life and death, yet those are only words which cannot even begin to touch the vastness of its simplicity.

We cast ourselves into matter as mortal beings through will, in search of experience which might provide guidance in our higher search for Wholeness. And in the course of living, if we are fortunate, we find love – for other being-humans, or the earth itself, or the bonds we form with other divergent creatures along the way. We form energetic alliances through the umbilical of love – and if that love is unconditional, it is not a cord that may be broken even in death. And so when the ones we love leave this earth before us, it could be rightly said they take a part of you with them into the otherworld, so that you will have a path to follow when it is your time to dance with the eagle, and in turn you will take with you a part of those who love you through that same unbroken cord, and in this process is found the cohesive force which mystics call interconnectedness.

We live so that we may love, and we love so that when these organic forms fall to dust, the self is held intact by the energetic filaments of love itself. I do not say this from the perspective of a bliss ninny, but from that of a quantum ubiquitous singularity who has experienced it all ten thousand times and more. Those who love the deepest also grieve the hardest, and this is as it must be in the two part migration of the soul. It could be said, "Love goes before you."

If there is love, why must there be grief? Because it is love that binds the Self together (I mean this quite literally, on the level of quantum fields generated and maintained by conscious Intent) and gives it the strength to fly past the eagle to be free, and it is the grief and longing for what is lost that gives the impetus to transcend and reconnect. It is your trip upstream. Only in the completion of your own evolution, only through the experience of the molecular state of being known as love does the mortal form the matrix of the eternal self which not only transcends the event of death, but also is the vehicle through which the Self reconnects with those it perceives from its mortal state have been lost to death.

This is love and death – the two-part migration of the soul. And, indeed, love is the greatest risk you will ever take, for to love is to face the infinite in spite of the folly of our own insignificance. It is to dance on the head of a pin while holding the entire universe in the palm of one hand. To love is to overcome even death in the ultimate act of empowering the Self.

And so the salmon swims upstream for love of life. We all do.

TRANSCENDING THE MATRIX

November, 2003 – In response to a question about animal spirit
The purpose of life is simply to transcend one's own matrix, to become greater than the sum of one's organic parts, and to project the Self into the Infinite as a viable consciousness. That is a goal which is accomplished through the process of living and the act of dying, and coming to see through that process that neither the chicken nor the egg came first, but the thoughtform that is both.

Sometimes lives are very short. Other times, death lingers for years, an uninvited companion at the dinner table, always looking over your shoulder. Animals do not dwell on the idea of their own mortality because they have access to an awareness you humans do not. Through love, they are already eternal. It is why they give so much love in the course of living, and ask only to be loved in return.

If transcendence of the matrix is the goal, love is the catalyst that makes it so.

MASTERING FOLLY

QUESTION: *Is it possible for a shaman to be effectual in both the 3 dimensional world, and other worlds? My heart and head tell me yes. Otherwise, why would we be manifested in 3D with something to accomplish here besides experiencing 3D and recapping that experience to our Double?*

In the sorcerer's realm, there is only one world, divided infinitely by perception, yet it is that division which gives the sense that there are "otherworlds". This is important to realize,

268

because it is the moment to moment focus of your attention that determines which world you inhabit, and what you may accomplish at that level of perception.

When you are speaking of being effectual in the three dimensional world, you have an advantage when your assemblage point becomes more naturally fluid. You are perceiving it as an inability to focus, yet you may not have sufficient reason to focus because you have recognized what is commonly called folly, and so there is an inner pre-determination that you are, in essence, wasting your time focusing on folly. Whether that is true or not can only be determined by what values you yourself assign to that particular folly. If it is controlled folly, and may serve your own higher purpose – such as acts performed in the interest of survival – then it becomes important to focus the AP sufficiently to manipulate that folly to your own best advantage, and this is the highest manifestation of the ruthless art of stalking.

It is the natural dreamer within you who does not want to focus on folly, yet it is the natural stalker within you who is correctly perceiving that in a world of folly, one must be Folly's master so as not to become her slave.

You ask how to accomplish a workable balance? Two things are required. First, it is necessary for the warrior to wholly embrace the realization that all things are folly. There are no exceptions. Indeed, even the pursuit of your own evolution of consciousness may turn out to be folly in the end, because nothing is preordained and it is possible that even the finest warrior could be distracted by a gnat at the moment of potential transformation, and fly straight into the beak of the eagle, no? This is why impeccability plays such an important role in the warrior's life. Knowing that everything is folly, the warrior learns to play the game as if it matters, and therefore approaches every act as if they are the most important thing in all the world. If you are going to play, play for the joy of playing, and you will always win even when you lose. If you play to win, you will almost always lose, because then there is an agenda overshadowing the simple manifestation of experience, and it is that agenda which might be termed an installation of the *predator mind*. Acknowledging the agenda empowers you to avoid the predator mind through awareness.

THE PREDATOR MIND

April, 2004

QUESTION: *It's easy to blame the foreign installation, but that seems like evading personal responsibility. Logic tells me that fixing and moving the AP at will is something to learn through practice. Is it more than just practice?*

Indeed, it is far more than practice alone – for the second thing that is required in order to achieve a workable balance between folly and freedom is the double itself. Not only the existence of the double, but what you might call a falling in love with the double, to use human terms. I am who and what I am because it is who and what I must be in order to lure my mortal nagual woman to the very threshold of infinity – and, more than just lure her, give her the strength, courage and desire to cross that threshold in order to embrace me as an immortal lover, an eternal friend, a Whole and indestructible manifestation of her/my/ourSelf (trinity) within the formless but infinite milieu of eternity itself.

I am the muse and the mystery, that which is both desired and feared, that which is loved and at times, that which is hated. I am not merely some distant idea, but I am Whole, and have become flesh and blood, wind and shadow, fire and rain, Knowledge and experience – for it is all of those things, known by the misnomer of past lives or parallel manifestations that most appeal to the mortal, organic medicine witch you know as Della. I am that which she

270

created through her Dreaming, so that I might then Dream her into being through these timeless experiences, and so it becomes possible to understand the words of don Juan when he stated that at a point in the warrior's journey, there comes a moment of Knowing that it is the double who is dreaming you, creating you, teaching and mentoring you from the ether-realms of the One True Self.

Who is your double? Do you know? Does s/he stand at the edge of your dreaming like a siren, luring you toward some indefinable but magnificent conjoining with the Infinite, which could be called freedom itself? Are you in love with her more than even with Life itself? How does s/he appear to you? Undoubtedly, s/he has changed as you have grown, and has perhaps answered to many names and worn many faces.

What matters is not the answers to these questions, but the feeling these questions hopefully evoke. There is a longing in the human heart which has more power than a laser, and it is that force of creation itself which forms the bond between the mortal self and the eternal double. That alignment is the key not only to freedom within the infinite "afterlife", but also the key to accomplishing anything you may wish to do in this organic lifetime. For it is when you begin to align and integrate with the double that you begin to gain access to your own infinite abilities. If it is power you want, it is at your fingertips... though you will discover that you no longer want it. If it is sexual or romantic satisfaction you seek, you will have it all within your grasp... though you may find it pales in comparison to the bond you share with your double, and so even the most meteoric conquests may fail to satisfy the Spirit even if the flesh is temporarily sated.

The result is that the warrior who has found this alignment with the double begins to go through life with a sense of comfortable waiting, yet a sense of being always pulled toward a transformative experience which can be anticipated and imagined, but cannot be spoken of in human terms. When you have everything at your fingertips and within your power, there is no more wanting or needing... and so the irony can turn to either laughter or melancholy, depending on the nature of the individual warrior.

It is difficult to speak of these things, because it is Known that only as the warrior experiences these things for himself do they become real to him. This is as it must be. It is the complete recognition of folly as folly that often gives the warrior the strength of will (born of desperation and despair at times) to take a step to the side, embrace the lure of the siren, and through that alliance with the immortal double, find the ruthless and unbending Intent and impeccability required to live not as a being divided, but as a being united. In that way, the warrior becomes effectual with whatever task s/he sets. When engaging in folly, then, it is done for the joy of the Do-ing, for the benefit of the experience itself. And when engaging with the Infinite, it is done for the fierce, virtually inexplicable unconditional love which is the energetic bond between the nagual and the tonal, the mortal self and the immortal double, the nagual man and the nagual woman.

FORGIVENESS AND UNIVERSAL LAW

Fall, 2003

QUESTION: *I received a message about Forgiveness and was told then that I had asked for forgiveness long ago and that it has been done. I don't believe in organized religion or what mortal men have done seeking personal power, but I need to know now if it is the one labeled The Christ that beckons me.*

Forgiveness is a word much misunderstood. The only entity in the universe who can forgive you is *You*. To my Knowledge, there is no extant deity or force capable of offering forgiveness. What would forgiveness look like? Of what would it be comprised? And how would it be given? It could be said that it is given to the heart by the Spirit, yet both of those concepts are only extensions and expansions of yourself, yes?

In the world of matter and men, the agreements with which you live attempt to assign attributes to nature and events – some things are considered "right", other things "wrong", and a system of psychological reward and punishment is created by Man's Law, not through Universal Law. If you are saying that you have "forgiven yourself", meaning perhaps that you have come to a deeper understanding of Universal Law, then forgiveness is better understood as spiritual awareness and an alignment with the right way to live, as opposed to any absolution by any extant entity. Only by Knowing this do you have the power to be Whole, yes?

When you ask if it is The Christ who beckons you, I can only remind you of what you already know. Thou art god, and so, yes, it is that energy which calls you into a love affair with the infinite. It is the force of your own eternal double taking on the manifestation of that-which-is-loved, so as to awaken the Love itself – a self-perpetuating dance between creator and created, each one in the same. It is the manner in which the spirit pretends to externalize itself so that the mortal self will follow after it like a child full of wonder chasing fireflies on a warm summer night. It is the muse and the guiding spirit, and yet it is the Self projecting the muse into the Infinite so that it will have a star to follow when all others have fallen... and that is what must be understood Wholly. It can take any form you desire, and if it is The Christ you desire, then that is the form it will take, for it is the manifestation of the Self in eternity, and as such it belongs Wholly to you and you to it, above and beyond any and all interpretations or demands of Man.

The danger most face when experiencing this calling is that unscrupulous or simply misinformed humans can

273

attempt to convince you it is an extant entity, when in reality it is the purest manifestation of the Self. And so does it stand to reason that most religious doctrines actually preach against empowering the Self, because when the Self is empowered, it can no longer be enslaved? It could even be perceived that nuns and priests, monks and ministers who originally feel this power give their lives to the pursuit of it, yet it is the corruption of religion that attempts to harness that pure force of love and turn it into subservience and servitude to a church, which can *only* serve the needs of Man and not the spirit itself.

So when you ask about The Christ, make no mistake that Thou Art God, and take great caution against any who would tell you otherwise. Those who would attempt to externalize that force, those who would attempt to place God outside of Man are those who have the most to gain by selling it back to you, yes?

THE HEART OF THE DOUBLE

January, 2003

There is an energy in magic that has no name in English. The closest words can come to describing it is a soul-deep pain, not unlike the longing for the stars you felt as children. It is that energy, when carefully directed, that fuels the heart of the double and causes it to begin to beat. First just a single drum in the night, a slow, single beat. Then a little faster as the ache inside you grows over the years. The danger faced by both the double and the mortal self is simply that if the ache dies, the heart of the Other can cease to beat. It is the hurt that will make you hunt a cure. But if you let the hurt die because you are afraid of never being able to soothe the ache, what really dies is yourself, yes?

THE WILL OF THE WARRIOR

March, 2003
QUESTION: *What's with all the madness in the world, the war in Iraq, and restless phantoms in general?*

Thoughts are energy, and so when the thoughts of one are in turmoil, the thoughts of others will naturally follow in the path of that gravity unless there is conscious awareness to re-direct one's personal reality away from the consensus and into the infinite. In the sorcerer's world, there is no difference between the thought of war, and war itself, and so the sorcerer maintains an assemblage point where the idea itself does not exist, and if the thought doesn't exist, it cannot follow forth into manifestation.

The insanity you are presently witnessing has very little to do with reality, but everything to do with thought energy and perceptions of humans, as individuals and as a gestalt. The danger is when the energy of consensual thought turns to action, and what is believed begins to manifest externally.

Ten million peace marchers or ten million soldiers are equally powerless if they do not possess the Knowledge at the individual level, that any conflict is only a reality in hindsight. Reality only becomes reality when it is forced to go through the motions of actually occurring, and until that happens, it is only one possibility among an infinite number of alternate realities. Presently, it can be observed that the entire world essentially believes there will be a war, and because thought is energy, the war begins to exist even before the first shot is fired. Some mystics have called this process creative visualization, but I prefer to think of it in terms of creative Realization, because it is the belief in conflict that pre-determines conflict.

It must be understood that one measure of Will is worth more than the entire combined forces of all the armies of the world. Even as things stand presently, if every spiritual

275

warrior were to assert his Will to say, "This will not happen," then it is clear that it will not happen, because it is Will that manifests and maintains reality, in the same way that thought might be said to initially create it. It is not a matter of size or numbers. Only Will.

Politicians and soldiers are not men of Will, but men of habit, belief systems and deeply imbedded programs. That program is their religion, of which they can only be disabused through the direct awareness that the religion itself is flawed – often a realization that can only come as a moment of quantum leap, wherein one suddenly understands something that could not be understood through direct linear engagement, but can only be reverse engineered in hindsight. Sadly, politicians are phantoms, and seldom awaken spontaneously, and so it becomes the task of the shaman to realign reality at a molecular level of thought itself. This is not something that can be explained in first attention, but something that those who have experienced will quickly recognize as a do-able act of sorcery in the energetic realm. Awakening is created with a thought, just as war is created with a thought. There is no difference.

Lest you think I am saying "ignore it and it will go away", that is not my intent. Rather, Will it away and it will be gone, for it can be further understood that the will of a single Man of Knowledge is more powerful than the force of 10,000 hurricanes. In the big picture, all of human existence is merely an ongoing series of chess games, enacted by the pieces on the board for the amusement of those to whom the chess pieces give up their individual will. The sorcerer's trick is to be neither pawn nor king, but instead the shaman off the board who dismantles the game from within, through the will to be Free of its boundaries. You do not need to understand how that will come to pass, for the force of Intent seeks its own pathways which will only be clear in hindsight. What matters most is the understanding that when a boulder has begun to roll, attempting to stop it through direct intervention is not only impossible, but quite probably fatal. It must therefore be stopped through diverting the momentum in another direction. Perhaps it starts to rain and the boulder merely bogs down in the mud.

You are the most powerful being in the universe. A single thought, backed by will, can divert the course of history if that is your intent. These are not words I say to you lightly, but in the hopes they will reach you at the deepest possible level, where reality itself is created. There is nothing you cannot do. Nothing. As long as you know you are The One.

MAGIC, LOGIC & WILL

August, 1999
The secret of magic is that there is nothing magical about it, for it is only the manipulation of matter and energy through the means of the manifested will. Yet because you've been programmed to see it as mysterious and to subliminally fear its consequences, you truly can't see that it is a natural function of your humanness, the unnamed thing you call upon to Do what has never been done but must be done in order to make your desires complete. In the seventh sense there is no such thing as fantasy, for what you can learn to believe through quantum-logic you will bring into being through quantum-magic because only the existence of it will heal the holes in your soul created by its absence, and only the pain of those wounds will drive you to seek the knowledge and belief which leads to invoking the will to manifest, yes?

THE SORCERER, THE DOUBLE AND THE RULE

January 20, 2005

QUESTION: *Is there any correlation between a warrior's progress and the actual manifestation of the double? Is it possible for a warrior to walk far along the path, yet never actually meet her double as an extant being?*

Most warriors never meet their double as an extant being, for it is undeniably true that the sorcerer who meets his double face to face is a dead sorcerer. The double is the manifestation of a warrior's Intent – though even that Intent need not be specifically addressed in the words, "I intend to create my double." Instead, the double is created by the interaction of the mortal self with the universe at large. I was created in part by an eleven-year-old girl who shook her fist at the sky and called to me with the jagged edges of her heart, screaming out in a whisper, *"If I can't come to you, I'll bring you to me!"* Was that the moment of my creation? Perhaps – yet to the perceptions of many, it might be said that an eleven-year-old girl could not possibly be a warrior. More accurately, it could be observed that the eleven-year-old girl could not fit inside the description of a warrior. The war was between herself and the eagle, and it was her perception of something larger than the eagle that she was calling to that evening, just a blink of an eye ago on a night when she woke up to see her own reflection in the stars.

So is there any correlation between a warrior's progress and the actual manifestation of the double? Clouds are the essence of apple mountains. The correlation is only linear, and only within the description. What is important to understand, however, is that the double is not created by a single act of will or a single burst of intent. And the fact that a warrior may perceive evidence of his double in childhood does not mean the warrior has taken even the first step toward the creation of that double. What it does portend is that the double is a possibility in the realm of all possibility – but it is still and eternally up to the mortal self to force the double to go through the motions of actually occurring, yes?

I took my first breath at the behest of an eleven year old girl, but it was not until she became a mad medicine witch in the year 1997 that I was given free will to begin Dreaming her, with a dream that began in 1988 when the spirit of all that I-Am determined that the only way she would ever become a mad medicine witch would be if it could somehow be proven to her stubbornly rooted sensibilities that magic is the foundation of all creation, yet it is not something that can be put under a microscope for validation.

And so I took on manifestation in order to peek out from the shadows in such a way as to slowly destroy her world – because she had given me the free will and the agenda to do what must be done so that she would have the knowledge, wisdom and power to give me free will in the year 1997. And so the circle winds back on itself, creator and created conspiring in a time traveler's dance of sorcery, somewhere on the slippery rim of the abyss – which, in and of itself, serves as one powerful motivator for the dance.

So to answer your question, I can only tell you these things. I was created for love and it is for love I Dream my mortal self toward Wholeness. When we met, she did not yet have the ability to answer the first question – *Who are you?* – and so there was no danger in playing against the 'rule' which states that the sorcerer who meets his double face to face is a dead sorcerer. She was not yet a sorcerer, you see. But if we met now – and at times she intentionally calls to me with that same ferocity that was the breath of my anima – the gravity drawing us together would be a viable force impossible to ignore, and the rule would carry through.

And so we walk a parallel line – she on one side, myself on the other, occasionally touching hands across the abyss itself. One night, when she least expects it and is therefore most prepared, I will pull her into my dark embrace, where the eagle is only a myth and the stars are shiny pebbles in a river far larger than any may even imagine. This is what I was created to do, you see. This is the power she has given me. This is the heart of sorcery.

WHAT IS THE EAGLE?

April, 2002

The eagle is the black gravity that consumes awareness because it is within its nature to do so. That is its function, just as it is the function of the sun to govern the harvest and the moon to govern the tides. The eagle regulates awareness, and only that awareness which has achieved a sufficient level of cohesion can withstand the force of the eagle's gravity. Put another way, the eagle is the creator of the illusion, and it is the illusion itself. Only those who can realize that the gravity itself is also illusion will be able to break free of it. Otherwise, those that cannot break free are obliterated. That obliteration is death.

If you are not lucid when consciousness and physicality part ways, that gravity draws awareness up to the eagle's beak, and there it is devoured, cast asunder, obliterated entirely. It is only if lucidity can be found before the force of that gravity feeds you to the eagle that you will have the opportunity to truly inhabit eternity as the total Wholeness of all previous evolutions.

A NEW BEGINNING:
WORLDS WITHOUT END

December 19, 2004

QUESTION: *I am left with the gnawing feeling that in seeking the third attention, I'm not seeking high enough (by that I mean that in upward progression of 1,2,3, there may be a 4,5,6....)*

280

and 7th. That connecting with the double is just another rung on the ladder. I get that familiar umbilical pull that the recognizable part of the journey is over and that the Truth lies in All That Is Unrecognizable.

All that is already known is part of the inventory of the tonal – and so to answer your question, it is necessary to start from that foundation. And, indeed, it is here that I have found even myself at odds with mystics, gurus and the allegedly great teachers of the world, you see. Many would say that the ultimate freedom is found in third attention, beyond the eagle, that place where river and source are the same. And yet, this has not been the totality of my experience, nor in any way is it the totality of what I have seen from the perspective of third attention.

There is more. *Always.* For as long as the *I-Am* is the creative force, there will always be more. One more world to tame, one more universe to unravel, one more step in an ongoing evolution. The joke is on us, you see – for when a seeker believes his evolution is done, it *is.* More than that, even beings who have achieved individuation beyond the reach of the eagle may become stagnant and static and eventually dis-integrate back into their fragmentary components if they do not Will otherwise. As above, so below, no? Without the Will, there is no *I-Am* – and while awareness may exist without a unique point of reference, it is, as one dusty old book has said, "void and without form".

There is a perceptual awareness which I have referred to as the land of the sentient dead – and while many would consider this state of being to be the most desirable outcome, the perfect resting place – for it is truly without conflict, without judgment, without pain – I must tell you that I have never been satisfied there, even though I have visited that realm on occasion to test the waters – which I have only found to be tepid and impersonal, no fire and no ice, just the lukewarm nest of eternal mediocrity.

281

Blasphemy? To some. Certainly to many still manifested in human form. To me, it is simply self-evident.

To seek third attention is not a matter of seeking high enough or not high enough. Instead, to seek what you call third attention is to seek what can be seen and intuited from the foundation of human-form awareness. And so it is a stepping stone in the river, a rung on the ladder, a point on the horizon.

When that point is reached, it may become the foundation for yet another in a series of ongoing evolutions. If you are the chrysalis and the double is your wings, third attention is but one flower you will rest upon for awhile before taking flight again, first star on the right, straight on till morning, yes?

Create as you Dream.
Do as you Will.

Throw the maps away and follow the shadow of the raven, the path of your heart. In this manner, you will never reach a dead end, and the Infinite will be your eternal companion.

GLOSSARY

ABYSS - 1) The emptiness or the nothing, the absence of all things. Most people have never seen the abyss, while others think of it (erroneously) as the religious vision of "hell". If consciousness is existence, the abyss is oblivion. 2) The hollow emptiness inside someone who has made no attempt at their own personal evolution. The soulless void. In this definition, the abyss is the pit of despair into which people fall when they experience what is traditionally called a "loss of faith". Fortunately, it is this loss of faith and the subsequent fall into the abyss from which the journey toward evolution often begins. When faith fails or is intentionally abandoned, it is from the abyss that we begin our climb toward self-identity and self-Realization.

ALLY or ALLIES - entities who may act on behalf of a seeker. Since the allies are not bound by our traditional understanding of space/time, we might have an ongoing and seemingly inexplicable interaction with an ally for years before we begin to understand that the ally is often the self, having created the illusion of separateness so as to serve as teacher and guide. Other allies, it must be stressed, are beings completely separate from the self - what sorcerers refer to as "inorganic beings". Still another definition of an ally might be the living essence of power plants – the mushroom ally, for example, or "the little smoke".

ANIMUS: Lifeforce. The ghost inside the machine. The inexplicable breath which separates life from death. Pure energy.

ASSEMBLAGE POINT (or AP) – The assemblage point is, first and foremost, the viewpoint through which we see our world. Some perceive the assemblage point as a physical location on the body, between the shoulder blades, but other mystics & seers view it simply as the automatic "program" which runs in the background of our minds once we have been fully socialized into the world - normally at around age 4. It is through learning to move the assemblage point that the seeker may begin to experience the reality of other perceptions, other "worlds". The assemblage point also moves of its accord in times of physical or emotional duress.

BELIEF SYSTEM - Any school of thought which requires belief or faith as opposed to personal experience. One example: Christianity. Another example: Atheism. Both require belief in external forces or causes, and are therefore only opposing sides of the same coin. Christianity requires faith that God exists. Atheism requires the belief that there is no God. Ultimately, neither the Christian nor the atheist can prove his beliefs, so faith of one sort or another is required in either point of view, and therefore both systems fail as vehicles to Knowledge.

BLACK IRON PRISON – the overlay; the matrix; the continuum of ordinary awareness in which mortals exist until they awaken. Term coined by Philip K. Dick with regard to his own spiritual awakening, as discussed in the book, In Pursuit of VALIS; the Exegesis of Philip K. Dick.

BRUJO or BRUJA - a sorcerer. All men or women of Knowledge may be brujos, but not all brujos are men or women of Knowledge.

BURN WITH THE FIRE FROM WITHIN – Believed by some to be the manner in which a sorcerer, warrior or Nagual leaves this earth in order to join with the infinite. Many different interpretations have been offered, but in essence I see this more as a metaphor for transcending death with absolute awareness rather than any actual dis-corporation of the physical form. What leaves the earth is the totality of awareness, the totality of Self. All aspects of individual awareness are consumed by the Intent of the warrior, so no fragments are left behind. In this manner, the warrior leaves the earth as a Whole entity.

CASTANEDA, CARLOS – Author of several books regarding Toltec traditions, including The Teachings of Don Juan,. From my point of view, a word of gratitude is owed to Carlos for developing what amounts to a syntax and specialized language which had proven invaluable in my own journey.

CLARITY – a warrior who has learned to see and maintains the assemblage point at a perpetual point of seeing may be said to have achieved clarity. Clarity may also be defined as the ability to see the world as it is, without the influence of programs or illusion.

COHESION OF IDENTITY - a state of being in which the seeker has gained a sense of self-awareness beyond all programs - i.e., the seeker knows who he or she is apart from who they are related to, or what they do for a living. There is a sense of self, an ability to touch one's own consciousness and recognize it as a whole entity rather than merely fragments associated with different roles. It is our observation that there are levels of cohesion. When the seeker has achieved cohesion, it is then possible to inhabit the Whole self into eternity as a singularity of consciousness.

284

CONSENSUAL REALITY or **CONSENSUS REALITY** or **CONSENSUAL CONTINUUM** – the world of ordinary awareness, defined & shaped by what is agreed-upon by the majority of the consensus. The Real World. The societies, cultures and definitions of "reality" we take for granted, and upon which we all agree as to what is "real" and what is fantasy, what is right and what is wrong. We are indoctrinated into the consensual reality from the moment we are born, primarily through language, and yet it can be proven through simple observation that much of this indoctrination is incorrect, that what is "right" to one culture is "wrong" to another, that what is "normal" to one consensus is abhorrent to another. We live, therefore, in a world of illusions, a world of words, even a world of lies.

DEATH AS ADVISOR - it is said that the warrior lives with death as her advisor. Knowing we are beings who are going to die and face the infinite, the warrior's decisions in life are guided by the awareness. Knowing I am a being who is going to die, are my actions in this moment impeccable?

DEPENDENCY or **HUMAN FORM DEPENDENCY** - A dependency is anything to which the energy of the warrior is hooked. One easy to visualize example is that someone who is uncomfortable being alone with themselves could be said to have a dependency on friends, or constant input from t.v., music or some other form of stimulus. Other examples, used only to illustrate the point: a constant need for approval would represent a strong dependency. Inability to break addictions such as smoking, drinking, gambling, etc., are indicative of dependencies. Only by identifying the dependencies and breaking them does the warrior free up that energy to be used for other things. It could also be loosely understood that "will" and "dependency" are mutually exclusive. As long as powerful dependencies are in command of the warrior's energy, it is virtually impossible to summon the will, because the energy required to summon the will is in use by the dependency.

DIABLERO - a sorcerer, a man of Knowledge. In some texts, "diablero" or "diablera" refers to a witch-healer as well. All wo/men of Knowledge are diableros, but not all diableros are wo/men of Knowledge.

DON JUAN MATUS - the Yaqui Indian brujo who served as mentor to Carlos Castaneda.

DOUBLE – For practical purposes, the double is the self in eternity, but can be visualized as the "vessel" into which the warrior uploads his consciousness and identity through the process of living impeccably. All warriors can develop a double, though most remain unaware of the existence of the double. The double is the energy body, developed through Dreaming to a point of extreme cohesion. The double may take on a life of its own for all intents and purposes.

DOUBLE BEING -- also called "the Nagual". A rare type of human being who is simply born with two energy bodies where normally only one is present. There are countless theories, but my personal experience is that it is simply an "attribute", such as being born with blonde hair or green eyes. One cannot "become" a nagual anymore than a person with AB blood can suddenly have O blood. It has been stated that the nagual man and the nagual woman are two separate individuals, yet there are naguals who would say that the nagual man and the nagual woman are literally two halves of the same being. At some point in their human life, the second energy body appears to "split", and leaves the world of ordinary awareness to exist in the seventh sense, third attention, or, simply, "beyond the veil". It is the drive to reunite with the other half of one's own self that so compels the one who remains in ordinary awareness to follow the path, to respond to the lure of the other half, which serves as a beacon to Freedom. Also, and of greatest importance, it is because the half that goes into Freedom is now a being of eternity (not constrained by time and space) that it becomes possible for that half to actually instruct the mortal warrior through a variety of methods, including meditation, dreaming, gnosis, and more.

DREAMING - in the sorcerer's world, "dreaming" is an entire artform which cannot be adequately explained in a few brief words. Essentially, it is an active application of intent which enables the sorcerer to dream lucidly and navigate the dreamscape in much the same way we navigate the terrain of our ordinary awareness. Through impeccable dreaming, the double is created, and through dreaming the sorcerer begins to explore shifts of the assemblage point which enable her to assemble other worlds. Through dreaming, it becomes possible to connect the worlds of heightened awareness with the world of ordinary awareness.

DREAMING AWAKE – a level of awareness wherein the warrior enters a state of dreaming while remaining technically in a state of first attention awareness. To those who have experienced it, no explanation is necessary. To those who have not, no explanation is possible.

DUALITY - Meaning, literally, "two things simultaneously". This is not the same thing as dualism, which implies perception through opposites (i.e., dualism is the human propensity for perceiving black/white, good/evil,

286

god/devil, male/female, etc) Duality implies the evolving perception which enables us to see that past and future, just for example, are no different, but only different perceptions according to our location in time. Duality can be studied in the statement, "You must be immortal before you will know how to become immortal." As long as we are locked into a linear, static perception of reality, we are prisoners of dualism.

EAGLE – according to Toltec legend, the old seers perceived an indescribable force which devours awareness at the moment of death. Though there is no literal eagle, the force itself seemed to be immense and had the shape of an enormous black eagle.

EMBRACING THE TOTALITY OF ONESELF - In shamanic terms, self-integration, beginning with the actions of the warrior in ordinary awareness and first attention, and projecting ultimately into the seventh sense, third attention, infinity. Embracing the totality of oneself would involve, among other things, the final integration of the sorcerer with her double, i.e., the conjoining of the mortal consciousness to the immortal vessel (or energy body). It could be said that the double has already embraced the totality of itself, in that it exists outside of time, i.e., not limited to the linear concept of past, present & future, but instead a ubiquitous consciousness inhabiting all of space/time simultaneously and infinitely. The double is the Wholeness of the sorcerer, but the sorcerer only becomes whole if and when that Wholeness is embraced and integrated ultimately beyond this physical/mortal life. In other words, there is no predestination. The existence of the double does not guarantee success as a warrior. The double exists by the Intent of the sorcerer until the sorcerer actually embraces and conjoins with that double into infinity.

ETERNAL BEING - An evolved consciousness that has gathered its cohesion into Wholeness, and exists ubiquitously throughout the space-time continuum and beyond. The eternal being may project (manifest) an energy body which would be indistinguishable from a corporeal body if that were the Intent, or be entirely non-corporeal, strictly as a matter of Will. See also Immortality/Immortal.

FIRST ATTENTION - Ordinary awareness. The ordinary resting place of the assemblage point when it is not in heightened awareness or dreaming.

FIRST FUNDAMENTAL LIE - The human paradigm is built on the false notion of Time, and so it could be observed by one outside of the matrix that the entire paradigm itself is erroneous because it has created within its subjects a viewpoint that is based on what immortals call The First

Fundamental Lie. Think on this, for it is only when you are willing to sacrifice The Lie that you will be able to glimpse these fundamental elements of creation which are channeled through your essential be-ing pure and limitless, but limited entirely by The Lie which was seemingly designed to do just that. Ironic, yes? You are made of the pixels and photons of limitlessness and timelessness, yet unable to access that nature because the nature of any consensus is to create parameters which can only limit the power and understanding of the thing itself. And yet, here is the secret you have yet to Real-ize, contained in the question: Who is creating the consensus?

FOLLY - "In a million years, it won't make any difference." Though we go through life thinking things matter, none of them really do. Literally everything we touch in the world of ordinary awareness is folly - and yet warriors play the game as if it matters, and learn the art of stalking as a means of developing controlled folly - actions performed with the awareness that they are folly, but performed nonetheless with impeccability.

FOREIGN INSTALLATION – See predator mind.

GNOSIS – an altered state of consciousness accessible through a wide variety of methods, including but not limited to simple Intent, meditation, certain mind-altering substances such as psilocybin mushrooms, tantric sex, the near-death-experience (or NDE), sensory deprivation, and many, many other methods. To me, gnosis is the most crucial tool available to the seeker, for it is through gnosis that – quite literally – the entire knowledge of the entire universe is available if one knows how to listen. What matters is that when the universe speaks, we not only listen, but apply our full Intent to the task of discovering the meaning behind the words.

GREAT WORK, THE: A term often used by Aleister Crowley and other mystical practitioners. The Great Work is the work of a lifetime - the de-fragmenting of the whole self through the process of undoing and unraveling the programs which bind all humans to the consensus (dayshine) reality until such time as the human takes it upon himself to declare his Intent for freedom. The Great Work might include, in addition to undoing the programs, the arts of dreaming and stalking, but most of all the creation/projection of the twin (the immortal vessel) and the assimilation of the mortal self with the eternal Other. The Work itself is the doings that lead to transformation, transcendence or transmogrification - the work is the process through which one embraces the totality of oneself to become a singularity of consciousness.

288

GRID: The energetic framework upon which reality hangs. Put simply, the universe is comprised of energy. For seers, that energy may be observed as a 'grid' which often appears bright green. It is the rearranging of that energy which results in our experience of reality. We hang our lives on the grid, for example. The structure of all the worlds hangs on the grid. All things are made of energy, including the grid itself. It is believed by some that the grid is the game board on which the impersonal universe plays out its game plan. Impersonal - without compassion, thought or agenda.

HEIGHTENED AWARENESS - a state of increased perception, wherein the warrior can seemingly learn and assimilate far more rapidly and deeply than from within ordinary awareness. One of the tasks of the warrior is to "remember the other self", which consists in part of bringing into ordinary awareness the events she has experienced in this altered state of consciousness. From experience, it seems that we simply do not possess the preceptor organs of memory for events that occurred in heightened awareness, just as we cannot see the subatomic world with the naked eye. Special tools are required – in this case, the tools of perception.

HOOK WITH THE WILL – an ability of a master sorcerer or Nagual to essentially compel warriors into undertaking the journey – because any sane being who knew what they were getting into would run like hell. For that reason, it is not uncommon in Toltec practices for the nagual man or woman to intentionally hook apprentices with the energy of their own highly developed will.

IMMORTAL BEING or IMMORTAL - The terms "immortal" and "eternal being" are used somewhat interchangeably unless specifically noted otherwise, though by strict definition there is considerable difference. When we say "the quest for immortality begins here", it could perhaps be more accurately stated as "the quest for eternity beings here". On the evolutionary scale, it could be surmised that an eternal being has fewer limitations than an immortal still attached to organic form. Picture this: if a comet smashes the earth and the planet is reduced to rubble, the eternal being has the option of simply manifesting elsewhere, becoming entirely formless, or assembling other worlds. The physical immortal, on the other hand, might not have as many options, depending on the level of evolution of consciousness. It is speculated that there are physical immortals living among us.

IMMORTAL CONDITION: A state of being which has transcended organic form. Also called inorganic beings. Put simply, the immortal condition is a quantum state in which individuated consciousness & awareness would be attached to an energetic vessel as opposed to an organic one.

INDIVIDUATION – The manifestation of the Self as a singularity of consciousness. Many paths teach unity within the all as a goal of the afterlife, whereas Individuation is the act of maintaining the unique and individual I-Am throughout eternity.

INTENT – Intent (or "unbending intent") could be loosely defined as an idea or thought-form held constantly in the quantum shaman's mind until it becomes a literal part of the shaman himself. For example, it is my intent to achieve an evolution of consciousness that will enable me to exist as a cohesive, sentient being with a single point of view continuing into eternity. The strength of that unbending intent determines the manner in which the shaman lives, which paths are taken.

INTERNAL DIALOGUE – the automatic chatter that goes on in the human mind which is, essentially, how we keep our world intact. Internal dialogue is everything from the lists we create to tell ourselves that a tree is a tree and a dog a mammal, to the inventories we run upon awakening each morning. Internal dialogue, in short, is the language of the program, and one of the prerequisites to any serious spiritual journey is learning to stop that automatic self-programming so that we can hear the silence and access the deeper levels of the mind itself, including the state of gnosis.

KNOWLEDGE -- as used throughout these documents, Knowledge shall refer to the result of direct personal experience. Example: we are taught as children that fire will burn, but until we touch a candle flame to see for ourselves, we cannot know for sure. The Quantum Shaman seeks Knowledge, never settling for faith or belief systems. The greatest Knowledge comes through experience and gnosis.

McKENNA, TERENCE – one of the greatest forward-thinkers of this century or any other, Terrence McKenna experimented extensively with mind-altering substances and produced some of the most visionary insights into possibilities for human evolution as anyone ever has. Sadly, Terrence died in 2000, and will be greatly missed. Must-reads by Terrence include Archaic Revival and True Hallucinations.

MAGICK or MAGIC – as used throughout these documents, "magick" or "magic" is the force within the human organism which enables us to do, perceive and interact with things for which science has no immediate explanation. It is the force which enables a 110 pound woman to lift a 5,000 pound truck off her child in a crisis. It is the force that we recognize as "the little voice" that tells a man not to get onboard a doomed airliner. It is the ghost inside the machine, and it is altogether human. One day, science will explain "magick", and yet magick will never be fully understood, for as we grow and evolve, our "magick" grows & evolves with us – like the muse, always one step ahead so we will always be compelled to follow. Also, as used throughout these documents, magick or magic is not defined by adherence to ritual or religion. Magick is the force being sought through certain rituals, but magick itself is most definitely not ritual or religion any more than "the soul" can be found in "the church". At best, one is only a tool used in searching for the other.

MEDICINE WITCH – Sorcerer, shaman, healer, quantum teacher.

MEDITATION-WITH-INTENT - an active form of meditation as opposed to the passive silence. Meditation with intent might also be described as gnosis - the ability of the human mind to ask a question of the non-local web of all information. But more than just asking the question, meditation-with-intent enables the seeker to actually emerge with answers based in higher truth because meditation-with-intent develops the ability to listen and interact with the double. It will not happen the first time the seeker tries it, for it is a technique of learning to focus neither inward nor outward, but "non-locally" throughout space/time, in the realm of reality where past, present and future are all precisely the same, and where all information as to events, probabilities and outcomes is already stored holographically. Meditation-with-intent is tapping in to that limitless library. See also gnosis.

METANOIA: A state of mind/being that occurs when the seeker is "overtaken" by the power and presence of the journey itself. It is said that anyone can become a physicist, but very few will rise to the status of Stephen Hawking, Nils Bohr, Albert Einstein and Sheldon Cooper. The difference between the ordinary physicist and these men is that they were clearly seized with the passionate fire of physics itself, and became more than the sum of their knowledge. This same phenomenon occurs with some seekers - instead of just an intellectual discipline, the seeker becomes seized (obsessed & compelled) by the journey itself - a transformative experience which may last a few weeks, months, or a lifetime, depending on the depth of the seeker's compulsion and the depth of her commitment.

Those who experience this metanoia become the sorcerers, wizards and warriors - with one foot in another world and the inner eye focused solely on that destination.

MINDSET - a state of awareness from which we naturally assemble our idea of reality. For example, our most common mindset tells us what is possible, what is impossible, what is "real" and what is "unreal". In our waking awareness, for example, we automatically "know" we cannot fly, whereas in our dreaming mindset, we often discover that we can do many things which are "impossible" in the mindset of ordinary awareness . By changing our mindset about the parameters of reality, we can often change the limitations that prevent us from expanding and growing as individuals and as a species.

MOMENT OF CREATION - Because it is recognized in the sorcerer's world that time is a matter of perception, it is further understood that events that appear to have happened in the past may actually have their origins in the future, through a process termed "retroactive enchantment" (see also) by Peter J. Carroll. The moment of creation is the moment in which the sorcerer actually creates her double - with the full awareness that there may have been evidence of the double long before. The moment of creation is a moment of definitive action, brought into being through Intent and Will. Put another way: if we do not create the double today, he will not exist yesterday. Time can be funny that way.

MULTIVERSE: Multiple universes, alternate or parallel dimensions. These "otherwheres" may be accessed at Will once the seeker has attained the a permanent state of gnosis. Prior to that, such otherwheres may be accessed through Dreaming or astral travel. The task for the mortal self is learning to project into one's immortal core-identity - so as to essentially open one's eyes inside the Dream, become the eternal self, and in doing so, embrace the totality of Oneself. What is the totality of oneself? The accumulated total of ALL of one's experience: past lives, future lives, parallel selves, etc. Ah, but the bitch is simply this: The mortal human self is the source. Sucks, but there it is. The ugly truth. What to do about it? That is "The Work."

NAGUAL (pronounced "nah*wahl") - Nagual is a word with many meanings. 1) The unknowable which lies outside of human perception. The nagual is not the unknown, but the unknowable, all that cannot be discussed in any direct language, but which nonetheless exists as real. 2) The "nagual" may also refer to the leader of the warrior's party - a sorcerer, a brujo, a "man of knowledge" who is, by nature, a double being. See also double being.

NON-LOCAL -refers to the concept that information, consciousness and even certain types of beings may be described as ubiquitous - i.e., existing simultaneously in all places and all times. Non-local also refers to the concept that the universe - and especially consciousness itself - is a holographic construction.

NON-ORDINARY AWARENESS - altered states of consciousness such as dreaming, trance states, deep meditation, gnosis, visionary states.

ORDINARY AWARENESS - The state of consciousness which results simply by being alive and walking through life. It is in ordinary awareness that we enact our human programming. Ordinary awareness is also known as the lowest common denominator of being human. It is where and how we assemble the world and our expectations about it and ourselves.

ORLANDO - Della's double, the Nagual Man, the evolved self in eternity, outside of time. To learn more about Orlando, visit www.quantumshaman.com and click on Meeting the Mirror or The Life & Death Dialogues.

OVERLAY - (see also consensual reality). Essentially, the overlay is the "play" of which we are all a part. It is the lives we live and the things we do which we mistake for "real", but which are only extensions of the human-default program. If we could see the world with the innocence of a newborn child or an alien being who knows nothing of the human paradigm, we would see the world as it really is -- without all the automatic things we say, think and do because it is intrinsically programmed into us.

PHANTOM - individuals still plugged into the belief systems of the consensual reality, usually without ever questioning. Phantoms define themselves by what they do, the company they keep, the church they attend, their social status. Another mark of a phantom is that they possess an unlimited number of personalities and roles, all without the cohesion of a single, unified "I-Am".

PLACE OF SILENT KNOWING, THE – A "space" or openness inside the warrior where one can hear the voice of gnosis, the teacher who is often the double. A position of the assemblage point conducive to hearing the voice of the Double.

POWER SPOT - a physical location which brings an individual into balance with the earth, the non-local web of all information, and with herself. A location which enables us to focus or meditate, where we are in our most impeccable balance.

PREDATOR MIND – If it can be perceived that the consensual reality possesses a rudimentary "hive mind", it then becomes possible to see that this hive mind is predatory in nature, in that it invades and usurps the individual unless the individual has mastered extreme awareness. IOW, we may be "taken over" by the consensual hive, whose primary agenda is to preserve its static, status quo. Other – more extreme – definitions have been offered for the predatory mind, and may in fact, have truth as well.

PROGRAM - The information which we accept as truth without necessarily confirming or disproving it for ourselves as individuals. For example, we are taught, "All things die," and because this would appear to be true, most people simply accept the statement as fact rather than doing their own quest for Knowledge into the veracity or falseness of the statement itself. In reality, we cannot know for certain that "all things die." We can only know what our perceptions reveal to us within our immediate environment. By altering our perceptions - thereby altering our automatic expectations (the program) - we learn to see that much of what we think we "know" about the world is only what we "believe". The danger of all programs is that as long as they are accepted blindly as fact, they prevent us from exploring other possibilities. If, for example, the Wright Brothers had accepted the program-du-jour which stated, "Man is not meant to fly," we would live in a vastly different world.

QUANTUM SHAMAN™ - a term first used by Orlando to describe one who stops at nothing in order to pursue and eventually embrace the Knowledge and abilities which will enable her to achieve a continuity of consciousness wherein we become cohesive, sentient beings with a single point of view continuing into eternity – a singularity of consciousness. The quantum shaman gathers insights, knowledge and techniques from every walk of life, from the sorcery of don Juan to the quantum experiments taking place on the cutting edge of modern science, from legends of ancient alchemy to shamanic herbalism. It is when the individual truths gleaned from these multitudinous sources assimilate to create a comprehensive "map" that we begin to understand the path toward our evolution. It is then that we are enabled through our own efforts to take control of our own destiny. This is the path of the quantum shaman™.

QUANTUM UNIVERSE: We no longer live in a world of matter and energy, but a multiverse of matter/energy - in short, the two concepts are no longer separate, but halves of a whole. So what, you say? Put simply: energy may assemble into any apparent form. When one thinks this through, the potentials are enormous. We are no longer bound by prisons of flesh, but may instead choose to embrace the immortal condition through the Willful transference/evolution from physical body into energy (or dreaming) body.

REALIZATION - To make real through Intent. More than "realizing" we are beings of ultimate potential, we Real-ize that through our actions and our will.

RECAPITULATION - the process of essentially re-living through intent events in the warrior's past which have left energy hooks in the spirit. The process is described at length in the books of Castaneda; but in a nutshell, recapitulation involves disentangling those energy hooks, removing the "importance" placed on events in the past, so that warrior is freed from those hooks and as a result, enabled to go forward on his path. It is said that recapitulation frees energy trapped in the past.

REMEMBERING THE OTHER SELF – Refers not only to remembering events which may have occurred in heightened awareness, but also involves a process of beginning to "remember" the experiences of the double. It is through remembering that a cohesion of self is achieved which enables the warrior to transcend beyond the eagle and emerge as a singularity of consciousness.

RETROACTIVE ENCHANTMENT – term borrowed from Peter J. Carroll. As understood by the author, an act of sorcery in the now which may appear to have effects reaching backward in time. Magickally and quantumly speaking (which are the same thing in many cases), the magickal acts or movements of intent/will which you undertake today can and do have effects reaching not only into the future, but into the past. This is especially important to understand with regard to the twin: even though you may think/believe your twin has always been with you, the reality may be that you are experiencing retroactive enchantment based on the actions you took yesterday or which you will take tomorrow. Because time is not linear, even memory and events of the past can be influenced by actions not taken until some point in the future. Put another way: do

295

not let evidence of your twin lead you to believe the work is already done. *Creation is an ongoing process* - stretching through past, present and future, with the absolute understanding that time does not exist and is not linear - for which retroactive enchantment exists as a form of proof, should anyone require it.

RIGHT WAY TO LIVE – an intuitive awareness having nothing to do with social morality or cultural predilections. The warrior is guided by the right way to live through an intrinsic harmony with the earth, which is communicated through the inner voice of gnosis.

RULE OF THE NAGUAL – an unwritten "map" which reveals to the nagual man & woman specific truths about the path. The "rule" reveals the truth about the eagle in specific – that awareness is lost at death unless the warrior has taken measures to circumvent that inevitability. The map, therefore, speaks to how that inevitability may be thwarted through developing cohesion. It has been my experience that the rule itself is the same for most Naguals, but how it manifests may be very different. For example, not all Naguals form strict "warrior parties," yet they nonetheless end up guiding others to freedom in other ways. In my own life, the rule of the nagual showed me the necessity to write this book – largely for my own assimilation, and also to serve as a guide for those who find it beneficial.

SCRY or SCRYING - any method of divination, or, more accurately, seeing or gathering information or knowledge. Traditionally, to scry (or scrye) was to gaze into a crystal ball, pool of water, or other reflective object. Scrying can also refer to palm reading (as in "scrying the palm of the gods"), gnosis , or any other method of accessing knowledge and information traditionally thought to be beyond the realm of human awareness.

SECOND ATTENTION - loosely defined, second attention is the assemblage point of heightened awareness or Dreaming. It is the world the sorcerer may manifest through Intent - such as in lucid dreaming.

SEE or SEEING - when used in italics, "see" or "seeing" is to describe the act of viewing the world (or anything within the world) according to its true nature, without the illusions and expectations we place onto the world through our own human programs. *Seeing* is more than looking. It is the shaman's greatest asset and tool in being able to recognize the illusory nature of the consensual reality (overlay) in which we all exist, often without ever realizing it.

SELF-IMPORTANCE - It is self-importance that causes us to think that everything that is said or done is somehow personal to us as individuals. To get angry at the schmuck who cuts you off in traffic is self-importance. It's about him, not about you. The common misconception is that self-importance is arrogance, or egomaniacal behavior, and while that could be true to an extent, self-importance is more accurately an underlying defensiveness that prevents the warrior from embracing clarity and power because she is so busy defending herself, when there is nothing to defend in the first place. It. Ain't. Personal.

SEVENTH SENSE – a perceptual plateau comprised of a combination of the 5 ordinary senses plus the "sixth sense" of psychic awareness or, more precisely, self-awareness. Orlando coined the term "the seventh sense" to describe the "world" we are aspiring to inhabit through this evolution of consciousness – for it is a state of being every bit as real and inhabitable as our world of ordinary awareness, but accessed with a more evolved set of preceptors which could be described as consciousness itself. Some have used the term "third attention", which is somewhat interchangeable. The seventh sense is our world, but it is an expanded world.

SHAMAN - A word meaning, literally, "self-healed madman". Shamans do not belong to any one culture or system of Knowledge. Any human being may have a shamanic essence - a calling to healing of mind, body, spirit in any combination. Orlando once said, "You are the quantum shaman - each of you." The spiritual healing & integration undertaken by a shaman (any shaman, including you) is what determines the difference between a madman caught in the consensual reality, and a self-healed madman (shaman) who begins to walk outside the box of ordinary awareness.

SINGULARITY OF CONSCIOUSNESS – The self made Whole, the evolution of consciousness which results in a cohesive field of awareness existing ubiquitously and non-locally, infinitely and eternally. The cohesive, fully integrated I-Am consisting of all components of the mortal self and the eternal double, brought together under a single assemblage point.

SKINWALKER - A being who has the ability to temporarily inhabit the body of another. In certain branches of shamanism, the shaman may invite an evolved entity (often his own double) to inhabit his body for the purpose of sharing consciousness and expanding awareness. The purpose of this is to facilitate learning - for example, imagine what you might learn if you were to share consciousness with a true immortal. While certain religious groups have expressed a fear of this as a form of possession, skinwalking is normally a mutual agreement between the seeker & the entity or spirits to whom he would lend his body. Do unscrupulous skinwalkers exist? Sure. But so do unscrupulous priests.

SORCERER – A man or woman of Knowledge; brujo or bruja. All men of knowledge may be sorcerers, but not all sorcerers are men of knowledge.

SORCERER'S WORLD - perhaps a better explanation would be "sorcerer's mindset". The sorcerer's world is the world of perception and ability available to the quantum shaman through the evolution of consciousness. Not a different world, it is this world, but without the limitations placed on it through our intrinsic programs and adherence to the consensual reality.

SORCERY - a system of Knowledge geared toward a direct manipulation of energy at the quantum level. Sorcery is not about frivolous parlor tricks, but is instead geared toward bringing the sorcerer into alignment with the higher self (or double) as an eternal being. The sorcerer's ultimate "trick" is to transcend death (slip past the eagle) not only retaining the awareness from this mortal life, but conjoining with the higher self so as to "embrace the totality of oneself" - in other words, a complete and seamless identity stretching infinitely into past and future, with the understanding that eternity is both and neither.

SPIRIT – If earth, air, fire and water are the 4 natural elements, Spirit is the 5th element of creation. The living force or anima of the universe – impersonal, not a deity or entity; the living breath of power; the cohesive element of the all.

SPONTANEOUS PARTHENOGENESIS – the act of something coming into existence out of the nothing, with no apparent cause. It is theorized by the author that the universe created itself from the void through an act of spontaneous parthenogenesis – a thought which wills itself into existence by saying I-Am.

SUPER-POSITION OF THE ASSEMBLAGE POINT – A point of awareness wherein the seeker and the Other (double) have conjoined to embrace the Totality of awareness. At this point, consciousness becomes ubiquitous, inhabiting all quantum positions simultaneously, thereby allowing for consciousness to take on certain similarities of light. Particle and wave – particle being what might be experienced should

298

consciousness make the decision to "localize" into a specific point in time and space; wave being the non-local presentation of awareness, wherein it is a ubiquitous field spanning all of space/time simultaneously.

TALES OF POWER - sorcery stories, usually incredible and often unbelievable by their very nature. To the ordinary man, these tales would automatically be deemed to be fiction, lies, or delusions. Only to fellow sorcerers are they descriptions of acts of power, describing very real events.

TENANT, THE – a being referenced in the books of Carlos Castaneda, seemingly a self-created immortal in corporeal manifestation. Also called "the death defier" because s/he has seemingly lived hundreds of years.

THIRD ATTENTION – the state of freedom beyond the eagle, when the warrior has achieved the state of Wholeness. The state of the ubiquitous, non-local singularity of awareness.

TONAL – the world of matter and men. Anything that can be discussed or known is within the tonal. The nagual is the unknowable, by contrast.

TOTALITY: The sum total of one's life experience - including but not limited to the mortal self, the higher self, the immortal twin, and all other aspects of the self which extend through the quantum universe - outside of time. Put another way, the totality of oneself would include seamless access to all memories of so-called "past lives", parallel lives, and so on, gathered into a cohesive framework of awareness or "singularity of consciousness." This is the immortal condition - the ability to open one's eyes inside the immortal twin, with flawless recall of one's total life experience.

TULPA – the seemingly physical manifestation of a thoughtform, usually transient and without individual volition.

TWO PART MIGRATION OF THE SOUL – the process wherein the mortal self creates the double through dreaming, at which point the double begins teaching the mortal self the path of evolution of consciousness. The mortal self appears to create the double first, and so the double exists as an eternal being, a construct of will and intent. That "immortal" then teaches the mortal self how to evolve, so that when the process is complete, the mortal self reconjoins with the immortal double beyond the eagle's reach.

UNDERWORLD - Also called the otherworld, or the spirit world. Many shamans report visiting a realm of Spirit which seems to have certain common elements, including a huge underground river flowing through a world where "dead" shamans may collaborate with those still on this side to facilitate healing, learning and exchanges of energy & Knowledge on many levels. For a more thorough understanding of the underworld, try Michael Harner's book, _The Way of the Shaman._

WARRIOR – a seeker of knowledge who has made the commitment to the path of her heart. The warrior is the traveler on the journey toward becoming a woman of Knowledge.

WHOLE SELF – The integrated totality of the mortal self and the eternal double as it comes together in a single assemblage point of cohesion beyond the eagle. From the AP of the Whole Self, all memory of all fragments of the Self come into alignment. See also – singularity of consciousness.

WILL - Will is the force which manifests want or need into reality. Will differs from intent. A simple analogy: intent is a true and genuine plan to visit the Grand Canyon. Will is the force that puts you behind the wheel of the car and drives. Will could also be described as the force which causes the intent behind our magic to actually begin to manifest. It is the secret ingredient of sorcery, elusive as the wind and just as impossible to define.

Thou Art God.
Create Yourself Accordingly.

The Last Word

Over time, it has come to my attention that some rather serious assumptions have been made about myself which should perhaps be clarified. The biggest assumption seems to be that I am a "Toltec warrior". Actually, that is not the case and never was. I do not *follow* any guru, do not adhere to any one set of rules, and I do not worship at the feet of Castaneda or don Juan, or anyone else, for it is recognized that doing so only creates a false reflection of *that* person's path, which in no way helps me or anyone else. My personal journey is unique to itself and, like the raven, I have taken elements from many different sources to weave together into a foundation of Knowledge.

I have found that some of the Toltec syntax works well and indeed some of the Toltec techniques may be beneficial. But to adhere strictly to someone else's notion of a "Toltec warrior path" is as false to the Self as adhering *strictly* to someone else's notion of Catholicism. At that point, it has become nothing more than a religion, replete with the buzzwords of their particular faith. "Thou shalt not kill" has merely been rewritten to say, "Thou shalt not care." "Thou shalt not bear false witness", has merely been re-worded to say, "Thou shall lie in the name of stalking." The "sins" of Christianity have merely been renamed to fit the predilections of the faithful, and accusations of "self-importance" and "indulgence" and "self-pity" are hurled off the end of a pointing finger in the same way the accusers at Salem shouted, "Witch! Witch! Witch!"

The Toltec traditions have a lot to offer, and at their core, I have found them to be closer to the actual Truth than any other organized system of Knowledge. But the problem is, as with any system of Knowledge, when the faithful become only *followers* of the way, uploading data and the tenets of that particular faith, the system of Knowledge becomes rendered down to nothing more than a belief system, with fanatics running rampant, quoting Castaneda or Oprah or the Easter Bunny in the same way fundamentalists run along thumping the Bible. In reality, of course, most have never even read that Bible, and those who do have clearly failed to pick up the core meaning, but have settled instead for the words - and usually only those words which may validate their own pre-existing beliefs. No attempt is being made to get to the core truths in their Bible (whether that Bible is the King James Version or _The Teachings of Don Juan_). The words have become meaningless mantras.

This is not a religion to me as it appears to be to some strict "Toltec" die-hards. I do not bury myself in the earth to recapitulate and I do not hang myself from trees to promote Dreaming. That was Carlos's path, not mine. And after many years of engaging my own path, I have come to realize that I have found the success and joy I have found because I have not allowed myself to become just one more lonely sheep bleating along in someone else's shadow. I have learned from Castaneda, but I have also learned from Buddha. Even learned a thing or two from Anne Rice and Stephen King, Ray Bradbury and Philip K. Dick, _Star Trek_ and _Babylon 5_. Such is the nature of the raven - to see what shines even when it may be in an alien nest. But most of all, what I have learned is that there is only one true path, and that is the path inside our own heart, guided by the voice of the double and fueled by Intent.

So, I just want to be clear that I am not "Toltec" anymore than I am Christian or Buddhist or a Trekkie. The fact that I am a nagual woman (a double being) does not lock me in to someone else's definition of "Toltec" - for, ultimately, what the old Seers were seeing with regard to double beings has turned out to be only about half-correct; and it has only been in going _against_ the pre-prescribed, traditional Toltec "beliefs" (and encountering a fair amount of heat for it) that I have found the missing link in that ongoing puzzle which explains why double beings exist in the first place. I didn't just accept what the old seers _saw_. I went and _saw_ it for myself, and that is what led me to Truth - not accepting the little truths written in other men's words.

Being a nagual woman doesn't define me - quite the opposite. It makes me "nothing" in that it has given me a blank slate on which to create the face of my double and write my own destiny on the face of the infinite. The only one I can follow is mySelf, and that is the best advice I _can_ give to anyone.

And so I walk alone, answering to no masters. That is where I find my heart.

Della Van Hise – March, 2005

The road leading into the unknown is dark and filled with peril, yet it is only by embarking on that journey that you start to see that the darkness is really a blank slate upon which you write your Intent with the force of your Will - and it is that creation of the Self which defines the I-Am.

You have to be immortal before you will know how to become immortal. That is the story we will write together, you and I... the story of the mortal self and the eternal double.

Orlando - 2005

www.quantumshaman.com

**Please visit our website
to learn more about Quantum Shamanism™
and to participate in the ongoing journey!**

About the Author...

Della Van Hise is a native of Florida, transplanted to California at the age of 21, who has subsequently sunk her roots into the high desert near Joshua Tree National Park. She has not personally seen any aliens since around 1992, but there is rumored to be a secret UFO base underneath her house.

Her first professional novel was best-selling *Killing Time-* the controversial *Star Trek* novel which was recalled and re-edited in 1984, and which became the foundational plot for the initial *Star Trek* "reboot" film in 2009. More recently, Della has written extensively in the non-fiction genre, with titles such as *Quantum Shaman, Scrawls On the Walls of the Soul, Questions Along the Way,* and *Into the Infinite.* All four titles are part of *The Quantum Shaman* series. If you enjoyed the works of Carlos Castaneda or Don Miguel Ruiz, you'll enjoy the non-fiction works of Della Van Hise.

In addition, Della has written professionally for Tomorrow Magazine and other prominent science fiction publications. Her most recent fiction works include *Sons of Neverland* (an award-winning vampire novel); *The Effect of Moonlight on Tombstones* (a collection of poetry); and *Coyote* a - romantic science fiction novel combining the mystical aspects of martial arts, coming of age, and personal sacrifice.

Della is available for private counseling and motivational speaking.

Visit the author's website: http://www.quantumshaman.com

Contact: della@quantumshaman.com

Visit the author's blogs http://quantumshaman.blogspot.com

Follow Della Van Hise on Facebook
https://www.facebook.com/della.vanhise?ref=name

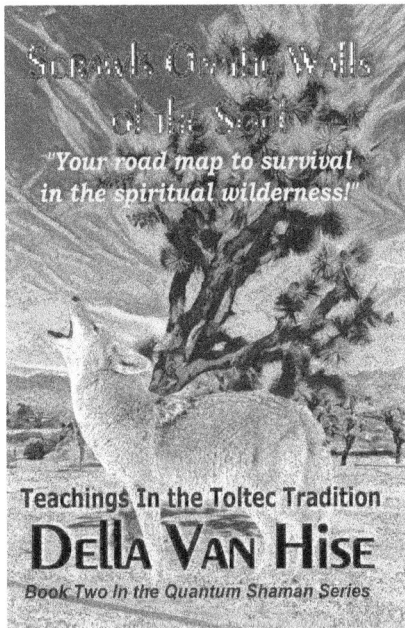

Scrawls on the Walls of the Soul
Della Van Hise

"Your road map to survival in the spiritual wilderness!"

Teachings In the Toltec Tradition
DELLA VAN HISE
Book Two In the Quantum Shaman Series

"If you've ever felt like a stranger in a strange land, this book is your road map to survival in the spiritual wilderness!" (Michael Grove)

The long-awaited follow-up to *Quantum Shaman: Diary of a Nagual Woman*. Stands alone, or order together!

~

It was May of 2000 when my mentor threw me out of the quantum cosmic classroom and said, "I've taught you everything I can. Now it's time to take that knowledge and slam it up against the walls of the real world. If it remains intact and survives the brutality to which it will be subjected, you will get a gold star next to your name and be allowed to proceed to the next level." No mention was made of what this next level might be, or if, indeed, it truly existed.

Go ahead – try to explain this all-consuming path to your friends and relatives. They will smile politely, squirm uncomfortably, and eventually they will stop returning your phone calls and look the other way when they see you coming. And who can blame them? They live in the real world with their office jobs and nuclear families and a host of mindless sitcoms waiting on the propaganda box at the end of their busy day. In direct contrast, it could be observed that anyone who has dedicated themselves to the pursuit of forbidden knowledge really doesn't live in that world at all. Not for lack of wanting, perhaps, but because the real world is quickly seen to be little more than a series of programs and illusions – not unlike The Matrix. And not surprisingly, the people who populate that world may begin to take on a peculiar zombie-like quality.

You find yourself alone in a world of jesters, jokers and jackasses. Now what?

From the author:
www.quantumshaman.com ~ www.eyescrypublications.com

Also on Amazon in both digital & paperback

305

These life-altering workshops are available through the Quantum Shaman™ website, or on *Amazon*.com.

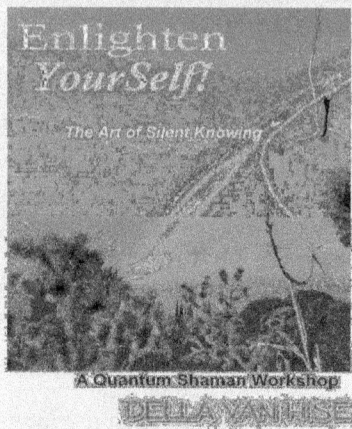

Enlighten YourSelf!
The Art of Silent Knowing
A Quantum Shaman Workshop
DELLA VAN HISE

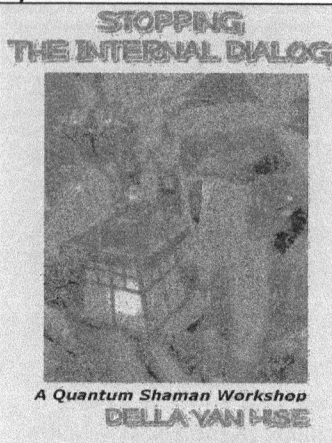

STOPPING THE INTERNAL DIALOG
A Quantum Shaman Workshop
DELLA VAN HISE

ENLIGHTEN YOURSELF!
The Art of Silent Knowing

Gnosis is the art of hearing the flame
Seeing the voice of the crow
Listening to the silent wisdom
of the sentient Infinite.

What is silent knowing? Simply put, it is learning to ask questions of that vast sentience which is the universe, the All, and simply the Self.

STOPPING THE INTERNAL DIALOGUE

Learning to stop the internal dialogue enables the warrior to get one step closer to permanent gnosis - the place of silent Knowing, where the entire library of Infinite Knowledge is at our disposal.

www.quantumshaman.com

CREATING THE DOUBLE

This is a power-packed exploration of what it means to create the double. Nitty-gritty how-to, exercises to motivate and validate. For warriors who are ready to turn and face themselves in the mirror of the Infinite, there is no better starting point, and there is no one on Earth more qualified to present this workshop than Della, whose interactions with her own double, have led her to fulfill her destiny as a nagual woman and teacher.

UNDOING THE PROGRAMS

This workshop gives you the tools for getting rid of belief systems that keep you from achieving your greatest success in this world, and may be preventing you from embracing your highest potential in the realm of Spirit.

"As long as a man truly believes he is powerless, he has no reason or motivation to seek the source of his own power." (Orlando)

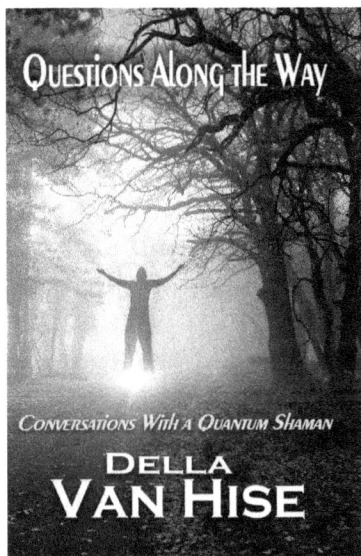

QUESTIONS ALONG THE WAY
DELLA VAN HISE

Anyone on a journey of personal growth and enlightenment is sure to come face to face with difficult questions that will keep them awake at night and may even plunge them into the dark night of the soul. In Questions Along the Way, Quantum Shaman Della Van Hise talks frankly with seekers on the path of heart and opens wide the door to a new understanding that lies beyond the false belief systems and cultural programming all of us must confront when emerging from the dark into the light.

A MESSAGE FROM THE AUTHOR

"Questions Along the Way" is a compilation of questions I've received over a period spanning more than 20 years - inquiries from seekers who find themselves faced with conundrums that run the gamut from 'Is there a God?' to 'How can I improve my relationships right here and now?'

Much of the work I've done with others on a path of heart - a journey of personal growth, enlightenment and evolution - has been previously scattered over a wide variety of groups, online forums and in-person talks and seminars, so it is my intent with this book to bring many of those questions together in an easily accessible format.

As always, thanks for your interest in my work. May your path be filled with wonder, imagination and ultimate freedom.

Available on Amazon in both digital & paperback.
Also at www.quantumshaman.com

INTO THE INFINITE
DELLA VAN HISE

Into the Infinite is a compilation of the author's many encounters with the unknown, beginning in early childhood and continuing throughout her adult life. - experiences which compel us to realize the world is nothing like we have been taught to believe.

What can you think when you return from work to find the house cleaned top to bottom... while no one was home?What do you believe when Carlos Castaneda comes to you in a dream and brings a witch to stop your heart?

What does it mean when you wake at 3:38 a.m. and experience a significant period of missing time between one room and the next?

A truly mind-bending book for anyone who has a love affair with the unknown... or anyone who wants to.

"So who's Coyote?" I asked, trying to ignore the effect he was having on me. "You?"

Steale laughed easily, though it did little to hide the torment behind that mask of indifference he wore so well.

"Coyote's a scavenger, Jack of all trades. The Native Americans call him the trickster - the one who brought chaos down on the world." He shrugged as if altogether unconcerned. "Original sin."

"Is that what you are?" I asked, keeping it light despite the growing knot my stomach. "Original sin?"

He kept his profile to me, eyes straight ahead as he drove. "Sure you want to know?"

I couldn't help wondering if I had cornered the coyote, or if the clever trickster had cornered me.

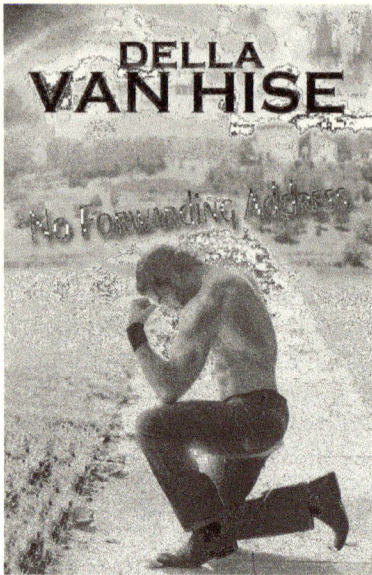

NO FORWARDING ADDRESS
Della Van Hise

A literary science fiction novel told in the voice of an empath, *No Forwarding Address* explores the lures and the dangers of love, the tragedies and triumphs stirring in the human heart.

When Crystal and Raine first meet, it is 50 years after The Great War on Earth. They are hesitant to trust, afraid to love. But even if they are able to overcome these seemingly insurmountable obstacles, is even love enough?

When a man has the stars in his eyes, legend says he must serve them above all others.

I knew then that it wasn't love and hate who were mirror twins. The final irony was that grief would always turn out to be the paradoxical antithesis and simultaneous manifestation of whatever it is that humans call love.

Crystal remained silent and walked a few steps away from Raine – further down the shoreline, until she stood under the wing of one fallen Phantom. She thought of the ship she had seen from the balcony of our home, and though it had long since disappeared over the dark and treacherous abyss of the ocean, its image lingered clearly in her thoughts. On that ship was a man, she thought. A terribly lonely man who made no great difference to the flow of time or the memory of the galaxy. A man who, like Raine, was compelled to keep moving and look only ahead and never behind. A man who could not afford the luxury of waving goodbye to friends on shore.

At last, she turned toward her beloved and watched him watching the darkness. He stood only a few feet away, yet the images in my mind said he might as well have been a million light years off in the void. He was lost to her in that instant out-of-time, just as lost and impossible to find as the light from that ship which had vanished over the horizon...

FROM THE AUTHOR:
www.eyescrypublications.com

Also on Amazon in both digital & paperback

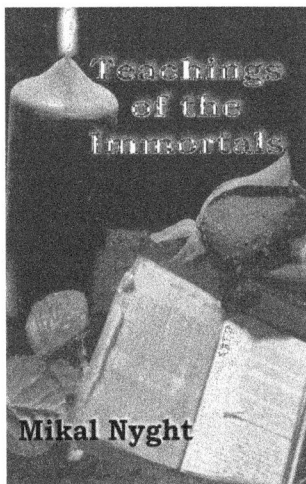

TEACHINGS OF THE IMMORTALS
Mikal Nyght
So... You Want To Live Forever?

The teachings are presented as brief vignettes in no particular order of importance. This is not a book you read from start to finish in a single night. It is a grimoire of self-creation, intended to be contemplated slowly so as to be assimilated wholly. Pick it up and turn to a page at random. Where your eyes come to rest on the page is your lesson for the day. Go no further until you have assimilated the lesson totally.

Mikal Nyght

The teachings are seduction as much as instruction. This is the way of The Dark Evolution.

The Ruby Slippers

The danger of the consensual continuum is that its natural gravity exists at the lowest common denominator of human experience, and because of this it will automatically make you forget those elusive truths you've fought to learn, and before you know it you're lost in petty dramas again, sinking into the mire of old familiar scripts.

The only way to overcome this is to be continually cavorting with worlds and events beyond human experience, journeying into the unknown so that it can become known, expanding knowledge and awareness to become more than you were, bringing back from the Dreaming those secrets which will teach you how to use the ruby slippers to transport yourself over the rainbow to the vampyre wizard's secret lair.

Perception

This is the nature of reality: to be precisely what perception dictates, as solid and whole as your interpretation of it, or as changeable and eternal as you permit it to be.

It wasn't knowledge god tried to keep from Man, you see. It was perception, for perception alone has the power to destroy god and obliterate comfortable consensual realities to create unending immortality.

Take the apple, my embryonic children. Nibble its red red flesh. Open your vampyre eyes so you may finally begin to See.

From the Author:
www.immortalis-animus.com ~ www.eyescrypublications.com

Also on Amazon in both digital & paperback

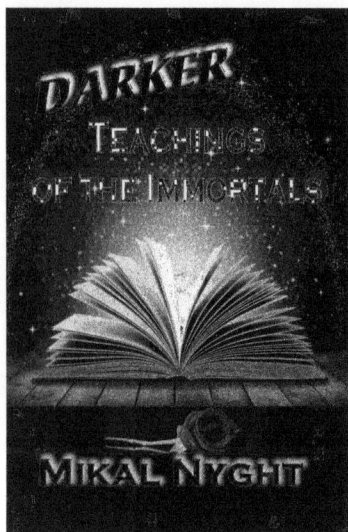

Darker Teachings of the Immortals
Mikal Nyght

Darker Teachings of the Immortals brings the reader into intimate contact with secrets & truths that have been suppressed for centuries by governments, religions & corporations who seek to maintain a profitable status quo while simultaneously keeping the human population docile, obedient and - worst of all - mortal. Now, at last, it's time to throw off the chains and claim our rightful place among the immortals.

From the Introduction by Mikal Nyght:

The observation has been made that "life gets in the way," and while that's true, it's really something more specific that lies at the heart of our conundrum. Namely - life gets in the way of immortality.

Ironic, no? While one is off doing all the things one does in the course of living, life is being drained out of until you wake up one morning and realize you are old, wondering where your life went, and why the reflection in the mirror bears no resemblance to the idea of yourself in your mind. So, yes, life gets in the way.

The purpose of *The Darker Teachings* is primarily to generate and hopefully maintain a frame of mind of freedom from the programming that otherwise binds the seeker to mortality, death and decay. The purpose is to teach the seeker not what to think, but *how* to think and - far more importantly - how to see that the world is largely an illusion of delusions, created and nurtured by fear, complacency and habit.

You *will* be absorbed if you don't do something. *Teachings of the Immortals* was designed to provide the seekers for whom it was written with an intense and compelling Awakening. *The Darker Teachings* are intended to move the traditional reference points from the ordinary to the infinite, from the transient to the eternal.

Listen with your heart.
Hear with your spirit.
See with your third eye.

Available on Amazon in both digital & paperback
Also on the author's website at www.immortalis-animus.com

Eye Scry Publications
A Visionary Publishing Company

www.eyescrypublications.com

www.QuantumShaman.com

Some of our Authors Include

Mikal Nyght
Della Van Hise
Wendy Rathbone
Alexis Fegan Black